Gas War

GAS WAR

Capt. R.K. Sirohi

PRASHANT PUBLISHING HOUSE
DELHI-110094

Published by :
Prashant Publishing House
C-34, 28 Foota Road, Gali-3,
West Karwal Nagar, Delhi-110094
Phone : 011-22963970, Mob. : 9810396373
e-mail.: prashantpublishinghouse@gmail.com

Gas War

First Published 2018

ISBN 978-81-938012-7-7

PRINTED IN INDIA
Published by Mr. R.K. Jha M/s Prashant Publishing House and Published at H.S. Offset House Press, Delhi.

Contents

Preface

Gas warfare is a method of war that employs weapons that are designed to cause casualties primarily through the use of harmful chemical agents. The First World War constitutes the most extensive incidence of gas warfare in the 20th century, and poison gas remains associated with the horrors of trench warfare in public memory.

The introduction of gas warfare during the First World War was anticipated insofar as the Hague Peace Conference of 1899 admonished nations "to abstain from the use of projectiles the object of which is the diffusion of asphyxiating or deleterious gasses." The scientific and industrial assets available to the belligerent nations, which sought to use their national resources for strategic advantage, made possible the mass-production of gas weapons.

The advent of gas warfare compelled nations to integrate a new method of war into their existing military organizations and doctrines. At times seeking to maximize the element of surprise or, alternatively, opting to create sustained hazardous conditions in areas for hours or days, military units in Europe experimented with a variety of techniques for the employment of gas in combat and fine-tuned the types of targets considered optimal over the course of the war. Producing gas weapons and defensive equipment required the creation of supporting scientific and manufacturing institutions, facilitating a diffusion of chemists into business and policy-making fields in First World War nations.

The Russia–Ukraine gas disputes refer to a number of disputes between Ukrainian oil and gas company Naftohaz Ukrayiny and Russian gas supplier Gazprom over natural gas supplies, prices, and debts. These disputes have grown beyond simple business disputes into transnational political issues—involving political leaders from several countries—that threaten natural gas supplies in numerous European countries dependent on natural gas imports from Russian suppliers, which are transported through Ukraine. Russia provides approximately a quarter of the natural gas consumed in the European Union; approximately 80% of those exports travel through pipelines across Ukrainian soil prior to arriving in the EU.

There are few weapons in war as nefarious as poison. One hundred years after the Germans first used chlorine gas during the Second Battle of Ypres, chemical weapons remain widely stigmatized and outlawed. Of all the technologies from World War I that went on to redefine combat in the 20th century, chemical weapons have the most sordid legacy.

Ultimately, however, the use of lethal and incapacitating gasses proved largely ineffective in conventional warfare. They were comparatively easy to counter, difficult to use and rarely achieved the desired or planned result. The impact of chemical weapons is less practical than it is psychological, which partly justifies the reluctance to use such measures but also explains why many countries still have chemical stockpiles.

This is a reference book. All the matter is just compiled and edited in nature, taken from the various sources which are in public domain.

This book will provide some of the tools for students to research the area of Gas War, chemical and biological warfare and, given that opportunity, to make their own judgments of the facts and opinions of many different agencies.

—*Editor*

1

Gas Warfare

Gas warfare is a method of war that employs weapons that are designed to cause casualties primarily through the use of harmful chemical agents. The First World War constitutes the most extensive incidence of gas warfare in the 20th century, and poison gas remains associated with the horrors of trench warfare in public memory.

The introduction of gas warfare during the First World War was anticipated insofar as the Hague Peace Conference of 1899 admonished nations "to abstain from the use of projectiles the object of which is the diffusion of asphyxiating or deleterious gasses." The scientific and industrial assets available to the belligerent nations, which sought to use their national resources for strategic advantage, made possible the mass-production of gas weapons.

The French army used rifle grenades filled with tear gas against the Germans beginning in August 1914, but the weapons proved extremely ineffective. In the early months of the war the British also researched the weaponized use of tear gas agents and more toxic gasses including sulfur dioxide. However, it was the German gas warfare program that achieved the earliest success.

The Germans developed and manufactured artillery shells filled with tear gas and other chemical irritants and used them first against the British at Neuve-Chapelle in October 1914 (not to be confused with the more famous battle fought there in March 1915) and then against the Russians at Bolimów in January 1915. In both cases the chemical agents in the weapons were ineffective. After these experiences, the Germans worked to innovate new methods of delivering poison gas.

The attack at Ypres on 22 April 1915 was the first successful instance of gas warfare during the First World War. Instead of using artillery shells or other projectiles, as had been done previously, German soldiers under the direction of Fritz Haber (1868-1934) released chlorine gas from storage cylinders and allowed the wind to carry the large gas cloud west across "No Man's Land."

The attack was devastating for the unprepared British, Canadian, French and Algerian defenders caught in the path of the chlorine, though German efforts to exploit the initial advantage were not ultimately successful.

Afterward, the German army conducted similar attacks against the Russians at Bolimów and, on 24 September 1915, the British launched their first chlorine gas attack at Loos, using Haber's method of releasing the gas and allowing it to drift with the wind.

DEVELOPMENT

Following the successful introduction of gas warfare, belligerent nations accelerated the development of protective masks and researched methods of manufacturing new war gasses. The Germans developed their *Gummischutzmaske* with an activated charcoal filter small enough to be worn on the face piece. The British developed the P Helmet in time for it to be issued to soldiers at Ypres during the first German phosgene gas attack in December 1915. The British Large Box Respirator and Small Box Respirator, French M2 gas mask, and Russian Zelinsky-Kumant Helmet were manufactured and issued to soldiers through 1916.

Germany remained consistently ahead of other gas warfare programs in the development of new war gasses, introducing diphosgene in May 1916 and mustard gas in July 1917. While phosgene accounted for the majority of gas casualties during the First World War, the use of mustard gas represented one of the most significant advances in gas warfare during the fighting.

Mustard gas is a vesicant that can burn any exposed skin, eyes, or other tissue, unlike other poison gasses that primarily affect the victim's lungs. The fact that mustard gas also took longer to dissipate than other types of war gasses - sometimes injuring soldiers who came into contact with the chemicals even days after employment - added to the difficulty of protecting soldiers against it.

Methods of deploying gas weapons changed over time, as systems that were less dependent on wind direction and speed were gradually developed. Most of the poison gas that was used in the Great War was delivered by artillery and mortar rounds. The British introduced Livens projectors to the battlefield in 1916, which were capable of blanketing target areas in large clouds of poison gas.

Effects

The advent of gas warfare compelled nations to integrate a new method of war into their existing military organizations and doctrines.

At times seeking to maximize the element of surprise or, alternatively, opting to create sustained hazardous conditions in areas for hours or days, military units in Europe experimented with a variety of techniques for the employment of gas in combat and fine-tuned the types of targets considered optimal over the course of the war. Producing gas weapons and defensive equipment required the creation of supporting scientific and manufacturing institutions, facilitating a diffusion of chemists into business and policy-making fields in First World War nations.

Data related to gas casualties is inherently inaccurate given the stringencies of war and the recording methods of the period. For some nations only generalized estimates exist.

Table : Estimated Gas Casualties (Killed and Wounded) for Nations with Dependable Data

Nation	Gas Casualties
France	130,000
Germany	107,000
United Kingdom	186,000
United States of America	73,000
Total	496,000

The diagnosis, evacuation and treatment of gas warfare casualties posed a substantial challenge to battlefield medicine and the long-term health effects of gas poisoning remained the subject of controversy after the war ended.

Following the Armistice, gas warfare continued to be a focus of international arms control efforts that resulted in the Geneva Gas Protocol (1925) and other subsequent agreements.

GAS AND CHEMICAL WARFARE IN WORLD WAR ONE

Gas represented one of the most horrific developments in military technologyproduced by World War One. These 10 facts tell part of the story of this terrible innovation.

Gas was first used at Bolimów by Germany

Gas first saw use in January 1915 at the battle of Bolimów. The Germans launched 18,000 shells of xylyl bromide in preparation to attack. The attack never took place though as unfavorable winds blew the gas back toward the Germans. Casualties were minimal, however, as the cold weather prevented the xylyl bromide fluid from evaporating fully.

Gas was climate dependent

In the wrong climate gases would disperse quickly, which reduced their chances of inflicting significant casualties on the enemy. Favorable conditions in contrast could sustain a gas' effect long after the initial attack; mustard gas could remain effective in an area over several days. Ideal conditions for gas were an absence of strong wind or sun, either of which caused the gas to dissipate quickly; high humidity was also desirable.

Gas was not officially lethal

The effects of gas were horrific and their consequences could take years to recover from, if you recovered at all. Gas attacks were, however, often not focused on killing.

Gases were divided into lethal and irritant categories and irritants were by far the more common including infamous chemical weapons like mustard gas (dichlorethylsulphide) and blue cross (Diphenylcyonoarsine). The fatality rate of gas casualties was 3% but the effects were so debilitating even in non-fatal cases that it remained one of the war's most feared weapons.

Gases were categorised by their effects

The Gases used in World War One came in 4 main categories: Respiratory Irritants; Lachrymators (tear gases); Sternutators (causing sneezing) and Vesicants (causing blistering). Often different kinds were used together to inflict the maximum possible damage.

Germany, France and Britain used the most gas in WWI

The most gas was produced by Germany, totaling 68,000 tons. The British and French were the closest after that with 25,000 and 37,000 tons respectively. No other nation came close to this volume of gas production.

Key to German advances at the 3rd Battle of the Aisne

In May and June of 1918 German forces advanced from the Aisne River toward Paris. They initially made swift progress aided by extensive artillery use. During the initial offensive 80% of long range bombardment shells, 70% shells in the barrage on the front line and 40% of shells in the creeping barrage were gas shells.

Gas was not the only chemical weapon of WWI

Although not as significant as gas, incendiary shells were deployed in World War One. These were launched mainly from mortars and comprised either of white phosphorous or thermit.

Gas was actually launched as a liquid

The Gas used in shells during WWI was stored in liquid form rather than as a gas. It only became a gas when the fluid dispersed from the shell and evaporated. This is why the effectiveness of gas attacks was so weather dependent. Sometimes gas was released in vapour form from canisters on the ground but this increased the chances of the gas blowing back at the army using it therefore making the liquid based shells the more popular system for deployment.

Gas was used to undermine enemy morale

As it was heavier than air gas could find its way into any trench or dugout in a way that other forms of attack could not. Consequently it impacted on morale by causing anxiety and panic, especially early in the war when no one had experienced chemical warfare before.

Gas usage was almost unique to World War One

The gas warfare of World War One was so horrific that it has rarely been used since. In the interwar period the French and Spanish used it in Morocco and the Bolsheviks used it against rebels.

After the 1925 Geneva Protocol prohibited chemical weapons their use further diminished. Fascist Italy and Imperial Japan also used gas in the 1930s, however, against Ethiopia and China respectively. A more recent use was by Iraq in the Iran-Iraq War 1980-88.

CHLORINE: THE GAS OF WAR CRIMES

On 2 August this year I noticed a small piece on the BBC news website about a gas attack in Syria. Accounts of the appalling situation in Syria and new devastating attacks seem to be almost a daily feature in the news. What I found especially depressing about the short item that made the news that day, was the alleged use of chlorine gas. Allegations of chlorine gas attacks have appeared again in the news on 11 August, this time resulting in the deaths of one woman and two children as well as a formal investigation by the UN.

Chlorine, the 17th element in the periodic table, is an industrially important chemical. Among other applications it is used in the dying industry and forms the basis for many household bleaches. But chlorine is perhaps most well known as an addition to swimming pools where, in small quantities, it reacts with the water to form hypochlorous acid that kills bacteria and prevents the growth of algae, resulting in safe, sanitary conditions for swimming.

Chlorine also has a much darker history in conflicts stretching back to the first world war. Its use at Ypres on 22 April 1915 marked a new era in chemical warfare. The possible threat of gas attacks had resulted in a treaty signed in 1899 prohibiting their use. The treaty did not stop the French from launching shells containing a primitive tear gas on German lines in 1914 but their aim had been disruption. The development of chlorine gas attacks were designed to kill. To avoid breaching the words of the treaty, though not the spirit, the pioneer of chemical warfare, Fritz Haber, planned the release of the gas from canisters – no projectiles would be involved.

The theory went that the pale green or yellow gas would be slowly pushed over no-mans-land towards the French lines by the wind. The heavier than air gas would then sink into the trenches. The hope was that the choking fumes would cause panic and chaos. French troops would simply run away and a gap would be left wide open for German troops, wearing gas masks, to advance and gain huge amounts of ground. Yes, there would be casualties, but reluctant German officials unsure of the technology were persuaded into trying Haber's innovative plan as he claimed it would shorten the war and thereby save countless lives in the long run.

Canisters of chlorine were amassed along a fifteen mile stretch of German lines. When the wind eventually turned in the Germans' favour (the prevailing wind was from the French trenches towards the German lines) the plan proceeded exactly as Haber had predicted. One hundred French troops died in the attack – a remarkably small number in a conflict that regularly saw the slaughter of thousands. But the Germans failed to capitalise on the gaping breach in French lines. As German troops tentatively advanced behind the gas, they were attacked by Canadian and British troops stationed alongside the French.

In the following months, the Allies also developed methods of deploying chlorine gas and both sides went on to develop even more toxic and devastating chemical agents to unleash on their enemies. Haber's hopes for shortening the war were hopelessly off the mark. After the first chlorine attack at Ypres, the war would continue to grind on for another three and a half years, and estimates of over a million people are thought to have died as a result of the use of poison gas.

The horrific results of poison gas in warfare have spurred the drafting of various treaties signed since the end of the first world war. Progressive agreements in this area have resulted in the banning of the use of chemical weapons in warfare as well as the production, transportation and stockpiling of these compounds. Sadly this has not brought an end to their use in conflicts.

The use of any chemical weapon is appalling. The indiscriminate nature of poison gas and the harrowing effects produced in the human body seems especially callous and inhumane. Chlorine can attack the body in a number of ways producing devastating chemical burns. A complex series of chemical reactions is involved as chlorine reacts with fats, proteins and other material of the body. Most of the damage is thought to be caused by the reaction with moisture in the body to produce acids. The human body contains a lot of water (we are all between two thirds and three quarters water). Breathing the gas in through the moist areas of the mouth and nose to reach the throat and lungs damages these areas in particular. The eyes can also be corroded. There is no antidote. Only supportive care and treatment of symptoms – supporting breathing, clearing affected areas – is possible. Death can be relatively quick or agonisingly slow, depending on the extent of the damage.

The most recent gas attacks in Aleppo are said to have come in the form of barrel bombs dropped from a helicopter. Medical workers on the ground claim the victims they have encountered show characteristic symptoms of chlorine poisoning. We will have to wait for the UN report for confirmation of what has happened and if chlorine, a relic of a historic and terrible war, really has made an unwelcome appearance in the current conflict in Syria. If the accounts are true then the perpetrators, whoever they may be, have committed a war crime.

US IN A GAS WAR WITH IRAN, RUSSIA, OWN ALLIES

The United States is flaunting its emerging energy prowess as a potential weapon as it draws a new line in the sand for global domination. On Thursday, Russian President Vladimir Putin signed off on a new state policy strategy that views the US as aspiring to dominate the world's oceans. The strategy pins down the potential areas of conflict, citing the Arctic where the US and its allies are striving "to reach an intimidating supremacy."

The issue of geopolitical rush for Arctic resources has been dominating debate in international relations for some time, with the five littoral states – Russia, the US, Canada, Norway and Denmark/Greenland – jockeying for position for its oil and gas interests. Putin's strategy outline, binding until 2030, reiterates the Arctic and the globe's resource-rich northernmost a priority development area for Russia in the face of the four other countries, all of whom are US allies.

The document states that the US and its allies are trying to "limit Russia's access to resources at sea and its access to vitally important naval transport communications."

'Great tool' to undermine foes

The claim is not without foundation. US military analyst James "Spider" Marks who has led many business ventures since retirement from the Army where he spent over 30 years and attained the rank of major general sums up America's possible designs for supremacy, including for countering Russia and its allies.

"If the United States is to counter the global influence of Russia, Iran, China and other hostile nations, we will need to find peaceful ways to advance our interests while undermining theirs," he wrote on the website of Washington-based Morning Consult company.

Marks singled out natural gas as "a great tool to use for this purpose," keeping in mind that Russia is the No. 2 producer of the fuel in the world, followed by Iran, and China as No. 6.

Global demand is rising across the world for natural gas which is viewed the big fuel of the next two decades. Gas consumption is on track to hit almost 4,000 billion cubic meters by 2022 and China is projected to account for almost 40 percent of growth.

Shale revolution

US advances in directional drilling and hydraulic fracturing has made the United States the world's No. 1 producer of natural gas. America's ability to extract energy from vast shale formations has put the country on the brink of being a global energy powerhouse.

President Donald Trump's refusal earlier this month to sign up to the communique pledging to implement the Paris climate accord has added new momentum to America's fracking activities. The Energy Department said on Monday that US shale production was set to rise for the eighth consecutive month in August.

"First, as we produce more of our own gas, we reduce our dependence on foreign sources of energy. Second, as our production grows, so does our ability to advance our interests abroad through exports," Marks wrote.

"This provides America unprecedented global flexibility, to engage internationally at a time and place of our choosing," he added.

Exerting power over allies

Marks identifies the target areas which Washington can use its natural gas as a double-edged weapon - exerting power over allies and countering enemies. He cites three Middle Eastern countries — Iran, Qatar and Saudi Arabia — which hold 40 percent of the world's natural gas reserves, with Iran projected to have the largest growth in natural gas production through 2040.

"Although the United States might not become an exporter to these countries, it can pump its own gas into the world market, keeping prices down and reducing reliance on the Middle East's dominant producers."

According to the International Energy Agency (IEA), the United States will challenge Qatar and Australia as the highest exporters by 2022 with more than half of the natural gas produced to be converted to liquefied natural gas (LNG) for export.

Three major LNG terminals are currently under construction in the US, which will double the number of US ports in use. The number of LNG consuming countries is expected to rise to 39 countries this year, making them amenable to fresh inroad and influence.

Rising liquefaction capacity is coming into a market already saturated, and the glut is driving down prices at the expense of traditional suppliers such as Qatar and Saudi Arabia, underlining their current diplomatic crisis.

US shale oil is already weighing down on the country's allies in the Persian Gulf, especially Saudi Arabia whose joint efforts with Russia to prop up prices have not produced intended results.

According to a UK-based consultancy, Riyadh which is hard pressed for oil revenues because of its war in Yemen and other expenses is now considering unilaterally cutting its oil exports 1 million barrels a day (bpd).

Targeting Russia and China

The next targets are Russia as the world's second gas producer and China as the sixth, both trying to increase their market share. "By maximizing its natural gas production and getting this gas to market efficiently and reliably, the United States can accomplish two goals. It can reduce its dependence on foreign energy while increasing its influence in global affairs at the expense of Russia and China," Marks noted.

"If we add to the global supply by increasing our exports, we further weaken Russia and China while strengthening our own alliances," he added.

OIL GEOPOLITICS AND IRAN'S RESPONSE

At first glance, last week's Vienna Group meeting—that is the Organization of Petroleum Exporting Countries (OPEC) plus non-OPEC producers including Russia—seemed to have resolved some thorny issues. The producer group confidently announced it would increase oil production to stabilize the global oil market. Iran, which had previously threatened to boycott any agreement in protest, appeared to acquiesce to the joint OPEC production increase communique. That may have seemed like a win for the Trump administration, which had hoped to box Iran in to the negotiating table on a host of issues, including conflict resolution in Yemen and Syria, when it cancelled the nuclear deal and reimposed sanctions on Iranian oil exports. Iran had suggested OPEC take a more strident stance on the U.S. policy. Not unexpectedly, U.S. Gulf allies, under pressure from U.S. President Donald Trump's tweets and back door diplomacy, offered a moderate approach, which will include significant production increases by Saudi Arabia, among others.

For those who might construe Iran's relatively mild public statements following the OPEC session as a sign that Iran had no real cards to play, a glance at regional conflicts might indicate otherwise. Immediately following the OPEC meeting, Syria's army, which has a history of on the ground collaboration with Iran, broke a standing cease fire agreement with the United States and Russia and advanced on the southern province of Daraa. At the same time, Iranian-backed Houthi rebels from Yemen fired missiles into the Saudi capital city of Riyadh. Both could be taken as a sign that pressure on Iran to deescalate its participation in regional conflicts isn't producing immediate results, increasing the probability that the Trump administration will actively press allies to buy less oil from Iran.

These events raise important questions about what Tehran's response will be in the coming days and months and what leverage the United States really has to alter facts on the ground.

Granted, a twitter report suggested that Iran was unhappy with Russia's collaboration with Saudi Arabia at OPEC and Russia's stated posture on southern Syria. Ironically (or maybe not ironically at all) the whole complex situation could be an oil win-win for Moscow. Russia's deal with Saudi Arabia to increase oil production achieves multiple benefits for the Kremlin. It demonstrates a willingness to consider U.S. interests but at a low cost to Russia. It helps preserve Russia's long run influence on Saudi Arabia. And the chances that Russia will lose revenue as a result look slimmer, if Iran is dissatisfied with the situation. Russia is likely making a good bet that frustration in Tehran could lead to an escalation of Mideast conflicts, which in turn keeps oil prices lofty, giving Russia even more money since it is increasing its export volumes. A disappointed Iran could also be less apt to participate in conflict negotiations with the United States, leading to tighter sanctions enforcement, which ultimately reduces competition to Russian oil and gas companies from Tehran in long term natural gas markets for Europe. In recent weeks, French firm Total, which is likely pulling the plug on its South Pars natural gas project in Iran as a result of U.S. sanctions, ventured to Russia to sign a deal to participate in Novatek's LNG-2 Arctic gas project. Europeans firms that are no longer active in Iran are also partners in the controversial Nord Stream 2 natural gas pipeline proposed to extend from Russia to Germany.

That begs the question: What next moves make sense for Iran? The Iranian government remains under pressure from its own citizens, who took to the streets again in large numbers this week. But even with this intense internal pressure, it's hard to see the logic behind the belief that the Iranian regime might simply just fold its cards on its regional ambitions. Even if Iran would consider reopening political negotiations with the United States and its neighbors to satisfy popular domestic sentiment—protesters have been chanting their government should spend more money at home than abroad—the ruling hardliners will likely want to gain negotiating leverage before doing so. That conflicts, for example, with the thesis that the battle for the Yemeni port of Al-Hodeida could set the stage for successful peace negotiations. Iran has many tactics at its disposal via its regional proxies and via asymmetric warfare that could be utilized to make its own interests appear more salient.

Oil prices jumped back up again early this week despite reports that Saudi oil production is surging to 10.8 million barrels a day (b/d), partly on news of an oil production snafu in Canada. But realistically, that loss of Canadian barrels was small at 350,000 b/d and temporary through July. More likely, markets are jittery because it's hard to construct a narrative on how Iran, Saudi Arabia, the United Arab Emirates, Israel, Russia, and the United States will navigate conflicts on the ground in the coming months.

OIL AS A LEADING CAUSE OF WAR

Although the threat of "resource wars" over possession of oil reserves is often exaggerated, the sum total of the political effects generated by the oil industry makes oil a leading cause of war. Between one-quarter and one-half of interstate wars since 1973 have been connected to one or more oil-related causal mechanisms. No other commodity has had such an impact on international security.

The influence of oil on conflict is often poorly understood. In U.S. public debates about the 1991 and 2003 Iraq wars, both sides focused excessively on the question of whether the United States was fighting for possession of oil reserves; neither sought a broader understanding of how oil shaped the preconditions for war.

Oil fuels international conflict through eight distinct mechanisms: (1) resource wars, in which states try to acquire oil reserves by force; (2) petro-aggression, whereby oil insulates aggressive leaders such as Saddam Hussein or Ayatollah Ruhollah Khomeini from domestic opposition, and therefore makes them more willing to engage in risky foreign policy adventurism; (3) the externalization of civil wars in oil-producing states ("petrostates"); (4) financing for insurgencies—for instance, Iran funneling oil money to Hezbollah; (5) conflicts triggered by the prospect of oil-market domination, such as the United States' war with Iraq over Kuwait in 1991; (6) clashes over control of oil transit routes, such as shipping lanes and pipelines; (7) oil-related grievances, whereby the presence of foreign workers in petrostates helps extremist groups such as al-Qaida recruit locals; and (8) oil-related obstacles to multilateral cooperation, such as when an importer's attempt to curry favor with a petrostate prevents multilateral cooperation on security issues. These mechanisms can contribute to conflict individually or in combination.

The linkages between oil and international conflict are growing increasingly important in light of three transitions under way in global energy markets. The first is the shift in patterns of global oil production away from traditional suppliers in the Middle East and toward (1) suppliers of unconventional oil reserves in North America and (2) new suppliers of conventional oil, especially in Africa. As many as sixteen developing countries will become oil exporters in the near future, creating a swath of new international security concerns. Second, the low oil prices of the 1990s have given way to higher and more volatile prices, increasing the magnitude of the consequences one can expect from oil-conflict linkages. Third, the relative decline of U.S. hegemony may reduce the provision of public goods such as security of shipping lanes and pipelines. Although these transitions alter some of the ways in which the oil industry contributes to international conflict, none eliminates linkages between the two or allows the United States to disengage from global markets.

The Role of Fracking

Understanding the eight mechanisms linking oil to international security can help policymakers think beyond the much-discussed goal of energy security, defined as reliable access to affordable fuel supplies. Achieving such an understanding is important in light of recent changes in the United States. As hydraulic fracturing—"fracking"—of shale oil and gas accelerates, energy imports are projected to decline, and North America could even achieve energy independence, in the sense of low or zero net overall energy imports, in the next decade. Yet the United States will continue to import large volumes of oil, and the world price of oil will continue to affect it. Moreover, so long as the rest of the world remains dependent on global oil markets, the fracking revolution will do little to reduce many oil-related threats to international security. The emergence of aggressive, revolutionary leaders in petrostates would likely continue to pose threats to regional security. Petrostates will continue to be weakly institutionalized and thus subject to civil wars, creating the kind of security problems that demand responses by the international community, as occurred in Libya in 2011. Petro-financed insurgent groups such as Hezbollah will persist, as will threats to the shipping lanes and oil transit routes that supply important U.S. allies, such as Japan.

In sum, energy autarky is not the answer. Self-sufficiency will bring economic benefits to the United States, but few gains for national security. So long as the oil market remains globally integrated, national oil imports matter far less than total consumption. Rather than viewing energy self-sufficiency as a panacea, the United States should contribute to international security by making long-term investments in research and development to reduce oil consumption and provide alternative fuel sources in the transportation sector. In addition to the economic and environmental benefits of reducing oil consumption, substantial evidence exists that military and security benefits will accrue from such investments.

Unexpected Sources of Conflict

Policymakers must also think systematically about oil-security linkages when monitoring emerging security threats as the global oil industry transforms itself. With sixteen additional countries potentially exporting oil in the near future, new international dynamics will materialize, especially in Africa. Furthermore, if oil prices remain high, incentives for resource grabs will grow. Resource wars are most likely to occur in unpopulated territories or naval zones, as oil can be extracted from these areas without the need to manage a populated, potentially hostile territory. Thus, policymakers should be most concerned about disputed territories in the East China and South China Seas and naval borders in the Caspian Sea. There are already competing sovereignty claims to territory in those regions, and considerable uncertainty about the magnitude of the energy resources located there, creating conditions ripe for miscalculation and mutual suspicion. Policymakers should be especially concerned about security threats that arise from unexpected sources, such as allies' energy needs or seemingly benign actions that prompt hostile responses from rivals.

RUSSIAN GAS VICTIMS-THE DAY OF THE GAS CLOUD OVER

The last German gas cloud to be discharged against the British Front was in August, 1916. In every way it was the greatest test to which our men had been put. It was the strongest cloud attack the Germans had made - not only were the individual waves of only ten minutes' duration but the boche had more cylinders in his line than usual. According to his own admissions the bottles were put in at the rate of three every two yards and in some places two per yard. Added to this he had brought up the proportion of phosgene to the maximum that can be used. The circumstances, too, were very unfavourable to us. It must be remembered that the Battle of the Somme was in full swing, and that for once in its war history the Ypres salient, where the gas attack took place, was a "quiet" sector where divisions used up in the battle went to "rest" and reorganise. The result was that the divisions attacked were composed very largely of fresh drafts. They had lost very heavily in officers and most of the company noncommissioned gas officers had been knocked out. Their gas training was therefore not at the high standard that it had attained previous to the battle.

Added to this, a relief was going on in the trenches. This, by the way, was the second time that our fellows were caught by a gas attack during a relief. Whether it was that the boche intelligence was particularly good or whether it was simply that his luck was in is not certain, but it meant that our trenches, both the front line and the communication trenches, had just twice the number of men in them that they would have had normally. And every man, both incoming and outgoing, was carrying his complete 'Christmas Tree" rig - rifle, ammunition, full pack, haversack, greatcoat, gas masks, and all the rest of it; in some places hardly able to squeeze through the trenches in his bulky marching equipment.

Into this congestion the boche let off his gas on the eighth of August about ten O'Clock P. M. It says worlds for the steadiness of our fellows that the total casualties from the three waves he sent over remained at the same low ebb that they had reached in the June attack. Of course but for the adverse circumstances they would undoubtedly have been still lower. It is interesting to note that the position on which the attack was made - namely, the line between Bellewarde Lake and the Yser Canal - included much of the line over which the first attack of all had been made a year and a half previously. The intensity of the cloud can be realised from the fact that helmets had to be worn at a division headquarters nine miles from the point of discharge, and the gas was perceptible, though not so dangerous, many miles beyond this point.

The most distinctive feature of the whole affair was the number of men who suffered from the delayed action of the phosgene and collapsed several hours after the attack, especially if they had taken any exercise or eaten a heavy meal in between. The latter is not very likely, though it does occur, for a man even slightly gassed with phosgene feels very depressed - "fed up" and not particularly inclined for a hearty meal. But the getting of the exercise is only too easy, what with the necessary work in the trenches and the possible walk back to the aid post or the march back to rest billets in the event of a relief. It was men who had done this kind of thing who suffered most.

After the attack we received official orders that no man suffering from the effects of the gas should be allowed to walk to the dressing station, and that if possible, after a gas attack troops in the front trenches should be relieved of all fatigue and carrying work for twenty-four hours. It was also ordered that during the passage of the gas all movement should be reduced to a minimum and there should be as little talking as possible. These were very wise orders, for there had been too many officers and noncommissioned officers gassed through moving up and down to control the positions of their men and from shouting orders through their helmets. A certain amount of talking is necessary, of course, but too much of it makes a man breathe more deeply and may be just the added strain sufficient to affect his heart and cause his collapse.

Of course after a gas attack there are always a certain number of malingerers, "Skrimshankers as we call them, who affect to be gassed in order to get away from the line for a bit. These are generally spotted easily enough by the doctor men. One medical officer I knew, harassed by the number of slightly "gassed " cases who would have to be evacuated, and suspicious about the genuine character of some of them, handed round cigarettes. All those who accepted and smoked their cigarettes were kept back. Later examination showed that he was right in every case.

A similar instance that I heard of, this time in a practice attack in a camp in England, concerned a very poor specimen who pretended to be badly gassed. He was taken to the orderly room on a stretcher; but unfortunately for him the medical corps sergeant recognised him as a man who had fallen out during a march a short time before, and knew all about him. Meantime the man was feigning unconsciousness, but the sergeant winked at the Medical officer and said: "It's a pity that order about sick leave prevents. men from going home in a case like this unless they live in London. What this poor fellow needs is a couple of weeks in his own home. "

The corpse thereupon sat up and said: "That's all right, sir. I live in Bow. When can I go? " As in all the previous attacks an analysis of the casualties showed that where the helmets had been kept in good condition and had been used properly and in time they had given perfect protection. The casualties were all due to preventable causes - some of them lamentable, others humorous, had it not been for their tragedy.

Many men were gassed through taking off their helmets too soon. It is really up to the officers and noncommissioned officers who have attended a course at a gas school to decide when the atmosphere is safe, and it is not nearly so risky to do this as it sounds. All that is necessary is to let a little air in from the outside by cautiously opening up the face piece of the mask - or the skirt of the helmet in the case of the old gas bag - and sniffing cautiously. Of course if it is not done cautiously and there happens to be a lot of gas about, the rash man suffers.

A number of men were gassed through going into unprotected dugouts before they had been ventilated or through wandering into pockets of the gas after the attack. They should have been on the lookout for these patches, as the gas notoriously keeps close to the ground at night, and sheltered places are bound to remain unhealthy for much longer periods than the open. It is curious that by some vagary of the wind the cloud farther back hopped over some houses that were used as billets and affected neither the inhabitants nor the unprotected animals on the ground, whereas some fowls that were roosting in the trees and on the tops of the houses were killed. One instance that shows how carelessness spells casualty in gas warfare was that of a working party of thirty or forty men who were busy on railway work a mile or two behind the line. They had taken off their coats and gas helmets and placed them on some trucks, but when the alarm was given and a rush was made for the helmets the trucks were found to have gone.

One thing that. was done after the August attack was definitely and finally to withdraw the Vermorel sprayers for use for clearing the gas out of the trenches and dugouts. These instruments, brought up for the work of spraying fruit trees and vineyards, had done some first-class fighting of the German gas, right in the front line, as long as the gas was chlorine. But with the introduction of large quantities of phosgene the work of the sprayers was gone. They could not touch the phosgene, and consequently Tommy's dependence on them was a snare and made things more dangerous for him than if they had not been used at all. For a dugout might be sprayed and tliought, therefore, to be quite healthy to sleep in and yet contain as much phosgene as would at any rate cause minor and delayed effects.

To clear out the gas recourse was had to ventilation by means of fires and by specially constructed canvas fans. These fans were the invention of an English lady named Ayrton - the widow of the physicist of that name - and were originally intended by her for fanning back the gas cloud to the German trenches. Of course they were quite incapable of doing any such thing, but during trials with them it was found that they were quite good, after an attack, for fanning the gas out of the trenches or creating such a draft of air into a dugout or cellar as to force out the impure air from the interior.

These anti-gas fans, or flapper fans as they were called, are made of canvas supported by braces of cane and attached to a hickory handle about two feet long. The blade of the fan which looks like an immense fly swat, is hinged in two places and measures about fifteen inches square. When the fan is brought down on the ground it bends over on the back hinge and produces a sharp puff of air, in just the same way that the sudden shutting of an open book does.

By working the fans in series, one man behind another it is possible to keep a current of air going which will ventilate a room or clear out a trench in remarkably quick time. In clearing out a trench the fan is brought back over the shoulder, and this helps to "shovel" the contaminated air put of the trench after it has been brought off the ground by the lower stroke, which is more like a smart slap.

These fans are kept as trench stores, which means that they are handed over on relief to the incoming unit taking over the line of trenches. They have proved very useful, especially in skilful hands their chief value being that, unlike the sprayers, they do not distinguish between different kinds of gases and they will deal as unceremoniously with tear gas and phosgene as they do with chlorine.

By the time of the last gas-cloud attack the organisation of the British Army for defence against gas had been brought to a pretty high state of efficiency. A special branch of the gas service had been detailed for the purpose and special gas officers were appointed to the staffs of the various formations, from army down to division.

The position of divisional gas officer is no sinecure. Besides having the job of screwing up the gas discipline of his division and having a general oversight of all gas-defence training and supplies, he is responsible to the divisional commander for the preparedness of the line to meet a German gas attack. He is the "intelligence" officer of his general as regards all things pertaining to gas and has to be a walking dictionary on the subject. He has to be a great part of his time in the front trenches and it is up to him to see that all enemy blind shells, and so on, are examined and brought in if they seem to be anything new. As he must deal direct with the battalion commanders he must know them and the senior officers of each regiment personally, so as to smooth the way in getting things done. Then if a gas attack or bombardment is made he must get there quick, so as to find out all about it from personal experience.

Altogether he is a very important and busy person, and to those acquainted with his work the following incident will appeal. I happened to overhear part of a conversation between two Cockney Tommies on the road:

What's this 'ere divisional gas officer, Bill? "

"Why, he's the bloke what goes round and blows up these observation balloons."

The divisional gas officer has a number of specially trained noncommissioned officers to help him, and each company of infantry and battery of artillery has at least one noncommissioned officer. It is the first and most important job of these noncommissioned officers to help the commander in everything pertaining to defence against German gas. He assists at drills and inspections, help in the arrangement and fitting up of alarms, in the taking of wind readings and the protection of the shelters and dugouts. In his charge are placed the gas fans and the sampliner apparatus. A good company gas noncommissioned officer is a real joy and can polish up the gas discipline of the company tremendously, as well as take a lot of responsibility off the overworked company commander's shoulders. A bad noncommissioned gas officer, on the other hand, can be the direct and indirect cause of the loss of many lives when the gas attack does come. This ended the British experience of German gas-cloud attacks, for though the 35th and 36th Pioneers made three subsequent visits to the Western Front it was each time to gas the French. The last cloud attack of all was made near Nieuport, at that time in the French lines, on April 23, 1917.

Since then the only cloud attacks have been made against the Russians and the Italians. Probably the chief reason that has caused the boche to hold back with his cloud attacks has been his conclusion that they were unprofitable against well-disciplined, highly trained and thoroughly protected troops. With a limited amount of gas available he naturally chose the method that would give him the best results. For the cloud attack his cheapest target was the Russians, who were incompletely equipped with gas masks of a modern kind and who for a long time were badly disciplined in anti-gas measures. Against such troops the gas cloud is just the thing, and the Germans have estimated that ten to fifteen per cent of all troops exposed to a successful gas cloud would become casualties. This was probably true on the Russian ' Front, but was certainly not true in the West.

Then the gas cloud has almost reached its apparent limit of development. There is a limit to the number of gases that can be used from cylinders, and there is a limit to the number of cylinders that'can be discharged at one time. Besides this the gas cloud is largely dependent on infantry labour for carrying and installation, and it is mighty difficult to bring off a complete surprise owing to the time it takes to prepare an attack.

On top of all this the whole procedure is wrong as regards efficiency, for it puts up the highest concentration of gas where the boche does not want it-just in front of his own trenches instead of in ours. For all these reasons the boche during the past year has specialised on the development of his gas shells. Of course he may come back with the cloud again, and we do not relax our vigilance or it certainly would reappear. But unless he discovers something new in the cloud line, and if we keep up a high standard of training, he will not do much damage, though for that matter the same thing is true about gas shells and trench mortar bombs.

2

Bolivian Gas Conflict

The Bolivian gas conflict was a social confrontation in Bolivia reaching its peak in 2003, centering on the exploitation of the country's vast natural gas reserves. The expression can be extended to refer to the general conflict in Bolivia over the exploitation of gas resources, thus including the 2005 protests and the election of Evo Morales as president. Before these protests, Bolivia had seen a series of similar earlier protests during the Cochabamba protests of 2000, which were against the privatization of the municipal water supply.

Overview

The conflict had its roots in grievances over the government's economic policies concerning natural gas, as well as coca eradication policies, corruption and violent military responses against strikes. On a larger scale, it can be traced to Bolivia's colonization since the 15th century and the subsequent exploitation of its natural resources (e.g., the mines of Potosí).

The "Bolivian gas war" thus came to a head in October 2003, leading to the resignation of President Gonzalo Sánchez de Lozada (aka "Goni"). Strikes and road blocks mounted by indigenous and labour groups (including the COB trade union) brought the country to a standstill. Violent suppression by the Bolivian armed forces left some 60 people dead in October 2003, mostly inhabitants of El Alto, located on the *Altiplano* above the capital city of La Paz.

The governing coalition disintegrated forcing Goni to resign and leave the country on October 18, 2003. He was succeeded by the vice president, Carlos Mesa, who put the gas issue to a referendum on July 18, 2004. In May 2005, under duress from protesters, the Bolivian congress enacted a new hydrocarbons law, increasing the state's royalties from natural gas exploitation. However, protesters, who included Evo Morales and Felipe Quispe, demanded full nationalization of hydrocarbon resources, and the increased participation of Bolivia's indigenous majority, mainly composed of Aymaras and Quechuas, in the political life of the country. On June 6, 2005, Mesa was forced to resign as tens of thousands of protesters caused daily blockades to La Paz from the rest of the country. Morales' election at the end of 2005 was met with enthusiasm by the social movements, because he was, as the leader of left-wing MAS, one of the staunchest opponents to the exportation of the gas without corresponding industrialization in Bolivia. On May 1, 2006, President Morales signed a decree stating that all gas reserves were to be nationalized: "the state recovers ownership, possession and total and absolute control" of hydrocarbons. The 2006 announcement was met by applause on La Paz's main plaza, where Vice President Alvaro Garcia told the crowd that the government's energy-related revenue would jump US$320 million to US$780 million in 2007, continuing a trend where revenues had expanded nearly sixfold between 2002 and 2006.

BACKGROUND

Gas reserves of Bolivia

The central issue was Bolivia's large natural gas reserves and the prospect for their future sale and use. The Bolivian gas reserves are the second largest in South America after Venezuela, and exploration after the privatization of the national oil company YPFB showed that proven natural gas reserves were 600% higher than previously known. The cash-poor, state-owned company could not afford the exploration costs. These reserves mainly are located in the southeastern Tarija

Department, which contains 85% of gas and petrol reserves. According to the United States Department of Energy, another 10.6% is located within the department of Santa Cruz and 2.5% in the Cochabamba Department. After further exploration from 1996 to 2002, the estimated size of the probable gas reserves was calculated to be 12.5 times larger, passing from 4.24×10^{12} cu ft (120 km^3) to 52.3×10^{12} cu ft (1,480 km^3). This number has declined somewhat to 48×10^{12} cu ft (1,400 km^3) probable reserves. The proven reserves are 26.7×10^{12} cu ft (760 km^3). With the declining importance of tin mines, those reserves accounted for the majority of foreign investment in Bolivia. The price which Bolivia is paid for its natural gas is roughly US$3.25 to Brazil and $US3.18 to Argentina.Other sources state that Brazil pays between US$3.15/MMBtu and US$3.60/MMBtu (not including US$1.50/MMBtu in Petrobras extraction and transportation costs). The price of gas in the US as a whole is between US$5.85/MMBtu (May 21, 2006), US$7.90/MMBtu (April 2006) & US$6.46/MMtu (June 2006), although several years ago the price of natural gas spiked at $14 in California due to lack of pipeline capacity to and within California as well as due to electricity outages. While according to *Le Monde*, Brazil and Argentina pay US$2 per thousand cubic meter of gas, which costs from $12 to $15 in California.

In 1994, a contract with Brazil was passed, two years before 1996's privatization of the 70-year-old, state-owned *Yacimientos Petroliferos Fiscales de Bolivia* (YPFB). The construction of the Bolivia-Brazil gas pipeline cost US$2.2 billion.

A consortium called Pacific LNG was formed to exploit the newly discovered reserves. The consortium comprised the British companies BG Group and BP, and Spain's Repsol YPF. Repsol is one of three companies that dominate the gas sector in Bolivia, along with Petrobras and Total. A plan costing US$6 billion was drawn to build a pipeline to the Pacificcoast, where the gas would be processed and liquefied before being shipped to Mexico and the United States (Baja California and California), through a Chilean port, for example Iquique. The 2003 Lozada deal was opposed heavily by Bolivian society, in part because of nationalism (Bolivia feels resentment after the territorial losses of the War of the Pacific in the late 19th century, which deprived it of the Litoral province and hence access to the sea).

Government ministers hoped to use the gas profits to bolster the sagging Bolivian economy and claimed the money would be invested exclusively in health and education. Opponents argued that under the current law, the exportation of the gas as a raw material would give Bolivia only 18% of the future profits, or US$40 million to US$70 million per year. They further argued that exporting the gas so cheaply would be the latest case of foreign exploitation of Bolivia's natural resources, starting with its silver and gold from the 17th century. They demanded that a plant be built in Bolivia to process the gas and that domestic consumption had to be met before export. As *Le Monde* puts it, "two reasons plead for the industrial exploitation of the gas, which the multinational companies now have the capacities of doing. The first is related to the necessity of satisfying the Bolivians' energy needs. The second demonstrates the interest of exporting a more profitable product rather than selling raw material". According to the French newspaper, only La Paz, El Alto, Sucre, Potosí, Camiri and Santa Cruz are now connected to the gas network; making an interior network which would reach all Bolivians would cost $1.5 billion, notwithstanding a central gas pipeline to link the various regions together. According to Carlos Miranda, an independent expert quoted by *Le Monde*, the best industrialisation project is the petrochemicalcomplex proposed by the Brazilian Braskem firm, which would create 40 000 direct or indirect jobs and cost $1.4 billion. This figure is equivalent to the amount so far invested by Repsol, Total and Petrobras.

Indigenous communities

Bolivia, like much of Latin America, is a highly class-segregated society, in this case along ethnic lines: European-Indio. European descendants tend to monopolize political and economic power and in fact the republican institutions are drawn along the lines of European schools of thought with little or no adjustment to the indigenous tradition. This makes it much harder for the indigenous to integrate into society and to achieve personal success. Since the late 1990s, the indigenous communities have become radicalized throughout the Andes, pressing for political reform in Peru, Ecuador and Bolivia, loosely coordinated in the Pachacuti movement. The Movement Toward Socialism (MAS) is perhaps the strongest political expression of this movement in Bolivia, coordinating a wide range of community-based organizations mostly reflecting Aymara political aspirations.

Santa Cruz autonomy movement

The wealthier, eastern departments of Santa Cruz, Beni, Tarija, and Pando recently had been mobilizing in favor of autonomy. Important issues were opposition to the seizure of resources though nationalization, the confiscation of land from local control by outside ethnic groups (mainly the Aymara and Quechua), and a greater share of taxes collected within Santa Cruz to support roads and schools. Community leaders are supported by the Comite Pro Santa Cruz, local co-ops, and by business organizations such as cattle ranchers and farmers. A strike against the new constitution was recently held which was observed in Santa Cruz, Beni, Tarija, and Pando. Tensions have been raised by the cultural and philosophical rift exposed by the push for a new constitution. As a basis for a new constitution, the western, Altiplano-based MAS party envisions a "council of indigenous peoples" along with a curtailment of private ownership, while Santa Cruz looks to western culture and capitalism. Cultural divisions exist because people in eastern Bolivia, called "Cambas" (meaning "friends" in Guarani), are primarily of mestizo descent (mix of European and several native tribes the largest of which are the Guaraní), while the western Altiplano is dominated by a small white elite and a historically oppressed Quechua and Aymara majority.

The first signs of the modern autonomy movement occurred in 2005 when a march for autonomy was attended by hundreds of thousands of people. A result of this was the change in law to allow the election of departmental prefects. Another area of tension was the result of ongoing population shifts and the resulting demands for proportionally greater representation in Bolivia's Congress to reflect these shifts by Santa Cruz. A compromise was reached to allow Santa Cruz to receive some of the seats warranted by population growth, and for the highlands to keep seats despite population losses.

Left-wing intellectuals Walter Chávez and Álvaro García Linera (the current Bolivian Vice President and MAS party member) published an article in the *Monthly Review* asserting that autonomy has been historically a demand of the Santa Cruz region, "contemporarily imbued with far-right, populist sentiments." They also qualified Santa Cruz autonomy as a "bourgeois ideology" of the "free market, foreign investment, racism, etc.", which pits the "modern", "whiter" Santa Cruz elite against the short, dark-skinned and anti-capitalistAymara and Quechua peoples of the western region of Bolivia.

Dispute over pipeline route

The dispute arose in early 2002, when the administration of President Jorge Quiroga proposed building the pipeline through neighboring Chile to the port of Mejillones, the most direct route to the Pacific Ocean. However, antagonism towards Chile runs deep in Bolivia because of the loss of Bolivia's Pacific coastline to Chile in the War of the Pacific (1879–1884).

Bolivians began campaigning against the Chilean option, arguing instead that the pipeline should be routed north through the Peruvian port of Ilo, 260 km further from the gas fields than Mejillones, or, better yet, first industrialized in Bolivia. According to Chilean estimates, the Mejillones option would be $600 million cheaper. Peru, however, claimed the difference in cost would be no more than $300 million. Bolivian proponents of the Peruvian option say it would also benefit the economy of the northern region of Bolivia through which the pipeline would pass.

Supporters of the Chile pipeline argued that U.S. financiers would be unlikely to develop processing facilities within Bolivia. Meanwhile, the Peruvian government, eager to promote territorial and economic integration, offered Bolivia a special economic zone for 99 years for exporting the gas at Ilo, the right of free passage, and the concession of a 10 km^2 area, including a port, that would be exclusively under Bolivian administration.

President Jorge Quiroga postponed the decision shortly before leaving office in July 2002 and left this highly contentious issue to his successor. It was thought Quiroga did not want to jeopardize his chances of re-election as president in the 2007 elections. After winning the 2002 presidential election Gonzalo Sánchez de Lozada expressed his preference for the Mejillones option but made no "official" decision. The Gas War led to his resignation in October 2003.

Escalation

The social conflict escalated in September 2003 with protests and road blockages paralyzing large parts of the country, leading to increasingly violent confrontations with the Bolivian armed forces. The insurrection was spearheaded by Bolivia's indigenous majority, who accused Sánchez de Lozada of pandering to the US government's "war on drugs" and blamed him for failing to improve living standards in Bolivia. On September 8,650 Aymaras started a hunger strike to protest against the state detention of a villager. The man detained was one of the heads of the village, and was imprisoned for having sentenced to the death penalty two young men in a "community justice" trial. On September 19, the National Coordination for the Defense of Gas mobilized 30,000 people in Cochabamba and 50,000 in La Paz to demonstrate against the pipeline. The following day six Aymara villagers, including an eight-year-old girl, were killed in a confrontation in the town of Warisata. Government forces used planes and helicopters to circumvent the strikers and evacuate several hundred foreign and Bolivian tourists from Sorata who had been stranded by the road blockades for five days.

In response to the shootings, Bolivia's Labor Union (COB) called a general strike on September 29 that paralyzed the country with road closures. Union leaders insisted they would continue until the government backed down on its decision. Poorly armed Aymara community militias drove the army and police out of Warisata and the towns of Sorata and Achacachi, equipped only with traditional Aymara sling shotsand guns from the 1952 Bolivian National Revolution. Eugenio Rojas, leader of the regional strike committee, declared that if the government refused to negotiate in Warisata, then the insurgent Aymara communities would surround La Paz and cut it off from the rest of the country — a tactic employed in the Túpaj Katari uprising of 1781. Felipe Quispe, leader of the Indigenous Pachakuti Movement (MIP), stated that he would not participate in dialogue with the government until the military withdrew from blockaded areas. The government refused to negotiate with Quispe, claiming that he did not have the authority to represent the *campesino* movement.

As the protests continued, protesters in El Alto, a sprawling indigenous city of 750,000 people on the periphery of La Paz, proceeded to block key access routes to the capital causing severe fuel and food shortages. They also demanded the resignation of Sánchez de Lozada and his ministers, Yerko Kukoc, Minister of Government, and Carlos Sánchez de Berzaín, Minister of Defense, who were held responsible for the Warisata massacre. Protesters also voiced their opposition to the Free Trade Area of the Americas agreement that was at the time under negotiation by the US and Latin American countries (since the November 2005 Mar del Plata Summit of the Americas, it has been put on stand-by).

MARTIAL LAW IN EL ALTO

On October 12, 2003 the government imposed martial law in El Alto after sixteen people were shot by the police and several dozen wounded in violent clashes which erupted when a caravan of oil trucks escorted by police and soldiers deploying tanks and heavy-caliber machine guns tried to breach a barricade. On October 13, the administration of Sánchez de Lozada suspended the gas project "until consultations have been conducted [with the Bolivian people]." However, Vice President Carlos Mesa deplored what he referred to as the "excessive force" used in El Alto (80 dead) and withdrew his support for Sánchez de Lozada. The Minister of Economic Development, Jorge Torrez, of the MIR party, also resigned.

The United States Department of State issued a statement on October 13 declaring its support for Sánchez de Lozada, calling for "Bolivia's political leaders [to] publicly express their support for democratic and constitutional order. The international community and the United States will not tolerate any interruption of constitutional order and will not support any regime that results from undemocratic means".

On October 18, Sánchez de Lozada's governing coalition was fatally weakened when the *New Republic Force* party withdrew its support. He was forced to resign and was replaced by his vice president, Carlos Mesa, a former journalist. The strikes and roadblocks were lifted. Mesa promised that no civilians would be killed by police or army forces during his presidency. Despite dramatic unrest during his time in office, he respected this promise.

Among his first actions as president, Mesa promised a referendum on the gas issue and appointed several indigenous people to cabinet posts. On July 18, 2004, Mesa put the issue of gas nationalization to a referendum. On May 6, 2005, the Bolivian Congress passed a new law raising taxes from 18% to 32% on profits made by foreign companies on the extraction of oil and gas. Mesa failed to either sign or veto the law, so by law Senate President Hormando Vaca Diez was required to sign it into law on May 17. Many protesters felt this law was inadequate and demanded full nationalization of the gas and oil industry.

The 2005 Hydrocarbons Law

On May 6, 2005 the long-awaited Hydrocarbons Law was finally approved by the Bolivian Congress. On May 17 Mesa again refused to either sign or veto the controversial law, thus constitutionally requiring Senate President Hormando Vaca Díez to sign the measure and put it into effect.

The new law returned legal ownership to the state of all hydrocarbons and natural resources, maintained royalties at 18 percent, but increased taxes from 16 to 32 percent. It gave the government control of the commercialization of the resources and allowed for continuous government control with annual audits. It also ordered companies to consult with indigenous groups who live on land containing gas deposits. The law stated that the 76 contracts signed by foreign firms must be renegotiated before 180 days. This has not yet been done. Protesters argued that the new law did not go far enough to protect the natural resources from exploitation by foreign corporations, demanding a complete nationalizationof the gas and process in Bolivia.

Due to the uncertainty over renegotiation of contracts, foreign firms have practically stopped investing in the gas sector. Foreign investment virtually came to a standstill in the second half of 2005. Shortages in supply – very similar to those observed in Argentina after the 2001 price-fixing – are deepening in diesel, LPG, and begin to be apparent in natural gas. The May–June social unrest affected the supply of hydrocarbons products to the internal market, principally LPG and natural gas to the occidental region. Brazil implemented a contingency plan – led by the Energy and Mines Minister – to mitigate any potential impact from gas export curtailment. Although the supply was never curtailed, the social unrest in Bolivia created a strong sensation that security of supply could not be guaranteed. Occasional social action has continued to affect the continuity of supply, especially valve-closing actions.

CARLOS MESA'S JUNE 2005 RESIGNATION

The protests

Over 80,000 people participated in the May 2005 protests. Tens of thousands of people each day walked from El Alto to the capital La Paz, where protesters effectively shut down the city, bringing transportation to a halt through strikes and blockades, and engaging in street battles with police. The protestors demanded the nationalisation of the gas industry and reforms to give more power to the indigenous majority, who were mainly Aymaras from the impoverished highlands. They were pushed back by the police with tear gas and rubber bullets, while many of the miners involved in the protests came armed with dynamite.

May 24, 2005 More than 10,000 Aymara peasant farmers from the twenty highland provinces came down from *El Alto*'s Ceja neighborhood into La Paz to protest. On May 31, 2005 residents of El Alto and the Aymara peasant farmers returned to La Paz. More than 50,000 people covered an area of nearly 100 square kilometers. The next day, the first regiment of the National Police decided, by consensus, not to repress the protests and were internally reprimanded by the government.

On June 2, as the protests raged on, President Mesa announced two measures, designed to placate the indigenous protesters on the one hand and the Santa Cruz autonomy movement on the other: elections for a new constitutional assembly and a referendum on regional autonomy, both set for October 16. However, both sides rejected Mesa's call: the Pro-Santa Cruz Civic Committee declared its own referendum on autonomy for August 12, while in El Alto protesters began to cut off gasoline to La Paz.

Approximately half a million people mobilized in the streets of La Paz, on June 6, and President Mesa subsequently offered his resignation. Riot police used tear gas as miners amongst the demonstrators traditionally set off dynamite in clashes near the presidential palace, while a strike brought traffic to a standstill. However, Congress failed to meet for several days owing to the "insecurity" of meeting as protests raged nearby. Many members of Congress found themselves unable to physically attend the sessions. Senate President Hormando Vaca Díez decided to move the sessions to Bolivia's alternate capital, Sucre, in an attempt to avoid the protesters. Radical farmers occupied oil wells owned by transnational companies, and blockaded border crossings. Mesa ordered the military to airlift food to La Paz, which remained totally blockaded.

Vaca Diez and House of Delegates president, Mario Cossío, were the two next in the line of succession to become President. However, they were strongly disliked by the protesters, and each declared they would not accept succession to the Presidency, finally promoting Edwardo Rodriguez, Supreme Court Chief Justice, to the Presidency. Considered apolitical and hence trustworthy by most, his administration was a temporary one until elections could be held. Protesters quickly disbanded in many areas, and like many times in Bolivia's past, major political upheavals were taken as a normal part of the political process.

Caretaker President Rodriguez proceeded to implement the Hydrocarbons Law. The new tax IDH has been levied from the companies that are paying 'under reserve'. A number of upstream gas companies have invoked Bilateral Investment Protection Treaties and entered the conciliation phase with the state of Bolivia. The treaties are a step towards a court hearing before the International Centre for Settlement of Investment Disputes (ICSID), dependent of the World Bank, which could force Bolivia to pay indemnities to the companies.

Concerns of possible US intervention

A military training agreement with Asunción (Paraguay), giving immunity to US soldiers, caused some concern after media reports initially reported that a base housing 20,000 US soldiers was being built at Mariscal Estigarribia within 200 km of Argentina and Bolivia, and 300 km of Brazil, near an airport which could receive large planes (B-52, C-130 Hercules, etc.) which the Paraguayan Air Forces do not have. According to the *Clarín*, an Argentinian newspaper, the US military base is strategic because of its location near the *Triple Frontera* between Paraguay, Brazil and Argentina; its proximity to the Guarani aquifer; and, finally, its proximity to Bolivia (less than 200 km) at the same "moment that Washington's magnifying glass goes on the *Altiplano* and points toward Venezuelan Hugo Chávez

— the regional demon according to Bush's administration — as the instigator of the instability in the region" (*Clarín*). Later reports indicated that 400 US troops would be deployed in Paraguay over 18 months for training and humanitarian missions consisting of 13 detachments numbering less than 50 personnel each. The Paraguayan administration as well as Bush's administration denied that the airport would be used as a US military base, or that there would be any other US base in Paraguay.

Other countries

The social conflicts of the last few years have paralyzed Bolivia's political life. The unpopularity of the neoliberal Washington consensus, a set of economic strategies implemented by Gonzalo de Lozada's administration, set the stage for the 2006 election of president Evo Morales, the country's first indigenous president. In the meantime, Chile promptly started to build several coastal terminals to receive shipments of liquefied natural gas from Indonesia, Australia and other sources. Other South American countries are contemplating other ways to secure gas supplies: one project aims at linking the Camisea gas reserves in Peru to Argentina, Brazil, Chile, Uruguay and Paraguay. Linking Pisco (south of Peru) to Tocopilla (north of Chile) with a 1200 km pipeline would cost $2 billion. However, experts doubt the Camisea reserves are enough for all the Southern Cone countries.

Another 8,000 km gas pipeline (Gran Gasoducto del Sur) has been proposed that would link Venezuela to Argentina via Brazil. Its cost is estimated between $8 and $12 billion.

While Argentina and Chile are large consumers of gas (50 percent and 25 percent respectively), other South American countries are a lot less dependent.

NATIONALIZATION OF NATURAL GAS INDUSTRY

On May 1, 2006 president Evo Morales signed a decree stating that all gas reserves were to be nationalized: "the state recovers ownership, possession and total and absolute control" of hydrocarbons. He thus realized his electoral promises, declaring that "We are not a government of mere promises: we follow through on what we propose and what the people demand". The announcement was timed to coincide with Labor Day on May 1. Ordering the military and engineers of YPFB, the state firm, to occupy and secure energy installations, he gave foreign companies a six-month "transition period" to re-negotiate contracts, or face expulsion. Nevertheless, president Morales stated that the nationalization would not take the form of expropriations or confiscations. Vice President Álvaro García said in La Paz's main plaza that the government's energy-related revenue will jump to $780 million next year, expanding nearly sixfold from 2002. Among the 53 installations affected by the measure are those of Brazil's Petrobras, one of Bolivia's largest investors, which controls 14% of the country's gas reserves. Brazil's Energy Minister, Silas Rondeau, reacted by considering the move as "unfriendly" and contrary to previous understandings between his country and Bolivia. Petrobras, Spain's Repsol YPF, UK gas and oil producer BG Group Plc and France's Total are the main gas companies present in the country. According to Reuters, "Bolivia's actions echo what Venezuelan President Hugo Chávez, a Morales ally, did in the world's fifth-largest oil exporter with forced contract migrations and retroactive tax hikes — conditions that oil majors largely agreed to accept." YPFB would pay foreign companies for their services, offering about 50 percent of the value of production, although the decree indicated that companies at the country's two largest gas fields would get just 18 percent.

Negotiations between the Bolivian government and the foreign companies intensified during the week leading up to the deadline of Saturday October 28, 2006. On Friday an agreement was reached with two of the companies (including Total) and by the deadline on Saturday the rest of the ten companies (including Petrobras and Repsol YPF) operating in Bolivia had also come to an agreement. Full details of the new contracts have not been released, but the objective of raising government share of revenues from the two major fields from 60 percent to 82 percent seems to have been achieved. Revenue share for the government from minor fields is set at 60 percent. During the six month negotiation period talks with the Brazilian company Petrobras had proven especially difficult. Petrobras had refused raises or reduction to a mere service provider. As a result of stalled talks Bolivian energy minister Andres Soliz Rada resigned in October and was replaced by Carlos Villegas. "We are obligated to live with Brazil in a marriage without divorce, because we both need each other", said Evo Morales in the contract signing ceremony underlining the mutual dependency of Brazil on Bolivian gas and of Bolivia on Petrobras in gas production.

Reaction

On December 15, 2007 the regions of Santa Cruz, Tarija, Beni, and Pando declared autonomy from the central government. They also moved to achieve full independence from Bolivia's new constitution.

THE PROTESTERS

Miners

Miners from the Bolivian trade union *Central Obrera Boliviana* (COB) have also been very active in the recent protests. Recently they have been active against propositions to privatize pensions. They have been known for letting off very loud explosions of dynamite in the recent protests.

Coca farmers

Shortly after the law passed, Evo Morales, an Aymara Indian, *cocalero*, and leader of the opposition party Movement Towards Socialism (MAS), took a moderate position calling the new law "middle ground". However, as the protests progressed, Morales has come out in favor of nationalization and new elections.

Protesters in Cochabamba

Oscar Olivera was a prominent leader in the 2001 protests in Cochabamba against the privatization of water in Bolivia and has also become a leading figure. Specifically the protesters in Cochabamba, Bolivia's fourth largest city, have cut off the main roads in the city and are calling for a new Constituent Assembly as well as nationalization.

Indigenous and peasant groups in Santa Cruz

Indians in the eastern lowland department of Santa Cruz have also become active in the recent disputes over nationalization of the gas and oil industry. They are composed of indigenous groups such as the Guaraní, Ayoreo, Chiquitano and the Guyarayos, as opposed to the highland Indians (Aymara and Quechua). They have been active in recent land disputes and the main organization representing this faction is known as the "Confederacion de pueblos indigenas de Bolivia" (CIDOB). The CIDOB after initially offering support to MAS, the party of Bolivia's new president, have come to believe that they were deceived by the Bolivian government. The MAS, which is based in the highlands, is no more willing to grant them voice than the previous governments whose power was also based from the highlands. Another smaller more radical group called the "Landless Peasant Movement" (MST) which is somewhat similar to the Landless Workers' Movement in Brazil, and is composed mainly of immigrants from the western part of the country. Recently, Guaraní Indians from this group have taken oil fields run by Spain's Repsol YPF and the United Kingdom's BP and have forced them to stop production.

Felipe Quispe and peasant farmers

Felipe Quispe is a radical Aymara leader who wishes to return control of the country from what he sees as the "white elite" to the indigenous Aymaran people who make up the majority of the country's population. Therefore, he is in favor of an independent "Aymaran state". Quispe is the leader of the Pachakutik Indigenous Movement, that won six seats in the Congress and the secretary general of the United Peasants Union of Bolivia in the 2002 Bolivian elections.

3

Russia–Ukraine Gas Disputes and Conflict

The Russia–Ukraine gas disputes refer to a number of disputes between Ukrainian oil and gas company Naftohaz Ukrayiny and Russian gas supplier Gazprom over natural gas supplies, prices, and debts. These disputes have grown beyond simple business disputes into transnational political issues—involving political leaders from several countries—that threaten natural gas supplies in numerous European countries dependent on natural gas imports from Russian suppliers, which are transported through Ukraine. Russia provides approximately a quarter of the natural gas consumed in the European Union; approximately 80% of those exports travel through pipelines across Ukrainian soil prior to arriving in the EU.

A serious dispute began in March 2005 over the price of natural gas supplied and the cost of transit. During this conflict, Russia claimed Ukraine was not paying for gas, but diverting that which was intended to be exported to the EU from the pipelines. Ukrainian officials at first denied the accusation, but later Naftogaz admitted that natural gas intended for other European countries was retained and used for domestic needs. The dispute reached a high point on 1 January 2006, when Russia cut off all gas supplies passing through Ukrainian territory. On 4 January 2006, a preliminary agreement between Russia and Ukraine was achieved, and the supply was restored.

The situation calmed until October 2007 when new disputes began over Ukrainian gas debts. This led to reduction of gas supplies in March 2008. During the last months of 2008, relations once again became tense when Ukraine and Russia could not agree on the debts owed by Ukraine.

In January 2009, this disagreement resulted in supply disruptions in many European nations, with eighteen European countries reporting major drops in or complete cut-offs of their gas supplies transported through Ukraine from Russia. In September 2009 officials from both countries stated they felt the situation was under control and that there would be no more conflicts over the topic, at least until the Ukrainian 2010 presidential elections. However, in October 2009, another disagreement arose about the amount of gas Ukraine would import from Russia in 2010. Ukraine intended to import less gas in 2010 as a result of reduced industry needs because of its economic recession; however, Gazprom insisted that Ukraine fulfill its contractual obligations and purchase the previously agreed upon quantities of gas.

On 8 June 2010, a Stockholm court of arbitration ruled Naftohaz of Ukraine must return 12.1 billion cubic metres (430 billion cubic feet) of gas to RosUkrEnergo, a Swiss-basedcompany in which Gazprom controls a 50% stake. Russia accused Ukrainian side of diverting gas from pipelines passing through Ukraine in 2009. Several high-ranking Ukrainian officials stated the return "would not be quick".

Russia plans to completely abandon gas supplies to Europe through Ukraine after 2018. Gazprom has already substantially reduced the volumes of gas it transits across Ukraine, and expressed its intention of reducing the level further by means of transit diversification pipelines (Nord Stream, Turkish Stream, etc).

HISTORICAL BACKGROUND

After the dissolution of the Soviet Union, oil import prices to Ukraine reached world market levels in 1993. However, gas import prices and transit fees remained below European levels for Russian exports to Europe through pipelines in Ukraine; these were set in bilateral negotiations. At the same time Ukraine remained the main transit corridor for Russia's gas export. In 2004–2005, 80% of Russian gas exports to the European Union were made through Ukrainian Territory. Two-thirds of Gazprom's revenue comes from the sale of gas that crosses Ukraine.

Ukraine's own annual gas consumption in 2004–2005 was around 80 billion cubic metres (2.8 trillion cubic feet), of which around 20 billion cubic metres (710 billion cubic feet) were produced domestically, 36 billion cubic metres (1.3 trillion cubic feet) were bought from Turkmenistan, and 17 billion cubic metres (600 billion cubic feet) were received from Russia in exchange for transport of Russian natural gas. The remaining 8 billion cubic metres (280 billion cubic feet) were purchased from Russia. The gas trading system differed substantially from the gas sale to the European Union and caused problems in the form of large-scale deliveries of relatively cheap Russian gas causing an increase of energy-intensive industries and supporting Ukraine's status as one of the world's least energy-efficient countries and largest gas importers, the accumulation of Ukrainian debts and non-payment of same, unsanctioned diversion of gas and alleged theft from the transit system, and Russian pressure on Ukraine to hand over infrastructure in return for relief of debts accumulated over natural gas transactions.

Gas trading was conducted under a framework of bilateral intergovernmental agreements which provided for sales, transit volumes, gas prices, gas storage, and other issues such as the establishment of production joint ventures. Commercial agreements were negotiated between the relevant companies within the guidelines and dictates of that framework and supplemented by annual agreements specifying exact prices and volumes for the following year. Gas sales prices and transit tariffs were determined in relationship to each other. Commercial agreements and trade relations have been nontransparent and trade has been conducted via intermediaries such as Itera, EuralTransGaz, and RosUkrEnergo. RosUkrEnergo's involvement in the Russian-Ukrainian gas trade has been controversial. There are allegations that the company is controlled by Semion Mogilevich and its beneficiaries include strategically placed officials in the Russian and Ukrainian gas industries and governmental structures related to the energy sector.Russian Prime Minister Vladimir Putin has made accusations that RosUkrEnergo is owned by a business ally of Ukraine's ex-president, Viktor Yushchenko. The Ukrainian investigation into RosUkrEnergo, during Yulia Tymoshenko's first term as Prime Minister, was closed after she was fired by Yushchenko in September 2005.

According to a contract between Gazprom and Naftohaz signed on 21 June 2002, payment for the transfer of Russian natural gas through the Ukrainian pipeline system had been made in exchange for no more than 15% of the gas pumped through Ukrainian territory to be taken in lieu of cash. This contract was supposed to be valid until the end of 2013. On 9 August 2004, the two companies signed an addendum to the contract, according to which the amount of gas given as a payment was calculated based on a tariff of US$1.09 for the transportation of 1,000 cubic meters of natural gas over a distance of 100 kilometres (62 mi); the addendum further stated the price of the natural gas supplied to Ukraine was to be $50 per 1,000 cubic meters (approximately $1.40 per million Btu). This price was constant notwithstanding the gas prices in the European markets.

According to the addendum the price was not subject to change until the end of 2009. Gazprom argued that this addendum was only applicable provided that the two countries sign an annual intergovernmental protocol that has higher legal status for specifying the terms of gas transit. According to Gazprom, the addendum becomes void as the annual protocol had not been signed for 2006 under the required terms. Russia claimed that Gazprom's subsidies to the Ukrainian economy amounted to billions of dollars.

According to the agreement of 2006, RosUkrEnergo was to receive no more than 20 percent of the total delivered gas, which in 2007 was 15 billion cubic metres (530 billion cubic feet) of 73 billion cubic metres (2.6 trillion cubic feet).

UKRAINE AS TRANSIT ROUTE OF NATURAL GAS

Ukraine remains the main transit route for Russian natural gas sold to Europe, which earns Ukraine about $3 billion a year in transit fees, making it the country's most lucrative export service. Following Russia's launch of the Nord Stream pipeline, which bypasses Ukraine, gas transit volumes have been steadily decreasing. In 2004 more than 120 bcm of Russian gas was transported through Ukraine; this figure dropped to just 84 bcm in 2012.

Russia–Ukraine gas disputes left many countries with a significant drop in their supplies when Russia cut off all natural gas supplies passing through Ukraine in 2009 and 2006.

Shale gas

Ukraine has Europe's third-largest shale gas reserves at 1.2 trillion cubic meters (tcm). There are two potentially large shale gas fields. The Yuzivska gas field located in Donetsk Oblast (province) and Kharkiv Oblast; and the Olesska field in Lviv Oblast and Ivano-Frankivsk Oblast.

Ukraine signed a shale gas 50-year production sharing agreement with Royal Dutch Shell on 25 January 2013 involving the Yuzivska gas field. The $10 billion deal was the largest foreign direct investment ever for Ukraine.

Full shale gas production depends on successful results from 15 test wells. Ukraine expects commercial shale gas extraction in 2017. On 13 September 2013 Ukrainian Prime Minister Mykola Azarov stated that the (containing all expenditures) price of shale gas will be $120–130 per 1,000 cubic meters.

By 2030 a production of 6-11 bcm of shale gas a year is wanted by the Ukrainian Government plans.

NEW RUSSIAN GAS EXPORT PROJECTS - FROM PIPE DREAMS TO PIPELINES

In the twelve months since the collapse of global oil prices and the imposition of Western economic sanctions against Russia, the number of new Russian gas export project announcements has skyrocketed. Only last month, Gazprom signed a memorandum of understanding (MOU) with three European companies to build a second large gas pipeline system under the Baltic Sea called Nord Stream II. This was preceded by the announcement in December by President Vladimir Putin himself of the cancellation of the ambitious South Stream gas pipeline under the Black Sea to be replaced by an equally grandiose project, soon to be dubbed Turkish Stream. Both Nord Stream II and Turkish Stream are designed to bypass the critical transit route through Ukraine utilized by 40 to 50 percent of Russia's current gas exports to Europe. Russia and Gazprom's position on whether gas transit through Ukraine will continue after the current agreement expires in the not-too-distant future flip-flopped within a matter of weeks recently – first proclaiming that all transit will cease after 2019, then declaring that negotiation of a new deal has been ordered by President Putin.

In the past year, we have also seen the supposed conclusion of not one but two large gas deals with China. Together with numerous previously proposed liquefied natural gas (LNG) and export pipeline projects, this picture is enough to make even a seasoned energy observer's head spin. To make matters worse, the mainstream press tends to report each one of these announcements, no matter how fanciful, as if they are all realistic projects that will be completed by the notional target dates even as Russia's financial position continues to deteriorate. The total cost of these projects is somewhere between $150 and $200 billion, and it is unlikely that Russia (even together with its prospective partners) could muster the necessary capital to complete most of them amidst Russia's low oil revenue, budget deficits, and falling GDP. Instead, the raft of announcements, postponements, and cancellations in June and July of 2015 suggest that Russia is groping for a viable gas export strategy.

To clarify this confusing picture, we present a list of yet-to-be completed gas export projects that Russia has announced to date, background information on each, and a simple assessment of their likelihood of success in ascending order of feasibility, from the most far-fetched to the most realistic. We focused our short analysis primarily on economic and commercial viability rather than political or geopolitical desirability. Obviously governments have the ability to subsidize selectively economically suboptimal projects (and Russia has an outstanding track record for doing so), but this is beyond the scope of this exercise. In contrast to alarmist geopolitical readings of recent Russian announcements, we hope to show which prospective projects make the most economic and commercial sense, and to demonstrate that because of the significant obstacles facing most of these projects, Russia's recent gas export expansionism does not pose the strategic threat that some Western policymakers perceive.

Vladivostok LNG (postponed) and the Sakhalin-Hokkaido Pipeline (hypothetical)

A Framework Agreement of Cooperation was signed between Gazprom and the Japanese Ministry of Economy, Trade, and Industry to build an LNG export terminal near the far-eastern Russian warm-water port of Vladivostok in 2005. Vladivostok LNG was estimated to cost roughly $7.5 billion, and was scheduled to begin exporting 5 million tons of gas annually (mmta) in 2018, eventually reaching a full capacity of 15 mmta. The facility would have shipped Gazprom gas from eastern Siberia and Sakhalin Island to Japanese LNG import terminals, but the project was postponed in June 2015 as Gazprom shifted its focus to supplying the Chinese market. The economic logic of shipping gas a great distance overland in order to liquefy it for export was never compelling. It doubles the cost of transporting gas to market, thus leading to much lower profits for gas producers.

Japanese lawmakers and companies have also expressed interest in several different undersea pipeline projects to supply Japan with gas from Sakhalin Island. The most recent proposal, reportedly made by Russia in November 2014, would link Sakhalin with Japan's northern Hokkaido Island. In May 2015, Tokyo Gas stated its interest in constructing a $3.5 billion gas pipeline from Russia to central Japan, likely passing through Hokkaido. While Russia's large natural gas supply and post-Fukushima Japan's growing demand make them natural trade partners, delivering Russian gas to areas of demand in Japan by pipe might be difficult. Some experts have claimed that seismic activity might endanger any undersea pipeline to Japan, and Japan currently lacks a domestic natural gas distribution network, relying instead on coastal power plants to convert imported gas to electricity and distribute it to consumers via the national power grid. This infrastructural gap favors Japan's continued reliance on LNG rather than pipe gas for its imports.

Trans-Korea Gas Pipeline (MOU signed)

A gas pipeline running from the Russian Far East through the Korean peninsula to supply both Koreas with Russian gas was first proposed in 1991, and Gazprom, South Korea, and North Korea signed a preliminary agreement to construct such a pipeline in 2011. Initial estimates suggested that the 12 billion cubic meters annually (bcma) pipeline would cost around $6.3 billion to construct. To secure North Korean support for the project, Russia suggested that the North would receive $100 million per year in transit payments if it allowed construction, and forgave 90 percent of the North's debt in 2014.

Though there have been no recent statements reassessing the viability of this project, there is obvious political complexity involved in delivering energy to South Korea via its northern rival. Until now, North Korea's impassability has made the South into an energy "island" like Japan, making coastal LNG import terminals a much less risky gas importation option.

Turkish Stream 3 and 4 (construction delayed) and the "South European Pipeline"

Following the cancellation of the 63 bcma Russia-Bulgaria South Stream pipeline in December 2014, Gazprom and the Turkish Botas Petroleum Pipeline Corporation signed a memorandum of understanding to build the Russia-Turkey "Turkish Stream."

This pipeline system is projected to cost $20 billion, and it would also have a total capacity of 63 bcma, made up of four 15.75 bcma strings to be built in phases. The first string would supply gas from Russia to Turkey, while the other three would serve the European market, allowing Russia to redirect gas flows currently transiting Ukraine.

While this project has fueled speculation that Turkey could become a gas re-export hub, Russia and Greece also recently signed a $2.24 billion "agreement" to send all of the EU-destined Turkish Stream gas – 47 bcma –to a newly-announced "South European Pipeline" in Greece, giving Greece the European gas hub role Turkey seeks.

Yet there are many reasons to doubt the feasibility of the third and fourth strings of Turkish Stream, and therefore of the South European Pipeline. As of this writing, Turkey and Russia have not yet agreed on a price for Turkish Stream's gas, and Gazprom canceled the contract for laying the first string of the pipeline under the Black Sea by Italian services company Saipem in early July.

Moreover, an expanded Turkish Stream competes directly with Nord Stream II for European gas demand. The recent announcement of Nord Stream II, with its more direct route to main European gas markets, signals Russia's lack of confidence in Turkish Stream 3 and 4 and South European Pipeline because these northern and southern expansions and extensions are redundant. Gazprom has also cancelled contracts with Russian companies on expanding the onshore pipeline system to the Black Sea that would feed gas to a Turkish Stream at full capacity.

Nord Stream II (MOU signed)

Nord Stream, which runs from Russia to Germany under the Baltic Sea, was completed in 2012 and its two lines can supply Western Europe with 55 bcma of natural gas.

A planned expansion was put on hold in January 2015, partly because of EU regulatory hurdles, but in June Gazprom signed an MOU with Shell and Nord Stream customers E.ON and OMV to build a new line (Nord Stream II) that would add another 55 bcma of export capacity. BASF/Wintershall, another Nord Stream customer, is also in talks to join the project. Despite a great deal of attention from the press, an MOU is very far away from a commercial agreement and project realization, especially given that Nord Stream itself is not yet operating at full capacity.

Nord Stream II offers Russia a more viable alternative to the Ukrainian transit route with direct access to major central and western European customers. However, the project is redundant with the South Europe Pipeline and the third and fourth strings of Turkish Stream, and Russia will very likely have to choose between them. None of these Ukraine bypass projects are likely to be in full operation by the time the current transit agreement between Russia and Ukraine expires in 2019.

Altai ("understanding" reached)

Negotiations between Gazprom and CNPC on the Altai pipeline route from Russia's West Siberian gas fields to western China began in 2004, and an "understanding" on the pipeline was reached between China and Russia in November 2014. The Altai route, which would cost between $11 billion and $14 billion, would ship 30 bcma of gas over the Altai Mountains to China, supplementing the 38 bcma Power of Siberia route to the east from eastern Siberia to northeastern China. According to official Chinese statements, a deal on the Altai line will be reached by the end of 2015.

Though this pipeline route makes great sense from a Russian perspective, it would be less than optimal for China. For Russia, the Altai route would provide a nearby alternative market for the massive West Siberia gas fields, which mainly supply Europe. For China, however, this route would require massive investments by China in a new domestic pipeline to bring the Russian gas thousands of miles from Xinjiang province in the far west to consumers in China's prime gas markets in the east. Russia's continual interest in this so-called western route distracts from China's prime focus on the eastern route.

Sakhalin-1 (agreement reached)

Exxon Neftegas, a consortium of ExxonMobil, Rosneft, Sodeco, and ONGC Videsh, began producing oil and gas from the Odoptu, Arkutun-Dagi, and Chayvo fields offshore of Sakhalin Island in 2005. In 2013, Rosneft agreed with ExxonMobil to develop a $15 billion, 5 mmta gas liquefaction facility on the island, with the goal of exporting to the growing Japanese gas market.

Despite the strong rationale for building out the infrastructure needed to export LNG to the large nearby market in Japan, complications with a major partner in the project and competition between major Russian gas companies may kill Sakhalin-1's LNG facility. Though ExxonMobil has not pulled out of the project over U.S. and European sanctions on Russia, in April the company filed a $500 million lawsuit claiming that Russia overcharged it in value added taxes on the Sakhalin-1 project. Perhaps more importantly, Rosneft indicated in May that it may move its LNG facility off Sakhalin island because Gazprom, which operates the nearby Sakhalin-2 LNG export terminal, is denying Rosneft access to the gas pipeline it would need to export its gas.

Turkish Stream1 and 2 (construction delayed)

The proposed second line of Turkish Stream would add 15.75 bcma capacity to serve Gazprom current gas customers in southeastern Europe while bypassing Ukraine. If Turkish Stream 3 and 4 are canceled, Turkish Stream 2 would be the only Russian pipeline delivering gas to Europe via Turkey. This would contradict agreements to route 47 bcma of Russian gas to the EU through Greece via Turkey, but this outcome seems more likely. While Turkish Stream 2 faces many of the same economic hurdles as lines 3 and 4, it would serve a more nearby market where Gazprom has a virtual monopoly on imported gas currently. However, once it passes through Turkey to EU soil, Turkish Stream will face the same regulatory hurdles on unbundling of gas production from transportation and open access to pipeline capacity that bedeviled the now cancelled South Stream project.

The first line of Turkish Stream would carry only 15.75 bcma of gas to the domestic Turkish market, supplementing the existing Blue Stream pipeline and replacing the Trans-Balkan gas pipeline, which together delivered 27.4 bcma to Turkey in 2014. Turkish Stream 1 is likely to be finished, though not necessarily by its projected December 2016 completion date. Most of the capital commitment to the first line of Turkish Stream is already sunk because it replaces the first line of the cancelled South Stream pipeline to Bulgaria. Russia and Turkey have extensive energy relations and the current impasse over gas prices may be temporary. The experience of the Blue Stream project which protected Turkey against supply disruptions stemming from Ukraine transit and Russia's interest to compete in the growing Turkish gas market may yet overcome any commercial obstacles.

Yamal LNG (construction underway)

Situated at the Arctic port of Sabetta near an estimated 22 trillion cubic meters (tcm) of gas reserves, the massive Yamal LNG project is one of the few Russian gas export projects not operated by Gazprom.

Novatek, Total, and CNPC jointly own the Yamal LNG export project, which has an anticipated construction cost of $27 billion and aims to eventually supply 16.5 mmta of LNG to European and East Asian markets, especially China. If exports begin in 2017, as scheduled, Russia will tap new gas reserves and be better able to circumvent Ukraine in its gas exports to

Europe, as well as diversifying the market for more of its gas to Asia.

Despite recent difficulties, it appears that Yamal LNG's stakeholders are committed to ensuring its completion. U.S. sanctions on Novatek and U.S.-EU financial sanctions on Russia have made borrowing difficult, but since January, Russia's National Wealth Fund and Russian and Chinese banks have committed roughly $20 billion to the project, and Novatek is reportedly seeking $5 billion from global export finance agencies. Yamal LNG also made deals to pre-sell some of its LNG in June, and Novatek Chief Executive Leonid Mikhelson aims to have the project's financing secured by the end of 2015.

Power of Siberia (construction underway)

A decade after beginning negotiations, Gazprom and CNPC signed a $400 billion, 30-year gas sale agreement that included a 38 bcma pipeline route from eastern Siberia to northeastern China. The Russian portion of the pipeline and the development of the two gas fields that feed it will cost an estimated $55 billion, and the system as a whole is projected to cost $77 billion.

Construction of the Russian portion of the pipeline began in September 2014, and the Chinese portion was underway as of June 2015. The system is scheduled for completion in 2018, and is planned to provide China with over 4 trillion cubic meters of gas over the following 30 years.

Uncertainty over gas price with the sharp decline in oil prices and spot LNG price in Asia after the contract was signed last May, as well as weaker Chinese gas demand with a slowing economy and the technical and financial challenges of complex gas field development raise doubts over the completion date. Though Power of Siberia may be delayed by one or two years, it is very unlikely that the route itself will be altered or canceled given the strategic interests of both countries. In addition to exporting gas, Power of Siberia is important for economically connecting eastern Siberia with the Russian Far East.

Sakhalin-2 LNG Expansion (agreement reached)

This project is the most feasible because it builds on an existing project. Gazprom, Shell, and Japanese companies Mitsui and Diamond Gas operate the Sakhalin-2 LNG export facility on the southern end of Sakhalin Island. The LNG terminal is fed by the Piltun-Astokhskoye and Lunskoye oil and gas fields, and export 10 mmta of gas mainly to Japan and South Korea. Gazprom and Shell's CEOs first agreed to upgrade the facility to 15 mmta at the 2014 Sochi Olympics, and committed to the expansion - estimated to cost somewhere between $5 and $7 billion – in June 2015. Given the relatively low cost of this incremental project and Gazprom's apparent intention to stifle Rosneft's rival Sakhalin-1 LNG facility, it seems more likely than any of the others to actually be completed.

This ranking is, of course, imprecise and subject to debate, which this commentary hopes to spark. One way of judging likelihood of economic success is to consider whether the export project:

a) Taps new gas supply through the most economic route, which makes good commercial sense – (Sakhalin-2 LNG expansion, Power of Siberia, Yamal LNG);
b) Redirects existing gas supply through a new, more expensive route, which makes economic sense only if the goal is to increase redundancy or meet future demand growth – (Turkish Stream, Nord Stream II, Altai, South Stream); or
c) Directs new supply through a more expensive route, which can be prohibitively expensive or uneconomic (Sakhalin-1, Vladivostok LNG, Sakhalin to Hokkaido pipeline; Trans-Korean pipeline).

To be sure, economic efficiency may not be the critical criterion for Russia on selecting which of the projects to fund. Yet given reduced financial capability and reduced access to external financing, economic efficiency is more important than in the days of $100+ oil price. Diversity of supply and supply routes are options to be pursued during times of plenty, not when capital discipline is required. Redirecting existing gas flows through new costly infrastructure leads immediately to lower profits, even if they are strategically desirable in the long term.

Russia's highly centralized political system and national champion oil and gas companies allow it to project the image of being able to make bold swift decisions on major projects.

However, this does little to help overcome the serious technical and economic challenges many of these projects face. Political decisionmaking may even compound difficulties and lead to costly delays, as history has demonstrated.

Moreover, protecting market share in Europe using existing routes has become more important for Gazprom in the current oil price and financial environment.

How Gazprom navigates the EU's evolving regulatory environment is more critical than how to ship gas to China, which is unlikely to start until the end of the decade in any case. Gazprom's reliance on existing European markets is evidenced by its recent contract flexibility with major customers on pricing, volume, and destination restriction.

Indeed, this path dependency even obtains in Ukraine, where Gazprom's recent gas price offer and admission that transit will continue after 2019 display uncharacteristic reasonableness. As in other spheres, Russia and Ukraine are stuck with each other on gas supply and transit in the short to medium term despite protestations to the contrary by both sides.

It therefore seems likely that Russia and Europe will continue to be tied together by the gas trade. It is consequently foolhardy for Western governments to attempt to supplant Russian gas in Europe with alternatives from the United States and elsewhere, as some who look at energy through a geopolitical lens have proposed.

This would bring Western governments and companies into a pipeline or LNG contest with Russia, even though natural gas infrastructure projects are challenging enough on their own, and Russia could defeat any effort to compete with its gas exports if it concentrates its resources and attention.

Western governments have neither the tools nor the strategic need to engage in major project development. Focusing on unglamorous efforts to advance market integration and increase open energy trade are more likely to achieve the policy objective of gas import supply diversification than would reviving fanciful, Western-backed projects like the Nabucco pipeline or LNG receiving terminals in parts of Europe where there is insufficient bankable demand to justify such costly projects.

Interpreting the shifting cross-currents guiding Russia's future gas exports will continue to be an adventure for those who make the attempt. It is best to ignore often misleading headlines and wait to understand fundamental industry drivers in order to judge each project's economic feasibility and the degree of political preference or government subsidy required.

DISPUTES OF THE 1990S

Initial disputes concerning gas debts and non-payment appeared immediately after the collapse of the Soviet Union. As a result of disputes over non-payments by Ukraine, Russia suspended natural gas exports several times between 1992 and 1994. This led to the illicit diversion of Russian natural gas exports from transit pipelines by Ukrainian companies and institutions in September 1993 and November 1994. The diversion of gas was acknowledged by Ukraine, while accusations of other diversions were disputed. In September 1993, at a summit conference in Massandra, Crimea, Russian President Boris Yeltsin offered to Ukrainian President Leonid Kravchuk to forgive Ukrainian debts in return for control of the Black Sea Fleet and Ukraine's nuclear arsenal. After a strong negative reaction from politicians in Kiev, the idea was abandoned. An intergovernmental agreement was drafted on gas issues, including a clause stating Ukraine would permit Gazprom to participate in the privatization of Ukrainian enterprises in gas and other sectors. In March 1994, a Ukrainian deputy prime minister agreed with Russia that Gazprom could acquire a 51% stake in the pipeline system. In early 1995, Russia and Ukraine agreed to create a joint company, Gaztransit, to operate Ukraine's natural gas transit infrastructure in exchange for the cancellation of a substantial portion of Ukraine's debts to Russia. These agreements were never implemented, and in November 1995, the Verkhovna Rada, Ukraine's parliament, adopted a law prohibiting the privatization of oil and gas assets.

In 1998, Gazprom and Naftohaz made a contract under which Gazprom would pay for the transit of volumes of gas, which established a link between gas prices and transit tariffs, but this contract did not resolve the issue of already incurred gas debts. In 1998, Gazprom alleged that Ukraine had illegally diverted gas meant for export to other European countries and suspended exports of oil and electricity to Ukraine in 1999. Gazprom also claimed that Ukraine's gas debt had reached $2.8 billion. In 2001, Deputy Prime Minister Oleh Dubyna acknowledged that in 2000 alone 8–7 billion cubic metres (280–250 billion cubic feet) of Russian natural gas had been diverted from export pipelines. The debt issue was settled on 4 October 2001, by the signing of an intergovernmental agreement on Additional Measures Regarding the Provision of Transit of Russian Natural Gas on the Territory of Ukraine (the 2001 Transit Agreement).

DISPUTE OF 2005–2006

In 2005, negotiations over gas prices for 2006 started. Gazprom insisted on a new price of $160 per 1,000 cubic meters. The Government of Ukraine agreed, with the stipulation that price increases were to be gradual, in return for increased gas transit fees and changing the method of payment for transit from payment in kind to cash. In May 2005, it was revealed that 7.8 billion cubic metres (280 billion cubic feet) of gas which Gazprom had deposited in Ukrainian storage reservoirs during the previous winter had not been made available to the company. It remained unclear if the gas was missing, had disappeared due to technical problems, or had been stolen. This issue was resolved in July 2005 by agreement between Gazprom, Naftohaz and RosUkrEnergo, according to which Naftohaz received 2.55 billion cubic metres (90 billion cubic feet) of gas as partial settlement of the Russian gas transit over 2005 services and 5.25 billion cubic metres (185 billion cubic feet) was sold by Gazprom to RosUkrEnergo who has to receive it from Naftohaz.However, the negotiations between Gazprom and Naftohaz over gas prices and a new gas supply agreement failed. On 1 January 2006, Gazprom started reducing the pressure in the pipelines from Russia to Ukraine.

Although Russia cut off supplies only to Ukraine, a number of European countries saw a drop in their supplies as well. The European Commissioner for Energy Andris Piebalgs and several affected member states warned that blocking of gas deliveries was unacceptable. Pascal Lamy, director general of the World Trade Organisation, expressed the opinion that all Post-Soviet statesshould pay market prices for their energy needs in order to improve the efficiency of their economies.

The supply was restored on 4 January 2006, after the preliminary agreement between Ukraine and Gazprom was settled. The five-year contract was signed, although with prices set for only six months. According to the contract, the gas was sold not directly to Naftohaz, but to the intermediary Russian-Swiss company RosUkrEnergo. The price of natural gas sold by Gazprom to RosUkrEnergo rose to $230 per 1,000 cubic metres, which, after mixing it in a proportion of one-third Russian gas to two-thirds cheaper supplies from Central Asia, was resold to Ukraine at a price of $95 per 1,000 cubic metres. The parties also agreed to raise the tariff for transit from US$1.09 to US$1.60 per 1,000 cubic meters per 100 km; this applied not only to the transit of Russian gas to Europe, but also Turkmen gas through Russia to Ukraine. On 11 January 2006, Presidents Vladimir Putin and Viktor Yushchenko confirmed that the conflict had been concluded.

One possible reason for this conflict is the more pro-NATO and European Union-style approach of the new "orange" government of Ukraine. Russia disagreed, stating they did not want to subsidize former Soviet republics.

DISPUTE OF 2007–2008

On 2 October 2007, Gazprom threatened to cut off gas supplies to Ukraine because of unpaid debt of $1.3 billion. This dispute appeared to be settled on 8 October 2007. On 5 January 2008, Gazprom warned Ukraine that it would reduce its gas supplies on 11 January if $1.5 billion in gas debts were not paid. Presidents Putin and Yushchenko announced on 12 February 2008, an agreement on the gas issue. Ukraine would begin paying off its debts for natural gas consumed in November–December 2007 and the price of $179.5 would be preserved in 2008. The presidents also decided to replace RosUkrEnergo and UkrGazEnergo with two new intermediaries, creating them as joint ventures of Gazprom and Naftogaz.

At the end of February 2008, Gazprom threatened to reduce the supply of natural gas to Ukraine beginning on 3 March 2008, unless the pre-payment for 2008 was paid. The Ukrainian government said it paid for the natural gas which was consumed in 2007, but refused to pay the bill for 2008. A Gazprom spokesman claimed that the bill for 1.9 billion cubic metres (67 billion cubic feet) of gas deliveries to Ukraine valued around $600 million remained unpaid. Ukraine disagreed as that debt accumulated in recent months when Russia used its own gas to make up for a shortfall in less expensive Central Asian gas. On 3 March, Gazprom cut its shipments to Ukraine by 25% and an additional 25% the next day, claiming that the $1.5 billion debt still was not paid, although Ukrainian officials stated it had indeed been paid. Gas supplies were restored on 5 March after Gazprom CEO Alexei Miller and Naftohaz CEO Oleh Dubyna agreed during negotiations by phone on a settlement. On 6 March, the Ukrainian cabinet refused to execute the gas agreements made by presidents Yushchenko and Putin. The

Ukrainian cabinet did not want to pay in advance for 2008, and it opposed the creation of a Naftohaz–Gazprom venture that would sell gas in Ukraine. Prime Minister Yulia Tymoshenko stated that Ukraine did not need any additional joint ventures, and as of 1 March 2008, UkrGazEnergo is no longer operating in Ukraine's domestic gas market.

DISPUTE OF 2008–2009

The gas crisis of 2009 began with a failure to reach an agreement on gas prices and supplies for 2009. Ukraine owed a debt of $2.4 billion to Gazprom for gas already consumed, and Gazprom requested payment before the commencement of a new supply contract. In December 2008, despite Ukraine's repayment of more than $1 billion of its debt, Gazprom maintained its position, intending to cut the supply of natural gas to Ukraine on 1 January 2009, if Ukraine did not fully repay the remainder of $1.67 billion debt in natural gas supplies and an additional $450 million in fines levied by Gazprom. On 30 December, Naftohaz paid $1.522 billion, of the outstanding debt, but the two parties were not able to agree on the price for 2009. Ukraine proposed a price of $201, and later increased their proposed price to $235, while Gazprom demanded $250 per 1,000 cubic meters. Negotiations between Gazprom and Naftohaz were interrupted on 31 December.

On 1 January 2009, exports to Ukraine of 90 million cubic meters of natural gas per day were halted completely at 10:00 MSK. Exports intended for transhipment to the EU continued at a volume of 300 million cubic meters per day. President Yushchenko requested that the European Union become involved in the settlement of this dispute in a letter to the President of the European Commission Jose Manuel Barroso. A Ukrainian delegation including Fuel and Energy Minister Yuriy Prodan, Deputy Foreign Minister Konstantin Yeliseyev, the President's Representative for Energy Issues Bohdan Sokolovsky, and Deputy Head of Naftohaz Vadym Chuprun visited the Czech Republic as the first stop on a tour of a number EU member states to hold consultations on the gas crisis.

On 2 January 2009, Hungary, Romania, and Poland reported that pressure in their pipelines had dropped. Bulgaria also reported that their natural gas supply was dropping, affecting the shipment of natural gas to Turkey, Greece, and Macedonia. Furthermore, the United Kingdom Government announced that it was preparing to enter its gas reserves after gas pressure had dropped from the continent. On 4 January 2009, both RosUkrEnergo and Gazprom filed lawsuits against Ukraine and Naftohaz respectively with the Stockholm Tribunal of the Arbitration Institute. Ukraine also filed lawsuits with the tribunal. According to Naftohaz, RosUkrEnergo owes the company $40 million for services in transportation of natural gas. On 5 January 2009, Kiev's economic court banned Naftohaz from transshipping Russian natural gas in 2009 at the price of $1.60 per 1,600 cubic meters per 100 kilometers. The court declared contracts made by Naftohaz for the transit of natural gas through Ukraine void because the contracts were signed by Naftohaz without authorization from the Cabinet of Ministers of Ukraine. On 30 March 2010, the Stockholm tribunal ordered Naftohaz to pay RosUkrEnergo around $200 million as a penalty for various breaches of supply, transit, and storage contracts. On 8 June 2010, the tribunal ordered Naftohaz to return 11 billion cubic metres (390 billion cubic feet) of natural gas to RosUkrEnergo. The tribunal further ordered that RosUkrEnergo would receive from Naftohaz a further 1.1 billion cubic metres (39 billion cubic feet) of natural gas in lieu of RosUkrEnergo's damages for breach of contract.

On 5 January 2009 Russian Prime Minister Vladimir Putin instructed Gazprom CEO Alexei Miller to reduce natural gas exports to Europe via transshipment through Ukraine by quantities equivalent to the amounts of gas which Ukraine had allegedly diverted from the pipelines since deliveries ended on 1 January 2009. On 7 January, all Russian natural gas exports via Ukraine were halted amid accusations between the two parties. Several countries reported a major fall in supplies of

Russian gas starting on 7 January; Bulgaria, Moldova, and Slovakia were among the most affected by these supply drops.

Talks between Naftohaz and Gazprom resumed overnight on 8 January 2009. Ukraine agreed to guarantee the unfettered transport of natural gas on the condition that Gazprom would guarantee and supply technical gas for Ukraine's gas transit system to function; this was denied by Russia. The supplies to Europe were not restored although the European Union, Ukraine, and Russia agreed to the deployment of an international monitoring group to the gas metering stations between Russia and Ukraine. Naftohaz blocked the transit of gas, blaming a lack of pressure in the pipeline system and saying the design of the Soviet-built pipeline meant it could not ship gas entering through the Sudzhametering station governing gas leaving through the Orlivka metering station without cutting off the Donetsk region, Luhansk region, and portions of the Dnipropetrovsk region of Ukraine. Naftohaz suggested a technically more feasible alternative through the Valuyki and Pisarevka metering stations but was refused.

On 17 January 2009, Russia held an international gas conference in Moscow. The EU was represented by the Presidency, the Czech Minister of Industry and Trade Martin Øíman, and the EU Energy Commissioner Andris Piebalgs, so that the European Union could speak with one voice. Ukraine was represented by the Prime Minister Yulia Tymoshenko. The conference did not achieve any solution to the crisis, and the negotiations continued bilaterally between Prime Ministers Putin and Tymoshenko. Early on 18 January 2009, after five hours of talks, Putin and Tymoshenko reached a deal to restore gas supplies to Europe and Ukraine. Both parties agreed that Ukraine would start paying European prices for its natural gas, less a 20% discount for 2009, and that Ukraine would pay the full European market price starting in 2010. In return for the discounts for 2009, Ukraine agreed to keep its transit fee for Russian gas unchanged in 2009. The two sides also agreed not to use intermediaries. On 19 January 2009, Gazprom CEOAlexei Miller and the head of Naftohaz Oleh Dubyna signed an agreement on natural gas supply to Ukraine for the period of 2009–2019. Gas supplies restarted on 20 January 2009, and were fully restored on 21 January.

According to the EU Commission and Presidency, the Russia–Ukraine gas disputes caused irreparable and irreversible damage to customers' confidence in Russia and Ukraine, causing Russia and Ukraine to no longer be regarded as reliable partners.According to reports, due to the gas crisis Gazprom lost more than $1.1 billion in revenue for the unsupplied gas. Ukraine also incurred losses as a result of the temporary closure of its steel and chemical industries due to the lack of gas. Ukraine also lost $100 million of potential revenue in transit fees from natural gas.

There were also accusations of illegal diversion of natural gas by Ukraine; however, these accusations were not confirmed. The issue of technical gas used to fuel compressor stations and to maintain gas pressure in the pipeline network remained unclear. Some sources asserted that the responsibility for providing the technical gas falls to Ukraine, while others say that this is the responsibility of Gazprom.

There were several theories as to alleged political motives behind the gas disputes, including Russia exerting pressure on Ukrainian politicians or attempting to subvert EU and NATO expansions to include Ukraine. Others suggested that Ukraine's actions were being orchestrated by the United States. Both sides tried to win sympathy for their arguments fighting a PR war.

In August 2009, it was agreed that loans worth $1.7 billion would be given to Ukraine to help it provide stable supplies of Russian gas to Europe by the International Monetary Fund, the World Bank, and the European Bank for Reconstruction and Development, in return for reforms in Ukraine's gas sector.

On 28 December 2009, the Slovakian government announced that Russia warned it would stop oil supplies to Slovakia, Hungary, and the Czech Republic over a transit price dispute with Ukraine. However, the next day, Ukraine's Naftohaz issued a statement confirming that Russia agreed to a 30% increase in the transit fees through Ukraine. The alleged rise in the tariff would be from $7.8 to $9.50 (or €6.6) per tonne of oil going through Ukraine in 2010. Additionally, unlike previous payments, new payments would be made in Euros as this was one of Ukraine's demands. Russia and Ukraine also agreed on the volume of oil to be transported through Ukraine. The overall amount of oil to be transported to Slovakia, Czech Republic, and Hungary through Ukraine in 2010 will be 15 million tonnes—a decrease from 17.1 million tonnes in 2008.

2010 NATURAL GAS AGREEMENT

Prologue

After meeting her Russian counterpart Putin, Ukrainian Prime Minister Tymoshenko declared on 3 September 2009, "Both sides, Russia and Ukraine, have agreed that at Christmas, there won't be [any halt in gas supplies], as usually happens when there are crises in the gas sector. Everything will be quite calm on the basis of the current agreements".Tymoshenko also said that the Ukrainian and Russian premiers had agreed that sanctions would not be imposed on Ukraine for the country buying less gas than expected and that the price of Russian gas transit across Ukraine may grow 65% till 70% in 2010. A week before Gazprom had said it expected gas transit fees via Ukraine to rise by up to 59% in 2010.

On 8 October 2009 Tymoshenko announced that Ukrainian 2010 natural gas imports will be significantly less than in previous years "because we have less need for natural gas". Because of its economic recession the industries require far less gas. In response to Tymoshenko Gazprom Chief Executive Alexey Miller stated that Ukraine should stick to the January (2009) contract for 2010.

On 16 November 2009 Commissioner for Energy at the European Commission Andris Piebalgs stated that Russia and the European Union do not expect another gas conflict with

Ukraine. According to him there were no gas price negotiations or questions other than that of gas payments.

On 20 November 2009, the gas deal of 18 January 2009, was altered after a meeting between Tymoshenko and Putin in Yalta; meaning Ukraine would not be fined for buying less gas then the old contract stipulated, this was done in view of the 2008–2009 Ukrainian financial crisis. On 24 November 2009 Gazprom and Naftohaz signed these supplements to the contract of 19 January 2009 on the purchase and sale of natural gas; according to the supplements, the annual contracted amount of gas to be supplied to Ukraine in 2010 has been set at 33.75 billion cubic metres (1.192 trillion cubic feet), instead of the 52 billion cubic metres (1.8 trillion cubic feet) contracted earlier. The documents signed by the sides also stipulated that there will be no fines related to the amount of gas consumed by Naftohaz in 2009. Over the first ten months of 2009 Naftohaz has purchased 18.85 billion cubic metres (666 billion cubic feet) of gas with the contracted volume being 31.7 billion cubic metres (1.12 trillion cubic feet).

On 15 December 2009, Russian Energy Minister Sergei Shmatko stated he expects no problems with Ukraine over gas supplies at New Year.

Agreement

Ukrainian Prime Minister Mykola Azarov and Energy Minister Yuriy Boyko were in Moscow late March 2010 to negotiate lower gas prices; neither clearly explained what Ukraine was prepared to offer in return. Following these talks Russian Prime Minister Vladimir Putin stated that Russia was prepared to discuss the revision of the price for natural gas it sells to Ukraine.

On 21 April 2010, Russian President Dmitry Medvedev and Ukrainian President Viktor Yanukovych signed an agreement in which Russia agreed to a 30 percent drop in the price of natural gas sold to Ukraine. Russia agreed to this in exchange for permission to extend Russia's lease of a major naval base in the Ukrainian Black Sea port of Sevastopol for an additional 25 years with an additional five-year renewal option (to 2042-47). As of June 2010 Ukraine pays Gazprom around $234/mcm (thousand cubic meter).

This agreement was subject to approval by both the Russian and Ukrainian parliaments. They did ratify the agreement on 27 April 2010. The Ukrainian parliament ratified it after several eggs were thrown towards the speaker, Volodymyr Lytvyn, by deputies and other incidents. Opposition members in Ukraine and Russia expressed doubts the agreement would be fulfilled by the Ukrainian side.

Yanukovych has defended the agreement as a tool to help stabilise the state budget. Opposition members in Ukraine described the agreement as a sell out of national interests.

DISPUTE OF 2013–2014

Annexation of Crimea

In February 2014, Ukraine's state-owned oil and gas company Naftogaz sued Chornomornaftogaz for delayed debt payments of 11.614 billion UAH (almost €1 billion) in the Economic Court of the Autonomous Republic of Crimea.

In March 2014, Republic of Crimea authorities announced that they would nationalize the company. Republic of Crimea deputy prime minister Rustam Temirgaliev said that Russia's Gazprom would be its new owner. A group of Gazprom representatives, including its head of business development, has been working at the Chornomornaftogaz head office since mid-March 2014. On April 1, Russia's energy minister Alexander Novak said that Gazprom would finance an undersea gas pipeline to Crimea.

On 11 April 2014 the U.S. Treasury's Office of Foreign Assets Control (OFAC) announced that it had added Chornomornaftagaz to the Specially Designated Nationals and Blocked Persons List as part of the third round of U.S. sanctions. Reuters quoted an anonymous U.S. official who explained that the United States wanted to make it impossible for Gazprom to "have dealings with Chornomorneftegaz", and if that were to happen, Gazprom itself could face sanctions.

The European Union followed suit on May 13, 2014, the first time its sanctions list has included a company (in addition to Chornomorneftegaz, a Crimean oil supplier called Feodosia was also included).

June 2014 gas supplies to Ukraine cut off

In an attempt at energy independence, Naftogaz signed a pipeline access deal with Slovakia's Eustream on April 28, 2014. Eustream and its Ukrainian counterpart Ukrtransgaz, owned by Naftogaz, agreed to allow Ukraine to use a never used (but aging, at 20 years old) pipeline on Slovakia's eastern border with Uzhhorod in western Ukraine. The deal would provide Ukraine with 3 billion cubic meters of natural gas beginning in autumn of 2014 with the aim of increasing that amount to 10 billion cubic meters in 2015.

On 1 April 2014 Gazprom cancelled Ukraine's natural gas discount as agreed in the 17 December 2013 Ukrainian–Russian action plan because its debt to the company had risen to $1.7 billion since 2013.

Later that month the price "automatically" jumped to $485 per 1,000 cubic meters because the Russian government annulled an export-duty exemption for Gazprom in place since the 2010 Kharkiv Pact (this agreement was denounced by Russia on 31 March 2014). On 16 June 2014 Gazprom stated that Ukraine's debt to the company was $4.5 billion. On 30 May 2014 Ukraine paid $786 million to Gazprom.

After intermediary (that had started in May 2014) trilateral talks between EU Energy Commissioner Günther Oettinger, Ukraine and Russia failed on 15 June 2014 the latter halted (after a deadline of 10 a.m. Moscow time passed without it receiving payment) its natural gas supplies to Ukraine the next day. Unilaterally Gazprom decided that Ukraine had to pay upfront for its natural gas. The company assured that its supplies to other European countries would continue. Ukraine vowed to "provide reliable supply of gas to consumers in Ukraine and we will provide reliable transit to the European Union". At the time about 15 percent of European Union's demand depended on Russian natural gas piped through Ukraine.

After trilateral months of talks between the European Union, Ukraine and Russia a deal was reached on 30 October 2014 in which Ukraine agreed to pay (in advance) $378 per 1,000 cubic metres to the end of 2014, and $365 in the first quarter (ending on 31 March) of 2015. Of its debts to Gazprom Ukraine agreed to pay of $1.45bn immediately, and $1.65bn by the end of 2014. It was agreed that the European Union will be acting as guarantor for Ukraine's gas purchases from Russia and would help to meet outstanding debts (using funds from existing accords with the European Union and IMF). The total package was worth $4.6bn. According to European Union officials the deal secured that there would be no natural gas supply disruptions in other European countries.

NOVEMBER 2015 GAS SUPPLIES STOP

On 25 November 2015 Gazprom halted its exports of Russian natural gas to Ukraine. According to the Ukrainian government they had stopped buying from Gazprom because Ukraine could buy natural gas cheaper from other suppliers. According to Gazprom it had halted deliveries because Ukraine had not paid them for the next delivery. Since then, Ukraine has been able to fulfill its gas supply needs solely from European Union states.

RUSSIA AND THE UKRAINE – THE WORRISOME CONNECTION TO WORLD OIL AND GAS PROBLEMS

What is behind the Russia/Ukraine problem? It seems to me that what we are seeing is Russia's attempt to fix a two-part problem:

1. Some oil and gas exporters, including Russia, are not receiving enough oil and gas revenue to meet their

needs. They are not able to collect enough taxes to provide the services they have promised to their citizens, plus allow the amount of reinvestment that is needed to maintain production. Russia is starting to experience economic contraction because of the low revenue situation. This situation very closely related similar problems I have written about previously. In one post I talked about major independent oil companies not producing enough profit to provide the revenue needed for reinvestment, and because of this, cutting back on new investment. In another, I talked about the problem of too low US natural gas sales prices, relative to the cost of extraction.

2. Some oil and gas importers, including Ukraine, are not using their imported oil and gas in productive enough ways that *they are able to afford to pay the market price* for oil and gas. Russia gave Ukraine a lower natural gas price because some of Russia's pipelines cross Ukraine, and Ukraine must maintain the pipeline. But even with this lower natural gas price, Ukraine is behind on its payments to Russia.

If a person thinks about the situation, it looks a lot like a situation where the world is reaching limits on oil and gas production. The marginal producers (including Russia) are being pushed out, at the same time that the marginal consumers (including Ukraine) are being pushed out.

Russia is trying to fix this situation, as best it can. One part of its approach is to make certain that Ukraine will in fact pay at least the European market price for natural gas. To do this, Russia will make Ukraine prepay for its natural gas; otherwise it will cut off its gas supply. Russia is also looking for new customers who can afford to pay higher prices for natural gas. In particular, Russia is working on a contract to sell LNG to China, quite possibly reducing the amount of natural gas it has available to sell to Europe. Russia is also signing a $10 billion contract with Iran in which it promises to construct new hydroelectric and thermal energy plants in Iran, in return for oil exports from Iran. This contract will increase the amount of oil Russia has to sell, and will increase the oil available on the world market. Russia's plan will do an end run around US and European sanctions.

Gradually, or perhaps not so gradually, Russia's exports are being redirected to those who can afford to pay higher prices. European Union purchases of natural gas imports have declined since 2008, presumably because they are having difficulty affording the current price of gas, so they are being relied on less for future sales.

The Russian approach seems to include building a new axis of power, including Russia, China, Iran and perhaps other countries. This new axis of power may threaten the US dollar's reserve currency status. With the dollar as reserve currency, the US has been able to buy far more goods from other countries than it sells to others. Putting an end to the US dollar as reserve currency would leave more and oil and gas for other countries. If purchases by the US are cut back, it will leave more oil and gas for other countries. The danger is that prices will drop too low because of the drop in US demand, leading to lower production. It this should happen, everyone might lose out.

I am doubtful that Russia's approach to fixing its problems will work. But if Russia is "between a rock and a hard place," I can understand its willingness to try something very different. It now has more power than it has had in the past because of its oil and gas exports, and is willing to use that power.

The US/European approach to this problem is to loan Ukraine $17 billion to pay for past natural gas bills. The hope is that with this loan, Ukraine will be able to make changes that will allow it to afford future natural gas bills. There is also the hope that the United States can step in with large natural gas exports to Europe and Ukraine. In addition, the US and Europe are trying to impose sanctions on Russia. I find it very difficult to believe that the US/European approach will work. The idea that the United States can start exporting huge amounts of natural gas to Europe in the near future borders on the bizarre. There are many hurdles that would need to be overcome for this to happen. Installing LNG export facilities is among the least of these hurdles.

In fact, the West badly needs both the oil and gas that Russia is producing, so it really is in a very precarious position. If Russia cuts off exports, or if Russia is forced to cut off exports because of financial difficulties, both the US and Europe will suffer. It is clear that Europe will suffer because of its dependence on pipeline exports of oil and gas from Russia. But the US will suffer as well, because the US is tied closely to Europe by financial ties, and by import and export arrangements with Europe.

Furthermore, the US/European approach involves a great deal of new debt, in an attempt to fix an inherent inability of the Ukrainian economy to afford high energy prices. Without a huge transformation, Ukraine will be in even more financial difficulty when it comes time to pay back the new debt–it will need make debt payments at the same time that it needs to pay for more expensive future natural gas. More debt doesn't necessarily fix the situation; it may make it worse.

The US powers that be do not understand what Russia (and the world) is up against, so the policies they propose are likely to make the situation worse, rather than better.

Background

We live in a world in which some countries use far more energy products than others. One question that the new proposed axis of power raises is whether this disproportionate share of energy use should be allowed to continue to exist.

The United States, Europe and Japan got to the position of using a disproportionate share of energy resources by way of being first with industrialization. This early industrialization set up a pattern of using energy for "frivolous" things–large, heated homes; private passenger automobiles for individual citizens; businesses that were not necessarily as energy-efficient as they might be. In the early days, imports were limited and cheap. As local supplies became depleted, imports rose. The cost of imported oil and imported gas (except for natural gas in the US) rose as well, making the imported fuel harder to afford. Now the early users–that is, the US, EU, and Japan, are the ones struggling to keep up past consumption levels.

In some ways, Ukraine is not too different from the EU is this respect. Ukraine also got to the position of using an above average share of energy resources, by being early in its industrialization, during the era of the Soviet Union. Ukraine, prior to the collapse of the Soviet Union, was using as much as energy on a per-capita basis as the US-Europe-Japan group, because of its heavy industry.

Once the Soviet Union collapsed, Ukraine had huge difficulties: Exports of oil and gas from Russia (upon which Ukraine's industry depended) collapsed. Ukraine's industry had been set up under the Soviet-Era model, and didn't produce the variety of goods, cheaply, that people outside the Soviet Union expected to buy. Ukraine also didn't have alternate sources of energy supply, if Russian supplies were cut off, because a major source of energy was pipelines of both oil and gas from Russia.

The Ukrainian economy has struggled for many years. Trying to transform it now to be successful competitor in the world economy is likely to be a difficult task. If Ukraine tries to make *goods* for the world market, it will find itself in competition with Asian competitors. The Asians are hard to outcompete, in part because their labour costs are low (because it uses workers with little energy use, so they can live on low salaries) and in part because their energy costs are low (often from coal). Safety standards are often low as well, adding to their low-cost structure.

If, instead of making goods for the world market, Ukraine decides to specialize in high-priced services, such as financial, medical, or educational services, it will find that it has a great deal of competition from the EU. It will also find that the EU is having difficulty making the service model work. The service model provides little for export, for one thing.

4

Chemical War and Weapons

For more than 2,000 years human ingenuity has turned natural and synthetic poisons into weapons of war. Three substances were responsible for most chemical-weapons injuries and deaths during World War I: chlorine, phosgene, and mustard gas.

Chlorine gas, used on the infamous day of April 22, 1915, produces a greenish-yellow cloud that smells of bleach and immediately irritates the eyes, nose, lungs, and throat of those exposed to it. At high enough doses it kills by asphyxiation.

Phosgene, which smells like moldy hay, is also an irritant but six times more deadly than chlorine gas. Phosgene is also a much stealthier weapon: it's colorless, and soldiers did not at first know they had received a fatal dose. After a day or two, victims' lungs would fill with fluid, and they would slowly suffocate in an agonizing death. Although the Germans were the first to use phosgene on the battlefield, it became the primary chemical weapon of the Allies. Phosgene was responsible for 85% of chemical-weapons fatalities during World War I.

Mustard gas, a potent blistering agent, was dubbed King of the Battle Gases. Like phosgene, its effects are not immediate. It has a potent smell; some say it reeks of garlic, gasoline, rubber, or dead horses. Hours after exposure a victim's eyes become bloodshot, begin to water, and become increasingly painful, with some victims suffering temporary blindness. Worse, skin begins to blister, particularly in moist areas, such as the armpits and genitals. As the blisters pop, they often become infected. Mustard gas could also contaminate land where it had been deployed. Exposure sensitized victims; further exposure even at lower doses produced symptoms. Mustard gas caused the highest number of casualties from chemical weapons—upward of 120,000 by some estimates—but it caused few direct deaths because the open air of the battlefield kept concentrations below the lethal threshold.

Timeline

Since the dawn of warfare people have sought new ways to kill one another. Here are some notable moments in chemical warfare through the ages.

600 BCE

The Athenian military taints the water supply of the besieged city of Kirrha with poisonous hellebore plants.

479 BCE

Peloponnesian forces use sulfur fumes against the town of Plataea.

1675

France and Germany sign the Strasbourg Agreement, the first international agreement to ban chemical weapons, in this case outlawing the use of poisoned bullets.

1845

During the French conquest of Algeria, French troops force more than 1,000 members of a Berber tribe into a cave and then use smoke to kill them.

1861–1865

During the American Civil War civilians and soldiers on both sides propose using chemical weapons. Among a multitude of unrealized ideas, New York City schoolteacher John Doughty recommends firing chlorine-gas projectiles at Confederate troops, and Confederate soldier Isham Walker suggests dropping canisters of poison gas from balloons.

1874–1907

A series of international treaties signed by most Western nations bans the use of poison and poisonous weapons in war.

1914

August

During the first month of World War I the French deploy tear-gas grenades, first developed in 1912 for police use.

October

German forces fire 3,000 shells containing dianisidine chlorosulfate, a lung irritant, at the British army at Neuve-Chapelle. The British are unaware that they had been subjected to a chemical attack because the chemical is incinerated by the explosive charge.

1915

January

The Germans fire 18,000 shells filled with the irritant xylyl bromide at Russian troops at Bolinow. The Russians are unharmed because the extreme cold keeps the liquid from vaporizing.

April 22

The German military launches the first large-scale use of chemical weapons in war at Ypres, Belgium. Nearly 170 metric tons of chlorine gas in 5,730 cylinders are buried along a four-mile stretch of the front. In the end more than 1,100 people are killed by the attack and 7,000 are injured.

September 25

The British military uses chemical weapons for the first time against the Germans at the Battle of Loos. They release chlorine gas from cylinders.

December 19

Six days before Christmas, Germans first use phosgene on Allied troops. More than 1,000 British soldiers are injured and 120 die.

1917

July 12

Mustard gas is used for the first time by German forces; it causes more than 2,100 casualties. During the first three weeks of mustard-gas use, Allied casualties equal the previous year's chemical-weapons casualties.

1918

May

U.S. research on mustard gas moves from a lab at American University in Maryland to a site called Edgewood Arsenal run by the newly created Chemical Warfare Service. Soon 10% of American artillery shells contain chemical weapons.

June

The Allies begin using mustard gas against German troops.

October 13–14

A young Adolf Hitler, an enlisted messenger in the trenches at Werwick near Ypres, is temporarily blinded during a gas attack. Hitler is evacuated to a military hospital in eastern Germany and spends the rest of the war recuperating.

November 11

World War I ends with 1.3 million casualties caused by chemical weapons, including 90,000 to 100,000 fatalities, primarily from phosgene.

1925

The Geneva Protocol is adopted by the League of Nations. The treaty bans the use of chemical and biological agents in war but does not prohibit the development, production, or stockpiling of such weapons. Many countries sign the treaty with reservations permitting them to respond in kind if attacked with chemical weapons.

1935–1936

Benito Mussolini drops mustard-gas bombs in Ethiopia to destroy Emperor Haile Selassie's army. Despite Italy being a signatory of the Geneva Protocol, the League of Nations does not stop its use of chemical weapons.

1936

German chemist Gerhard Schrader completes the synthesis and purification of tabun, a potent nerve poison. His intention is to build a pesticide, not a chemical weapon. The chemical he creates is so potent that army researchers call it taboo, or Tabu in German, from which it takes its name.

1939–1945

During World War II poison gases are used in Nazi concentration camps to kill civilians and by the Japanese army in Asia. Nerve agents are stockpiled by the Nazis, but chemical weapons are not used on European battlefields.

1943

The Nazis force prisoners at the Dyhernfurth concentration camp to produce tabun. Laborers are often denied medical treatment when exposed to lethal doses of the poison.

1953

British serviceman Ronald Maddison dies of sarin poisoning after being purposefully exposed to the toxin at Porton Down military facility.

1961–1971

The United States uses napalm and the herbicide Agent Orange during the Vietnam War, sparking national and international protest.

1963–1967

Egypt uses mustard gas and a nerve agent in Yemen to support a coup d'état against the Yemeni monarchy.

1972

The Biological and Toxin Weapons Convention is completed. Combined with the 1925 Geneva Protocol, the new accord bans the development, production, and possession of biological weapons. The accord has no mechanism to ensure compliance.

1980s

During the Iran-Iraq war Iraq uses chemical weapons, including tabun, against Iran and Iraq's Kurdish minority. United Nations experts confirm Iraq's use of chemical weapons, but there is little international outcry. Iran initiates its own chemical-weapons program in retaliation.

1993

The Chemical Weapons Convention is signed. Beginning in 1997, the disarmament agreement bans the development, production, stockpiling, and use of chemical weapons.

2013

The Syrian military uses sarin gas against civilians during the Syrian Civil War; hundreds are killed. Bashar al-Assad's government relinquishes its arsenal of chemical weapons after threats of U.S. air strikes.

Fritz Haber, Life and Death

In the early evening of April 22, 1915, a greenish-yellow fog wafted across the trenches near Ypres, Belgium, terrifying and asphyxiating unprepared French troops. This opening act of chemical warfare had been in planning for months and was carried out by many people: installing the nearly 6,000 gas cylinders alone required scores of German hands.

Yet Fritz Haber—and he alone—is the person we most identify with these weapons, and rightly so. Although many have invented, developed, or deployed chemical weapons throughout history, Haber used his considerable intelligence to militarize chemistry in World War I; in April 1915 at Ypres he witnessed the first fruits of this labor, the first large-scale use of chemical weapons in contemporary warfare. He remained an unfailing ambassador of such weapons, arguing until his death in 1934 that they are a more humane form of weaponry than modern artillery.

After World War I the Allies deemed Haber a war criminal for his work, and he lay low briefly in Switzerland until his name was removed from the wanted list. Haber continued to research and to promote chemical weapons after the war. As Dietrich Stoltzenberg describes in his comprehensive biography of the man, after World War I, Haber helped improve a one-step process for making mustard gas; aided Russia in developing its first chemical-weapons plant by recommending a colleague to Russian emissaries looking for advice; and until 1933 helped the German military in its secret chemical-weapon armament and research program, in direct contravention of the peace treaty signed in 1919.

Yet Haber's work has also deeply benefited humankind. His discovery of the Haber-Bosch reaction underpins the green revolution: the Nobel Prize–winning strategy for synthesizing ammonia paved the way for inexpensive fertilizers, with enormous benefits to agriculture. He also helped lay the foundations of 20th-century electrochemistry and physical chemistry.

Haber's Janus-faced scientific achievements were mirrored in his personal relationships. To some he was a great friend. According to one of his closest confidants, the chemist and fellow Nobel laureate Richard Willstätter, Haber was loyal, devoted, and entertaining. "The most beautiful trips were the ones I took with Fritz Haber," Willstätter wrote in his memoirs. "They were hours of friendship in which I came to know and understand his individuality, his noble mind, goodness of heart, wealth of ideas, and his boundless, extravagant drive." Haber also maintained strong bonds with Albert Einstein, despite their vast differences in opinion about everything from German politics and national pride to the ethics of chemical weapons. During his travels he wrote Einstein postcards in rhyme—as he did for many of his close friends—that were often humorous, ironic, or both.

Yet Haber's strong ego led to two failed marriages and rocky familial relationships. Haber's second marriage, to Charlotte Nathan, ended in divorce; his first, to Clara Immerwahr, ended when she committed suicide. Their son, Hermann, discovered his mother in a pool of her own blood, but Haber left the boy soon after for the eastern front to help deploy the chemical weapons he invented. In such ways Haber often prioritized his intellectual progeny over his biological offspring. It is perhaps no surprise that according to historian Ute Deichmann, years later Hermann and his wife declined an invitation to attend a scientific memorial for Haber. In a letter Hermann's wife remarked, "One has no right to celebrate a person *dead*, whom one would not tolerate *alive* today."

Haber's failures as a family man may have stemmed from his own rocky childhood and poor father figure. As Stoltzenberg notes, Haber's mother died in childbirth, and his father blamed the son for the loss of his new bride. The father-son relationship never recovered. Despite Haber's propensity for science, his father disapproved of his son's "chemical games" and wanted him to join the family dye trade business. Haber obeyed, but the two simply could not get along. In the end Haber was freed of his domineering father's influence and allowed to pursue his dream.

Haber's life ended cruelly. He deeply identified as a German and used his skills and intelligence to benefit his country in war and in peace. His Nobel Prize gave him fame, and he took pride in his status as a war hero. Yet by the end of his life his country saw him as little more than a dispensable Jew, even though Haber had converted to Christianity as a young man.

In 1933 Hitler ordered Jews removed from positions in the civil service. After trying but failing to help many of his Jewish colleagues, Haber stepped down from his founding position at the Kaiser Wilhelm Institute for Physical Chemistry and Electrochemistry. He spent the last year of his life wandering around Europe heartbroken—both literally and figuratively. He died in Basel, in 1934, of a heart attack.

TERRIBLE INGENUITY

The German soldier with the worrisome tale was captured by Allied forces in Tunisia on May 11, 1943. He told British interrogators that he was a chemist, far afield from the Berlin lab where he had been working on a new chemical weapon with "astounding properties." The poison was colorless and nearly odorless, and could asphyxiate its victims in less than 15 minutes—a tale that sounded straight out of a crime novel. But interrogators believed the story and sent a secret 10-page report to British military intelligence, notes Jonathan Tucker in *War of Nerves: Chemical Warfare from World War I to al-Qaeda.* Yet British intelligence officials doubted the truth of the report and did nothing—a blunder that could have had lethal repercussions for the Allies in World War II.

Not only had the Germans discovered a new family of chemical weapons—nerve agents called tabun, sarin, and soman—that were far more potent than anything the Allies had at their disposal; Hitler had already come close to approving their use on Allied forces after the German army's defeat in Stalingrad during the winter of 1943. The Nazis also had reconfigured the Dyhernfurth forced-labor camp in present-day Poland to produce thousands of metric tons of tabun.

Although many senior military officers encouraged Hitler to deploy their powerful new chemical weapon, he waffled, likely for two reasons. First, as a victim of gas poisoning during World War I, Hitler recoiled from using chemical poisons on troops—though he had no qualms about deploying poisons on concentration-camp prisoners. Second, German military intelligence was unsure whether the Allies had also discovered nerve agents since some of the foundational research had been done in England. Any Allied retaliation on German civilians could have been catastrophic. President Franklin D. Roosevelt said in June 1943 that "any use of gas by any Axis power will immediately be followed by the fullest possible retaliation upon munitions centers, seaports, and other military installations through the whole extent of the territory of such Axis country."

Yet the Germans overestimated Allied capabilities: the Allies had no nerve poisons at their disposal. The Germans had only acquired the new family of chemical weapons by serendipity. In 1936 a chemist named Gerhard Schrader first synthesized tabun at the German chemical company IG Farben. He was aiming to create an insecticide that would allow Germany to increase its food production. But after Schrader nearly poisoned himself and his lab mates with mere drops of his newly synthesized insecticide, the company realized that tabun was better suited to military applications and forwarded the discovery to German military researchers. Schrader experienced eye irritation, pupils constricted to pinpoints that dimmed the surrounding world, a runny nose, and shortness of breath. Luckily for him he avoided the next stage of nerve-agent poisoning: intense sweating, stomach cramping, muscle twitching, a loss of consciousness, and asphyxiation.

By 1943 a team of German military scientists developing tabun had also designed another nerve agent called sarin that was six times more potent than tabun. The German Nobel laureate Richard Kuhn was called on to help discern why the new poisons were so deadly. He soon discovered that these nerve agents interfere with a critical enzyme, cholinesterase. In the process Kuhn also discovered a third nerve agent: soman.

As the Nazis scaled up production of tabun at Dyhernfurth, they used 20 of the camp's prisoners as test subjects in nerve-agent experiments; a quarter of them died in agony. Dyhernfurth prisoners also were forced to travel alongside train shipments of the nerve agents—effectively used as human canaries to detect leaks of the poison gas. At the end of the war, after two-and-a-half years of production, the factory at Dyhernfurth had produced almost 12,000 metric tons of tabun. Some 10,000 tons were loaded into bombs for the Luftwaffe, and another 2,000 tons were encased in artillery shells. Meanwhile, Tucker writes that hundreds of forced laborers working at Dyhernfurth "had died of exhaustion, malnutrition and toxic exposure."

In February 1945, as the Russians marched toward Berlin, the Nazis quickly abandoned the Dyhernfurth factory. Hundreds of forced laborers were transferred by foot and in open wagons to another concentration camp, Mauthausen. Two-thirds of them died from exposure to freezing temperatures. The Gestapo tracked down the survivors at Mauthausen and killed them to get rid of witnesses.

Desperate to prevent the Red Army from capturing nerve-agent know-how, the Luftwaffe tried and failed to destroy the Dyhernfurth factory from the air. The Soviets discovered the tabun plant and a sarin pilot plant and carried the plant's machinery back home. British and U.S. military officials panicked when they learned of the existence of these nerve agents and that the Russians had nabbed an entire factory for making tabun. They hunted down German scientists familiar with nerve-agent production and used their know-how to create and stockpile these new weapons. Thus began a chemical arms race that for decades would parallel the nuclear arms race.

The Dark Side of British Chemical-Weapons Research

I believe it to be rather unlikely that any man in his right mind would have volunteered for such an experiment. — Ulf Schmidt, historical expert appointed to the public inquest into the 1953 death of Ronald Maddison

On May 6, 1953, Ronald Maddison, a 20-year-old British soldier, agreed to participate in a medical experiment at the Porton Down military research facility. The promised compensation was tempting: a three-day pass and 15 shillings, which Maddison wanted to use to buy an engagement ring for his girlfriend. But Porton Down officials did not disclose that they intended to use him as a human guinea pig to study the effects of the deadly nerve agent sarin.

Scientists placed 200 milligrams of pure sarin on a piece of flannel attached to Maddison's left forearm. Within half an hour Maddison was drenched in sweat and had lost his hearing; he then fell unconscious. At this point scientists injected him with atropine, a treatment for nerve agents, and took him to the hospital; but Maddison soon stopped breathing and was pronounced dead. Officials at the highest levels rushed to cover up the death. According to an inquiry conducted decades later, the home secretary had advised the coroner that an "inquest should be held in-camera [i.e., in private] on grounds of national security. Must not be published."

Maddison was just one among thousands of people used in chemical-weapons experiments at Porton Down. The facility was established by the British military in September 1915, just months after the surprise poison-gas attack at Ypres. Built on 3,000 acres of countryside about 85 miles southwest of London, Porton Down's aim was to test and research chemical weapons. Scientists at Porton Down, desperate to catch up with their German counterparts, examined 200 substances during World War I. Many of these experiments relied on living creatures, including dogs, goats, and humans.

By modern standards the tests seem absurdly irresponsible: they often took place outdoors, and given the nature of gases, the toxic chemicals tended to drift out of the facility's confines and into civilian areas, notes Rob Evans, author of *Gassed*. Another test required a fleet-footed cross-country runner to stand in a field near an arsenical smoke cloud. His job was to judge the cloud's potency by sniffing and, when the wind changed direction, to run after the cloud and get in front of it.

Evidence suggests many people were tested without consent or without full awareness of what was involved in the Porton Down trials. Major-General Charles Howard Foulkes, commanding officer at Porton Down, wrote that in the military station's first six months "the greatest difficulty was experienced in getting sufficient men to carry out the experimental work." Cooks, orderlies, and clerks were diverted from their usual jobs to participate in the experiments, Evans notes.

By the close of World War I, Britain had studied the effects on humans of 96 compounds. But the end of the war did not end the use of human guinea pigs. Instead their numbers rapidly increased. Through the 1950s more than 18,000 humans—mostly soldiers, often referred to by the sanitized euphemism "observer" in official reports—were exposed to a wide variety of established and prospective chemical weapons as well as psychoactive drugs. The nature and riskiness of the experiments were often withheld from these subjects.

In 1970 Porton Down's classified records began to reach the light of day. Maddison is the only known death, but many human experimental subjects suffered health problems after exposure, either immediately (for example, by falling into a coma) or years later (subjects had higher rates of cancer). In 2004 the jury of a public inquest into the Maddison case deemed that the young man was "unlawfully killed" at Porton Down. More than half a century after his death Maddison's family received £100,000 in compensation.

"Maddison's death was an accident waiting to happen that resulted from an inadequate level of disclosure and an understatement of risks, despite the fact that there was widespread consensus in the United Kingdom that the principles of the Nuremberg Code should govern these types of experiments," notes Ulf Schmidt, the historical expert appointed to the inquest.

"None of the evidence that I have seen indicates that any of the experimental subjects, including Maddison, was ever informed about the specific objective of the experiments," Schmidt adds. "And I believe it to be rather unlikely that any man in his right mind would have volunteered for such an experiment."

CHEMICAL WEAPONS IN WORLD WAR I

The use of toxic chemicals as weapons dates back thousands of years, but the first large scale use of chemical weapons was during World War I. They were primarily used to demoralize, injure, and kill entrenched defenders, against whom the indiscriminate and generally very slow-moving or static nature of gas clouds would be most effective. The types of weapons employed ranged from disabling chemicals, such as tear gas, to lethal agents like phosgene, chlorine, and mustard gas. This chemical warfare was a major component of the first global war and first total war of the 20th century. The killing capacity of gas was limited, with about ninety thousand fatalities from a total of 1.3 million casualties caused by gas attacks. Gas was unlike most other weapons of the period because it was possible to develop countermeasures, such as gas masks. In the later stages of the war, as the use of gas increased, its overall effectiveness diminished. The widespread use of these agents of chemical warfare, and wartime advances in the composition of high explosives, gave rise to an occasionally expressed view of World War I as "the chemist's war" and also the era where weapons of mass destruction were created.

The use of poison gas by all major belligerents throughout World War I constituted war crimes as its use violated the 1899 Hague Declaration Concerning Asphyxiating Gases and the 1907 Hague Convention on Land Warfare, which prohibited the use of "poison or poisoned weapons" in warfare.Widespread horror and public revulsion at the use of gas and its consequences led to a nearly-complete refusal by all combatants to use poison gas in World War II.

HISTORY OF POISON GAS IN WORLD WAR I

1914: Tear gas

The most frequently used chemicals during World War I were tear-inducing irritants rather than fatal or disabling poisons. During World War I, the French army was the first to employ gas, using 26 mm grenades filled with tear gas (ethyl bromoacetate) in August 1914. The small quantities of gas delivered, roughly 19 cm^3 per cartridge, were not even detected by the Germans. The stocks were rapidly consumed and by November a new order was placed by the French military. As bromine was scarce among the Entente allies, the active ingredient was changed to chloroacetone.

In October 1914, German troops fired fragmentation shells filled with a chemical irritant against British positions at Neuve Chapelle; the concentration achieved was so small that it too was barely noticed. None of the combatants considered the use of tear gas to be in conflict with the Hague Treaty of 1899, which prohibited the launching of projectiles containing asphyxiating or poisonous gas.

1915: Large-scale use and lethal gases

The first instance of large-scale use of gas as a weapon was on 31 January 1915, when Germany fired 18,000 artillery shells containing liquid xylyl bromide tear gas on Russian positions on the Rawka River, west of Warsaw during the Battle of Bolimov. Instead of vaporizing, the chemical froze and failed to have the desired effect.

The first killing agent used by the German military was chlorine. Chlorine is a powerful irritant that can inflict damage to the eyes, nose, throat and lungs. At high concentrations and prolonged exposure it can cause death by asphyxiation. German chemical companies BASF, Hoechst and Bayer (which formed the IG Farben conglomerate in 1925) had been making chlorine as a by-product of their dye manufacturing. In cooperation with Fritz Haber of the Kaiser Wilhelm Institute for Chemistry in Berlin, they began developing methods of discharging chlorine gas against enemy trenches.

According to the fieldpost letter of Major Karl von Zingler, the first chlorine gas attack by German forces took place before 2 January 1915: "In other war theatres it does not go better and it has been said that our Chlorine is very effective. 140 English officers have been killed. This is a horrible weapon ...".

By 22 April 1915, the German Army had 168 tons of chlorine deployed in 5,730 cylinders from Langemark–Poelkapelle, north of Ypres. At 17:30, in a slight easterly breeze, the liquid chlorine was siphoned from the tanks, producing gas which formed a grey-green cloud that drifted across positions held by French Colonial troops from Martinique, as well as the 1st Tirailleurs and the 2nd Zouaves from Algeria. Faced with an unfamiliar threat these troops broke ranks, abandoning their trenches and creating an 8,000-yard (7 km) gap in the Allied line. The German infantry were also wary of the gas and, lacking reinforcements, failed to exploit the break before the 1st Canadian Division and assorted French troops reformed the line in scattered, hastily prepared positions 1,000–3,000 yards (910–2,740 m) apart. The Entente governments claimed the attack was a flagrant violation of international law but Germany argued that the Hague treaty had only banned chemical shells, rather than the use of gas projectors.

In what became the Second Battle of Ypres, the Germans used gas on three more occasions; on 24 April against the 1st Canadian Division, on 2 May near Mouse Trap Farm and on 5 May against the British at Hill 60. The British Official History stated that at Hill 60, "90 men died from gas poisoning in the trenches or before they could be got to a dressing station; of the 207 brought to the nearest dressing stations, 46 died almost immediately and 12 after long suffering."

On 6 August, German troops used chlorine gas against Russian troops defending the Fortress of Osowiec. Surviving defenders drove back the attack and retained the fortress.

Germany used chemical weapons on the eastern front in an attack at Rawka, south of Warsaw. The Russian army took 9,000 casualties, with more than 1,000 fatalities. In response, the artillery branch of the Russian army organised a commission to study the delivery of poison gas in shells.

Effectiveness and countermeasures

It quickly became evident that the men who stayed in their places suffered less than those who ran away, as any movement worsened the effects of the gas, and that those who stood up on the fire step suffered less—indeed they often escaped any serious effects—than those who lay down or sat at the bottom of a trench. Men who stood on the parapet suffered least, as the gas was denser near the ground. The worst sufferers were the wounded lying on the ground, or on stretchers, and the men who moved back with the cloud. Chlorine was less effective as a weapon than the Germans had hoped, particularly as soon as simple countermeasures were introduced. The gas produced a visible greenish cloud and strong odour, making it easy to detect. It was water-soluble, so the simple expedient of covering the mouth and nose with a damp cloth was effective at reducing the effect of the gas. It was thought to be even more effective to use urine rather than water, as it was known at the time that chlorine reacted with urea (present in urine) to form dichloro urea.

Chlorine required a concentration of 1,000 parts per million to be fatal, destroying tissue in the lungs, likely through the formation of hydrochloric acid when dissolved in the water in the lungs ($2Cl_2 + 2H_2O$! $4HCl + O_2$). Despite its limitations, chlorine was an effective psychological weapon—the sight of an oncoming cloud of the gas was a continual source of dread for the infantry.

Countermeasures were quickly introduced in response to the use of chlorine. The Germans issued their troops with small gauze pads filled with cotton waste, and bottles of a bicarbonate solution with which to dampen the pads. Immediately following the use of chlorine gas by the Germans, instructions were sent to British and French troops to hold wet handkerchiefs or cloths over their mouths. Simple pad respirators similar to those issued to German troops were soon proposed by Lieutenant-Colonel N. C. Ferguson, the A.D.M.S. of the 28th Division. These pads were intended to be used damp, preferably dipped into a solution of bicarbonate kept in buckets for that purpose; other liquids were also used. Because such pads could not be expected to arrive at the front for several days, army divisions set about making them for themselves. Locally available muslin, flannel and gauze were used, officers were sent to Paris to buy more and local French women were employed making up rudimentary pads with string ties. Other units used lint bandages manufactured in the convent at Poperinge. Pad respirators were sent up with rations to British troops in the line as early as the evening of 24 April.

In Britain the *Daily Mail* newspaper encouraged women to manufacture cotton pads, and within one month a variety of pad respirators were available to British and French troops, along with motoring goggles to protect the eyes. The response was enormous and a million gas masks were produced in a day. The *Mail*'s design was useless when dry and caused suffocation when wet—the respirator was responsible for the deaths of scores of men. By 6 July 1915, the entire British army was equipped with the more effective "smoke helmet" designed by Major Cluny MacPherson, Newfoundland Regiment, which was a flannel bag with a celluloid window, which entirely covered the head. The race was then on between the introduction of new and more effective poison gases and the production of effective countermeasures, which marked gas warfare until the armistice in November 1918.

British gas attacks

The British expressed outrage at Germany's use of poison gas at Ypres and responded by developing their own gas warfare capability. The commander of II Corps, Lieutenant General Sir Charles Ferguson, said of gas:

> It is a cowardly form of warfare which does not commend itself to me or other English soldiers ... We cannot win this war unless we kill or incapacitate more of our enemies than they do of us, and if this can only be done by our copying the enemy in his choice of weapons, we must not refuse to do so.

The first use of gas by the British was at the Battle of Loos, 25 September 1915, but the attempt was a disaster. Chlorine, codenamed *Red Star*, was the agent to be used (140 tons arrayed in 5,100 cylinders), and the attack was dependent on a favourable wind. On this occasion the wind proved fickle, and the gas either lingered in no man's land or, in places, blew back on the British trenches. This was compounded when the gas could not be released from all the British canisters because the wrong turning keys were sent with them. Subsequent retaliatory German shelling hit some of those unused full cylinders, releasing gas among the British troops. Exacerbating the situation were the primitive flannel gas masks distributed to the British. The masks got hot, and the small eye-pieces misted over, reducing visibility. Some of the troops lifted the masks to get fresh air, causing them to be gassed.

1915: More deadly gases

The deficiencies of chlorine were overcome with the introduction of phosgene, which was prepared by a group of French chemists led by Victor Grignard and first used by France in 1915. Colourless and having an odour likened to "mouldy hay," phosgene was difficult to detect, making it a more effective weapon. Phosgene was sometimes used on its own, but was more often used mixed with an equal volume of chlorine, with the chlorine helping to spread the denser phosgene. The Allies called this combination *White Star* after the marking painted on shells containing the mixture.

Phosgene was a potent killing agent, deadlier than chlorine. It had a potential drawback in that some of the symptoms of exposure took 24 hours or more to manifest. This meant that the victims were initially still capable of putting up a fight; this could also mean that apparently fit troops would be incapacitated by the effects of the gas on the following day.

In the first combined chlorine–phosgene attack by Germany, against British troops at Wieltje near Ypres, Belgium on 19 December 1915, 88 tons of the gas were released from cylinders causing 1069 casualties and 69 deaths. The British P gas helmet, issued at the time, was impregnated with sodium phenolate and partially effective against phosgene. The modified PH Gas Helmet, which was impregnated with phenate hexamine and hexamethylene tetramine (urotropine) to improve the protection against phosgene, was issued in January 1916.

Around 36,600 tons of phosgene were manufactured during the war, out of a total of 190,000 tons for all chemical weapons, making it second only to chlorine (93,800 tons) in the quantity manufactured:

- Germany 18,100 tons
- France 15,700 tons
- United Kingdom 1,400 tons (also used French stocks)
- United States 1,400 tons (also used French stocks)

Phosgene was never as notorious in public consciousness as mustard gas, but it killed far more people, about 85% of the 90,000 deaths caused by chemical weapons during World War I.

1916: Austrian use

On 29 June 1916, Austrian forces attacked the Italian lines on Monte San Michele with a mix of phosgene and chlorine gas. Thousands of Italian soldiers died in this first chemical weapons attack on the Italian Front.

1917: Mustard gas

The most widely reported and, perhaps, the most effective chemical agent of the First World War was sulfur mustard, known as "mustard gas". It is a volatile oily liquid. It was introduced as a vesicant by Germany in July 1917 prior to the Third Battle of Ypres. The Germans marked their shells yellow for mustard gas and green for chlorine and phosgene; hence they called the new gas *Yellow Cross.* It was known to the British as *HS*(*Hun Stuff*), and the French called it *Yperite* (named after Ypres).

Mustard gas is not an effective killing agent (though in high enough doses it is fatal) but can be used to harass and disable the enemy and pollute the battlefield. Delivered in artillery shells, mustard gas was heavier than air, and it settled to the ground as an oily liquid. Once in the soil, mustard gas remained active for several days, weeks, or even months, depending on the weather conditions.

The skin of victims of mustard gas blistered, their eyes became very sore and they began to vomit. Mustard gas caused internal and external bleeding and attacked the bronchial tubes, stripping off the mucous membrane. This was extremely painful. Fatally injured victims sometimes took four or five weeks to die of mustard gas exposure.

One nurse, Vera Brittain, wrote: "I wish those people who talk about going on with this war whatever it costs could see the soldiers suffering from mustard gas poisoning. Great mustard-coloured blisters, blind eyes, all sticky and stuck together, always fighting for breath, with voices a mere whisper, saying that their throats are closing and they know they will choke."

The polluting nature of mustard gas meant that it was not always suitable for supporting an attack as the assaulting infantry would be exposed to the gas when they advanced. When Germany launched Operation *Michael* on 21 March 1918, they saturated the Flesquières salient with mustard gas instead of attacking it directly, believing that the harassing effect of the gas, coupled with threats to the salient's flanks, would make the British position untenable.

Gas never reproduced the dramatic success of 22 April 1915; it became a standard weapon which, combined with conventional artillery, was used to support most attacks in the later stages of the war. Gas was employed primarily on the Western Front—the static, confined trench system was ideal for achieving an effective concentration. Germany also used gas against Russia on the Eastern Front, where the lack of effective countermeasures resulted in deaths of over 56,000 Russians, while Britain experimented with gas in Palestine during the Second Battle of Gaza. Russia began manufacturing chlorine gas in 1916, with phosgene being produced later in the year. Most of the manufactured gas was never used.

The British Army first used mustard gas in November 1917 at Cambrai, after their armies had captured a stockpile of German mustard gas shells. It took the British more than a year to develop their own mustard gas weapon, with production of the chemicals centred on Avonmouth Docks.(The only option available to the British was the Despretz–Niemann–Guthrie process). This was used first in September 1918 during the breaking of the Hindenburg Line with the Hundred Days' Offensive.

The Allies mounted more gas attacks than the Germans in 1917 and 1918 because of a marked increase in production of gas from the Allied nations. Germany was unable to keep up with this pace despite creating various new gases for use in battle, mostly as a result of very costly methods of production. Entry into the war by the United States allowed the Allies to increase mustard gas production far more than Germany. Also the prevailing wind on the Western Frontwas blowing from west to east, which meant the British more frequently had favourable conditions for a gas release than did the Germans.

When the United States entered the war, it was already mobilizing resources from academic, industry and military sectors for research and development into poison gas. A Subcommittee on Noxious Gases was created by the National Research Committee, a major research centre was established at Camp American University, and the 1st Gas Regiment was recruited. The 1st Gas Regiment eventually served in France, where it used phosgene gas in several attacks. The Artillery used mustard gas with significant effect during the Meuse Argonne Offensive on at least three occasions. The United States began large-scale production of an improved vesicant gas known as Lewisite, for use in an offensive planned for early 1919. By the time of the armistice on 11 November, a plant near Willoughby, Ohio was producing 10 tons per day of the substance, for a total of about 150 tons. It is uncertain what effect this new chemical would have had on the battlefield, as it degrades in moist conditions.

Post-war

By the end of the war, chemical weapons had lost much of their effectiveness against well trained and equipped troops. At that time, chemical weapon agents inflicted an estimated 1.3 million casualties.

Nevertheless, in the following years, chemical weapons were used in several, mainly colonial, wars where one side had an advantage in equipment over the other. The British used poison gas, possibly adamsite, against Russian revolutionary troops beginning on 27 August 1919 and contemplated using chemical weapons against Iraqi insurgents in the 1920s; Bolshevik troops used poison gas to suppress the Tambov Rebellion in 1920, Spain used chemical weapons in Morocco against Rif tribesmen throughout the 1920s and Italy used mustard gas in Libya in 1930 and again during its invasion of Ethiopia in 1936. In 1925, a Chinese warlord, Zhang Zuolin, contracted a German company to build him a mustard gas plant in Shenyang, which was completed in 1927.

Public opinion had by then turned against the use of such weapons which led to the Geneva Protocol, an updated and extensive prohibition of poison weapons. The Protocol, which was signed by most First World War combatants in 1925, bans the use (but not the stockpiling) of lethal gas and bacteriological weapons. Most countries that signed ratified it within around five years; a few took much longer – Brazil, Japan, Uruguay, and the United States did not do so until the 1970s, and Nicaragua ratified it in 1990. The signatory nations agreed not to use poison gas in the future, stating "the use in war of asphyxiating, poisonous or other gases, and of all analogous liquids, materials or devices, has been justly condemned by the general opinion of the civilized world."

Chemical weapons have been used in at least a dozen wars since the end of the First World War; they were not used in combat on a large scale until Iraq used mustard gas and the more deadly nerve agents in the Halabja chemical attack near the end of the 8-year Iran–Iraq War. The full conflict's use of such weaponry killed around 20,000 Iranian troops (and injured another 80,000), around a quarter of the number of deaths caused by chemical weapons during the First World War.

Effect on World War II

All major combatants stockpiled chemical weapons during

the Second World War, but the only reports of its use in the conflict were the Japanese use of relatively small amounts of mustard gas and lewisite in China, Italy's use of gas in Ethiopia (in what is more often considered to be the Second Italo-Ethiopian War), and very rare occurrences in Europe (for example some mustard gas bombs were dropped on Warsaw on 3 September 1939, which Germany acknowledged in 1942 but indicated had been accidental). Mustard gas was the agent of choice, with the British stockpiling 40,719 tons, the Soviets 77,400 tons, the Americans over 87,000 tons and the Germans 27,597 tons. The destruction of an American cargo ship containing mustard gas led to many casualties in Bari, Italy, in December 1943.

In both Axis and Allied nations, children in school were taught to wear gas masks in case of gas attack. Germany developed the poison gases tabun, sarin, and soman during the war, and used Zyklon B in their extermination camps. Neither Germany nor the Allied nations used any of their war gases in combat, despite maintaining large stockpiles and occasional calls for their use. Poison gas played an important role in the Holocaust. Britain made plans to use mustard gas on the landing beaches in the event of an invasion of the United Kingdom in 1940. The United States considered using gas to support their planned invasion of Japan.

CASUALTIES

The contribution of gas weapons to the total casualty figures was relatively minor. British figures, which were accurately maintained from 1916, recorded that 3% of gas casualties were fatal, 2% were permanently invalid and 70% were fit for duty again within six weeks.

It was remarked as a joke that if someone yelled 'Gas', everyone in France would put on a mask. ... Gas shock was as frequent as shell shock. —*H. Allen, Towards the Flame, 1934*

Plate III, Pallid type of asphyxia from phosgene poisoning, with circulatory failure, American Red Cross and Medical Research Committee, *An Atlas of Gas Poisoning*, 1918

Death by gas was often slow and painful. According to Denis Winter (*Death's Men*, 1978), a fatal dose of phosgene eventually led to "shallow breathing and retching, pulse up to 120, an ashen face and the discharge of four pints (2 litres) of yellow liquid from the lungs each hour for the 48 of the drowning spasms."

A common fate of those exposed to gas was blindness, chlorine gas or mustard gas being the main causes. One of the most famous First World War paintings, *Gassed* by John Singer Sargent, captures such a scene of mustard gas casualties which he witnessed at a dressing station at Le Bac-du-Sud near Arras in July 1918. (The gases used during that battle (tear gas) caused temporary blindness and/or a painful stinging in the eyes. These bandages were normally water-soaked to provide a rudimentary form of pain relief to the eyes of casualties before they reached more organized medical help.)

The proportion of mustard gas fatalities to total casualties was low; 2% of mustard gas casualties died and many of these succumbed to secondary infections rather than the gas itself. Once it was introduced at the third battle of Ypres, mustard gas produced 90% of all British gas casualties and 14% of battle casualties of any type.

Estimated gas casualties

Nation	Fatal	Total
(Fatal & non-fatal)		
Russia	56,000	419,340
Germany	9,000	200,000
France	8,000	190,000
British Empire (includes Canada)	8,109	188,706
Austria-Hungary	3,000	100,000
United States	1,462	72,807
Italy	4,627	60,000
Total	90,198	1,230,853

Mustard gas was a source of extreme dread. In *The Anatomy of Courage* (1945), Lord Moran, who had been a medical officer during the war, wrote:

> After July 1917 gas partly usurped the role of high explosive in bringing to head a natural unfitness for war. The gassed men were an expression of trench fatigue, a menace when the manhood of the nation had been picked over.

Mustard gas did not need to be inhaled to be effective — any contact with skin was sufficient.

Exposure to 0.1 ppm was enough to cause massive blisters. Higher concentrations could burn flesh to the bone. It was particularly effective against the soft skin of the eyes, nose, armpits and groin, since it dissolved in the natural moisture of those areas.

Typical exposure would result in swelling of the conjunctiva and eyelids, forcing them closed and rendering the victim temporarily blind.

Where it contacted the skin, moist red patches would immediately appear which after 24 hours would have formed into blisters. Other symptoms included severe headache, elevated pulse and temperature (fever), and pneumonia (from blistering in the lungs).

Many of those who survived a gas attack were scarred for life. Respiratory disease and failing eyesight were common post-war afflictions. Of the Canadians who, without any effective protection, had withstood the first chlorine attacks during Second Ypres, 60% of the casualties had to be repatriated and half of these were still unfit by the end of the war, over three years later.

Many of those who were fairly soon recorded as fit for service were left with scar tissue in their lungs. This tissue was susceptible to tuberculosis attack. It was from this that many of the 1918 casualties died, around the time of the Second World War, shortly before sulfa drugs became widely available for its treatment.

British casualties

British forces gas casualties on the Western Front

Date	Agent	Casualties (official)	
		Fatal	Non-fatal
April –May 1915	Chlorine	350	7,000
May 1915 – June 1916	Lachrymants	0	0
December 1915 – August 1916	Chlorine	1,013	4,207
July 1916 – July 1917	Various	532	8,806
July 1917 – November 1918	Mustard gas	4,086	160,526
April 1915 – November 1918	Total	5,981	180,539

A British nurse treating mustard gas cases recorded:

They cannot be bandaged or touched. We cover them with a tent of propped-up sheets. Gas burns must be agonizing because usually the other cases do not complain even with the worst wounds but gas cases are invariably beyond endurance and they cannot help crying out.

A postmortem account from the British official medical history records one of the British casualties:

Case four. Aged 39 years. Gassed 29 July 1917. Admitted to casualty clearing station the same day. Died about ten days later. Brownish pigmentation present over large surfaces of the body. A white ring of skin where the wrist watch was. Marked superficial burning of the face and scrotum. The larynx much congested. The whole of the trachea was covered by a yellow membrane. The bronchi contained abundant gas. The lungs fairly voluminous. The right lung showing extensive collapse at the base. Liver congested and fatty. Stomach showed numerous submucous haemorrhages. The brain substance was unduly wet and very congested.

Civilian casualties

The distribution of gas cloud casualties was not limited to the front. Nearby towns were at risk from winds blowing the poison gases through. Civilians rarely had a warning system to alert their neighbours of the danger and often did not have access to effective gas masks. When the gas came to the towns it could easily get into houses through open windows and doors. An estimated 100,000-260,000 civilian casualties were caused by chemical weapons during the conflict and tens of thousands (along with military personnel) died from scarring of the lungs, skin damage, and cerebral damage in the years after the conflict ended. Many commanders on both sides knew that such weapons would cause major harm to civilians as wind would blow poison gases into nearby civilian towns but nonetheless continued to use them throughout the war. British Field Marshal Sir Douglas Haig wrote in his diary: "My officers and I were aware that such weapon would cause harm to women and children living in nearby towns, as strong winds were common on the battlefront. However, because the weapon was to be directed against the enemy, none of us were overly concerned at all."

Countermeasures

None of the First World War's combatants were prepared for the introduction of poison gas as a weapon. Once gas was introduced, development of gas protection began and the process continued for much of the war producing a series of increasingly effective gas masks.

Even at Second Ypres, Germany, still unsure of the weapon's effectiveness, only issued breathing masks to the engineers handling the gas. At Ypres a Canadian medical officer, who was also a chemist, quickly identified the gas as chlorine and recommended that the troops urinate on a cloth and hold it over their mouth and nose. The first official equipment issued was similarly crude; a pad of material, usually impregnated with a chemical, tied over the lower face. To protect the eyes from tear gas, soldiers were issued with gas goggles.

The next advance was the introduction of the gas helmet — basically a bag placed over the head. The fabric of the bag was impregnated with a chemical to neutralize the gas — the chemical would wash out into the soldier's eyes whenever it rained. Eye-pieces, which were prone to fog up, were initially made from talc. When going into combat, gas helmets were typically worn rolled up on top of the head, to be pulled down and secured about the neck when the gas alarm was given. The first British version was the Hypo helmet, the fabric of which was soaked in sodium hyposulfite (commonly known as "hypo"). The British P gas helmet, partially effective against phosgene and with which all infantry were equipped with at Loos, was impregnated with sodium phenolate. A mouthpiece was added through which the wearer would breathe out to prevent carbon dioxide build-up. The adjutant of the 1/23rd Battalion, The London Regiment, recalled his experience of the P helmet at Loos:

> The goggles rapidly dimmed over, and the air came through in such suffocatingly small quantities as to demand a continuous exercise of will-power on the part of the wearers.

A modified version of the P Helmet, called the PH Helmet, was issued in January 1916, and was impregnated with hexamethylenetetramine to improve the protection against phosgene.

Self-contained box respirators represented the culmination of gas mask development during the First World War. Box respirators used a two-piece design; a mouthpiece connected via a hose to a box filter. The box filter contained granules of chemicals that neutralised the gas, delivering clean air to the wearer. Separating the filter from the mask enabled a bulky but efficient filter to be supplied. Nevertheless, the first version, known as the Large Box Respirator (LBR) or "Harrison's Tower", was deemed too bulky — the box canister needed to be carried on the back. The LBR had no mask, just a mouthpiece and nose clip; separate gas goggles had to be worn. It continued to be issued to the artillery gun crews but the infantry were supplied with the "Small Box Respirator" (SBR).

The Small Box Respirator featured a single-piece, close-fitting rubberized mask with eye-pieces. The box filter was compact and could be worn around the neck. The SBR could be readily upgraded as more effective filter technology was developed. The British-designed SBR was also adopted for use by the American Expeditionary Force. The SBR was the prized possession of the ordinary infantryman; when the British were forced to retreat during the German Spring Offensive of 1918, it was found that while some troops had discarded their rifles, hardly any had left behind their respirators.

Horses and mules were important methods of transport that could be endangered if they came into close contact with gas. This was not so much of a problem until it became common to launch gas great distances. This caused researchers to develop masks that could be used on animals such as dogs, horses, mules, and even carrier pigeons.

For mustard gas, which could cause severe damage by simply making contact with skin, no effective countermeasure was found during the war. The kilt-wearing Scottish regiments were especially vulnerable to mustard gas injuries due to their bare legs. At Nieuwpoort in Flanders some Scottish battalions took to wearing women's tights beneath the kilt as a form of protection.

Gas alert procedure became a routine for the front-line soldier. To warn of a gas attack, a bell would be rung, often made from a spent artillery shell. At the noisy batteries of the siege guns, a compressed air strombus horn was used, which could be heard nine miles (14 km) away. Notices would be posted on all approaches to an affected area, warning people to take precautions.

Other British attempts at countermeasures were not so effective. An early plan was to use 100,000 fans to disperse the gas. Burning coal or carborundum dust was tried. A proposal was made to equip front-line sentries with diving helmets, air being pumped to them through a 100 ft (30 m) hose.

The effectiveness of all countermeasures is apparent. In 1915, when poison gas was relatively new, less than 3% of

British gas casualties died. In 1916, the proportion of fatalities jumped to 17%. By 1918, the figure was back below 3%, though the total number of British gas casualties was now nine times the 1915 levels.

DELIVERY SYSTEMS

The first system employed for the mass delivery of gas involved releasing the gas cylinders in a favourable wind such that it was carried over the enemy's trenches. The Hague Convention of 1899 prohibited the use of poisons gasses delivered by projectiles. The main advantage of this method was that it was relatively simple and, in suitable atmospheric conditions, produced a concentrated cloud capable of overwhelming the gas mask defences. The disadvantages of cylinder releases were numerous. First and foremost, delivery was at the mercy of the wind. If the wind was fickle, as was the case at Loos, the gas could backfire, causing friendly casualties. Gas clouds gave plenty of warning, allowing the enemy time to protect themselves, though many soldiers found the sight of a creeping gas cloud unnerving. Gas clouds had limited penetration, only capable of affecting the front-line trenches before dissipating.

Finally, the cylinders had to be emplaced at the very front of the trench system so that the gas was released directly over no man's land. This meant that the cylinders had to be manhandled through communication trenches, often clogged and sodden, and stored at the front where there was always the risk that cylinders would be prematurely breached during a bombardment. A leaking cylinder could issue a telltale wisp of gas that, if spotted, would be sure to attract shellfire.

A British chlorine cylinder, known as an "oojah", weighed 190 lb (86 kg), of which 60 lb (27 kg) was chlorine gas, and required two men to carry. Phosgene gas was introduced later in a cylinder, known as a "mouse", that weighed 50 lb (23 kg).

Delivering gas via artillery shell overcame many of the risks of dealing with gas in cylinders. The Germans, for example, used 5.9-inch (150 mm) artillery shells. Gas shells were independent of the wind and increased the effective range of gas, making anywhere within reach of the guns vulnerable. Gas shells could be delivered without warning, especially the clear, nearly odourless phosgene — there are numerous accounts of gas shells, landing with a "plop" rather than exploding, being initially dismissed as dud HE or shrapnel shells, giving the gas time to work before the soldiers were alerted and took precautions.

The main flaw associated with delivering gas via artillery was the difficulty of achieving a killing concentration. Each shell had a small gas payload and an area would have to be subjected to a saturation bombardment to produce a cloud to match cylinder delivery. Mustard gas did not need to form a concentrated cloud and hence artillery was the ideal vehicle for delivery of this battlefield pollutant.

The solution to achieving a lethal concentration without releasing from cylinders was the "gas projector", essentially a large-bore mortar that fired the entire cylinder as a missile. The British Livens projector (invented by Captain W.H. Livens in 1917) was a simple device; an 8-inch (200 mm) diameter tube sunk into the ground at an angle, a propellant was ignited by an electrical signal, firing the cylinder containing 30 or 40 lb (14 or 18 kg) of gas up to 1,900 metres. By arranging a battery of these projectors and firing them simultaneously, a dense concentration of gas could be achieved. The Livens was first used at Arras on 4 April 1917. On 31 March 1918 the British conducted their largest ever "gas shoot", firing 3,728 cylinders at Lens.

UNEXPLODED WEAPONS

Over 16,000,000 acres (65,000 km^2) of France had to be cordoned off at the end of the war because of unexploded ordnance. About 20% of the chemical shells were duds, and approximately 13 million of these munitions were left in place. This has been a serious problem in former battle areas from immediately after the end of the War until the present. Shells may be, for instance, uncovered when farmers plough their fields (termed the 'iron harvest'), and are also regularly discovered when public works or construction work is done.

Another difficulty is the current stringency of environmental legislation. In the past, a common method of getting rid of unexploded chemical ammunition was to detonate or dump it at sea; this is currently prohibited in most countries.

The problems are especially acute in some northern regions of France. The French government no longer disposes of chemical weapons at sea. For this reason, piles of untreated chemical weapons accumulated. In 2001, it became evident that the pile stored at a depot in Vimywas unsafe; the inhabitants of the neighbouring town were evacuated, and the pile moved, using refrigerated trucks and under heavy guard, to a military camp in Suippes. The capacity of the plant is meant to be 25 tons per year (extensible to 80 tons at the beginning), for a lifetime of 30 years.

Germany has to deal with unexploded ammunition and polluted lands resulting from the explosion of an ammunition train in 1919.

Aside from unexploded shells, there have been claims that poison residues have remained in the local environment for an extended period, though this is unconfirmed; well known but unverified anecdotes claim that as late as the 1960s trees in the area retained enough mustard gas residue to injure farmers or construction workers who were clearing them.

LONG-TERM HEALTH EFFECTS

Soldiers who claimed to have been exposed to chemical warfare have often presented with unusual medical conditions which has led to much controversy. The lack of information has left doctors, patients, and their families in the dark in terms of prognosis and treatment. Nerve agents such as sarin, tabun, and soman are believed to have the most significant long-term health effects. Chronic fatigue and memory loss have been reported to last up to three years after exposure. In the years following World War One, there were many conferences held in attempts to abolish the use of chemical weapons all together, such as the Washington Naval Conference (1921–22), Geneva Conference (1923–25) and the World Disarmament Conference (1933). The United States was an original signatory of the Geneva Protocol in 1925, but the US Senate did not ratify it until 1975.

Although the health effects are generally chronic in nature, the exposures were generally acute. A positive correlation has been proven between exposure to mustard agents and skin cancers, other respiratory and skin conditions, leukemia, several eye conditions, bone marrow depression and subsequent immunosuppression, psychological disorders and sexual dysfunction.

Chemicals used in the production of chemical weapons have also left residues in the soil where the weapons were used. The chemicals that have been detected can cause cancer and can affect the brain, blood, liver, kidneys and skin.

Despite the evidence in support of long-term health effects, there are studies that show just the opposite. Some US veterans who were closely affected by chemical weapons showed no neurological evidence in the following years. These same studies showed that one single contact with chemical weapons would be enough to cause long-term health effects.

RISK OF EXPOSURE IN CHEMICAL WARFARE

Injury from chemical weapon agents, known as CWAs, may result from industrial accidents, military stockpiling, war, or a terrorist attack.

Industrial accidents are a significant potential source of exposure to chemical agents. Chemicals such as phosgene, cyanide, anhydrous ammonia, and chlorine are used widely. These chemicals are frequently transported by industry. The accidental release of a methylisocyanate cloud (composed of phosgene and isocyanate) was implicated in the Bhopal, India, disaster in 1984.

- Chemical weapons first were used in 1915, when the German military released 168 tons of chlorine gas at Ypres, Belgium, killing an estimated 5,000 Allied troops.
- Two years later, the same battlefields saw the first deployment of sulfur mustard. Sulfur mustard was the major cause of chemical casualties in World War I.
- CWAs have been used in at least 12 conflicts since, including the first Persian Gulf War (Iraq-Iran War). The Iraqi military also used chemical weapons against the Iraqi Kurds during the second Persian Gulf War.
- Civilians also have been exposed inadvertently to chemical weapons many years after weapon deployment during war. Some 50,000 tons of mustard shells were disposed of in the Baltic Sea following World War I. Since then, numerous fishermen have been burned accidentally while hauling leaking shells aboard boats. Leaking mustard shells also have injured collectors of military memorabilia and children playing on old battlefields.

Although a number of international treaties have banned the development, production, and stockpiling of chemical weapons, these agents reportedly are still being produced or stockpiled in several countries.

Within the last decade, terrorists deployed chemical weapons against civilian populations for the first time in history. The release of sarin in Matsumoto, Japan, in June 1994 by the extremist Aum Shinrikyo cult left 7 dead and 280 injured. The following year, the Aum Shinrikyo cult released sarin vapour in the Tokyo subway system during morning rush hour, leaving 12 dead and sending more than 5,000 casualties to local hospitals.

Several characteristics of chemical weapon agents lend themselves to terrorist use.

- Chemicals used in CWAs are widely available, and recipes for CWA production may be found on the Internet.

- CWAs are transported easily and may be delivered by a variety of routes.
- Chemical agents often are difficult to protect against and quickly incapacitate the intended targets.
- Most civilian medical communities are inadequately prepared to deal with a chemical terrorist attack.

Types of Chemical Weapon Agents

- Chemical weapon agents are hazardous substances. Major categories of CWAs include the following:
  - o Nerve agents (such as sarin, soman, cyclohexylsarin, tabun, VX)
  - o Vesicating or blistering agents (such as mustards, lewisite)
  - o Choking agents or lung toxicants (such as chlorine, phosgene, diphosgene)
  - o Cyanides
  - o Incapacitating agents (such as anticholinergic compounds)
  - o Lacrimating or riot control agents (such as pepper gas, chloroacetophenone, CS)
  - o Vomiting agents (such as adamsite)
- Physical properties: CWAs generally are stored and transported as liquids and deployed as either liquid aerosols or vapors. Victims usually are exposed to agents via 1 or more of 3 routes: skin (liquid and high vapour concentrations), eyes (liquid or vapour), and respiratory tract (vapour inhalation). In general, some liquids may be harmful whether inhaled into the lungs or absorbed into the skin. Vapors can be affected by winds. Even a slight breeze can blow a nerve agent vapour away from its intended target. The effects of vapour are enhanced when used within an enclosed space.
- Clinical effects: Depending on the agent and the type and amount (concentration) of exposure, CWA effects may be immediate or delayed. Large inhalation

exposures to nerve agents or mustards are likely to kill people immediately. Small exposures on the skin to nerve agents and mustards are more dangerous than they seem at first. People exposed to such agents need to be carefully observed for slowly developing or delayed effects. A chart of signs and symptoms is available from the North Carolina Statewide Program for Infection Control and Epidemiology.

- Medical management: Ideally, emergency personnel will wear personal protective equipment, decontaminate the victims immediately, provide medical support to the victims and provide specific antidotes to counteract the harmful effects.
- Personal protective equipment: First responders to a chemical attack are at serious risk themselves from the chemically contaminated environment (known as the hot zone). They can come in direct contact with the CWA or inhale the vapour. They are also at risk if they handle skin and clothing of victims if a liquid chemical agent was used. Vapors pose little added risk for anyone outside the hot zone.
- Decontamination: Decontamination is the physical process of removing the remaining chemicals from people, equipment, and the environment. Residual hazardous chemicals on those who have been exposed directly are a source of ongoing exposure to others and pose a risk of secondary exposure to first responders and emergency care personnel. Immediate decontamination is a major treatment priority for those with CWA exposure.
    - o Initial decontamination involves removing all contaminated clothes and jewellery from the affected person and then washing the body thoroughly with warm water and soap.
    - o Hot water and vigorous scrubbing may actually worsen the effects by increasing chemical absorption into the skin.

- o Vapour exposure alone may not require decontamination. But if it is not known whether the exposure was to a vapour or liquid, or if exposed people have symptoms, they should undergo decontamination.
- o Ideally, decontamination will take place as close as possible to the site of exposure to minimize duration of exposure and prevent further spread. Hospitals receiving contaminated people may establish an area outside the Emergency Department in which to perform initial decontamination before people and equipment are allowed entry. Portable decontamination equipment with showers and run-off water collection systems are commercially available. All hospitals should have the capacity to safely decontaminate at least 1 person.

- Supportive and specific therapy: Doctors will first make sure exposed victims are able to breathe. For many chemical warfare agents, doctors can only treat the symptoms they produce. But specific, well-established antidotes are available for nerve agent and cyanide exposures. Lab tests are not widely available in hospitals to rapidly confirm exposure to chemical agents.

CHEMICAL WARFARE AGENTS IN THE ENVIRONMENT

When addressing the requirement for chemical agent detection at the scene of a terrorist incident, it is important to consider who really has the responsibility for detection operations. Is it the police, the fire department, the Hazmat team, or the EMS units? If the responsibility falls on medical assets, how will the use of detection equipment increase the efficiency of the health care team in preserving life and preventing further injury? Furthermore, will the absence of more sensitive equipment somehow inhibit their performance? These are important questions that must be addressed by policymakers and incident response planners.

Because of their physical properties, CWA use in a domestic terrorist incident may not be associated with a high-explosive event. Rather, these agents may well be dispersed in a manner that would involve a vapour hazard within a confined space.

The type of incident seen in Tokyo, while minimized by the inefficient release of the CWA, is an excellent example of the type of incident expected as a result of terrorist use of CWA. The highest probability of detecting the presence of CWA occurs in cases in which there is a continuing source of vapour.

By the time emergency medical personnel arrive at an incident, inevitably the agent will have dispersed significantly. In the case of cyanide and phosgene, and most nerve agents, detection in the environment may not be possible by the time monitoring equipment is in place at the scene.

In fact, once casualties of a vapour CWA incident are outside the area of the attack and accessible to medical personnel, the signs and symptoms of the patients may be the only detection method available, and the threat of spread of the CWA hazard from casualties may be minimal.

However, in the case of the Tokyo sarin attack, it has been reported that up to 9 percent of EMS workers and a significant number of hospital staff experienced acute symptoms of nerve agent toxicity due to exposure to casualties in unventilated areas (Okumura et al., 1998b). Given the increased threat of CWA terrorism and the various CW agents that can be used, emergency responders must have accurate and timely detection information or the ability to detect and identify a CWA at the time of their response.

Again in the case of the Tokyo subway attack, the first identification made was inaccurate, and it was not until three hours post incident that accurate detection of sarin was made and the information disseminated. The medical personnel on site will require equipment capable of detecting the widest range of chemical agents. For medical personnel, detection equipment may include rapid, minimally invasive or noninvasive clinical assays for various chemical agents or for the effects of the chemical agents, that is, cholinesterase inhibition. Without this ability, more individuals may be exposed, including emergency response and hospital personnel attempting to care for casualties.

Chemical agent detection will be an essential part of both medical crisis and consequence management. Detection and identification of the chemical agent or agents at the scene of a terrorist incident must not be accomplished at the expense of rapid and appropriate medical treatment of chemical casualties.

An emergency response incident that involves the release of any chemicals or toxic materials will typically be categorized as a hazardous materials (Hazmat) incident. The response to a Hazmat incident is somewhat standardized across the country. Specialized Hazmat teams are normally called in to address these situations. Hazmat teams are typically part of the fire services and will possess a majority of the locality's chemical detection equipment. The emergency responders who arrive on the scene first, however, must be capable of determining that a Hazmat incident has occurred. These first responders will be the individuals responsible for determining whether the Hazmat team should be called for assistance. Most emergency response vehicles do not carry any chemical detection equipment.

Chemical detection equipment currently used by Hazmat teams varies considerably by locality. For large metropolitan areas, current detectors range from adequate instrumentation to absolutely no capability for CWA detection. Hazmat teams are routinely equipped with a variety of chemical detectors and monitoring kits, primarily chemical-specific tests indicating only the presence or absence of the suspected chemical or class of chemical.

A negative response of the test means only that a specific substance is not present in significant quantity; a positive response says nothing about the possible presence of other hazardous agents. Colorimetric tubes, designed for the detection of known and unknown gases, are commonly used by Hazmat teams. There are over 200 different tubes available that can detect a variety of chemicals. The tubes used by responders are sold in basic detection sets typically consisting of the tubes and a hand or mechanical pump. The pump, used to draw the air sample through the tube, will simultaneously carry out a volume measurement with each stroke.

Direct reading detector tubes can be used for both short-term measurement and long-term measurement. The long-term tubes consist of two types: one requiring a constant flow pump, and the other a diffusion detector tube. Hazmat team analytical capabilities commonly include tests for chlorine, cyanide, phosgene gas, and organophosphate pesticides.

The last of these tests may respond to the military nerve agents, but the requisite validation studies have not been conducted. Colorimetric tubes for the detection of CWA are not standard issue items for Hazmat teams and rarely include a means of detecting the chemical vesicants, such as sulfur mustard or Lewisite.

Many modern detection devices used by Hazmat teams have not been thoroughly tested for their utility and reliability to detect CWA. There is an ongoing effort under the sponsorship of the U.S. Army-managed Domestic Preparedness Program to test currently used Hazmat detection systems against classical CW agents.

Preliminary analysis, for example, has shown that combustible gas indicators and pH paper, which are available to most Hazmat teams, will not serve as CWA detectors. The combustible gas detector was designed to detect and measure concentrations of combustible gases and/or vapors in the air, such as carbon monoxide, oxygen, and hydrogen sulfide, while pH paper is simply too generic to be useful as an indicator of CWA.

CHEMICAL WEAPONS : BEHIND TRUMP'S DECISION TO ORDER AIRSTRIKES IN SYRIA

When President Donald Trump announced on Friday night that he had ordered airstrikes on Syria, he explained the decision with an appeal to a longstanding international consensus that the use of chemical weapons — such as were used a week ago on Syrian opposition forces and civilians in Douma, per the assessment of the U.S., despite denials from the Syrian regime — is a wrong that merits such a forceful response. France's President Emmanuel Macron and Britain's Prime Minister Theresa May have made it clear that they essentially feel the same. "Following the horrors of World War I a century ago, civilized nations joined together to ban chemical warfare," Trump noted in his speech, later adding that the world never wants to see the "ghastly specter" of those weapons return.

The indications that such an announcement might be coming had been present for days since the initial report of the attack, which left Trump once again considering how such news might change his plans, as he had formerly expressed a desire to get the U.S. out of Syria.

Many dead, including women and children, in mindless CHEMICAL attack in Syria. Area of atrocity is in lockdown and encircled by Syrian Army, making it completely inaccessible to outside world. President Putin, Russia and Iran are responsible for backing Animal Assad. Big price...

The news follows a similar pattern to the events of about a year ago, when the use of chemical weapons in Syria and the resulting horrific imagery of the dead seemed enough to prompt a reversal in President Trump's stated aversion to U.S. intervention there.

And yet noncombatants are killed in the course of war in countless other fashions, and attempting to rank the cruelest ways to kill is an exercise in both futility and inhumanity. So why is it that chemical weapons spark such automatic revulsion when years of bombs and bullets have not? Though Trump correctly pinpointed World War I as a turning point, in fact the story is even older than that.

Early Developments

Chemical and biological weapons predate even our modern understanding of what those terms mean; there's evidence of the use of noxious gas as a weapon in the ancient world and, as TIME has pointed out, the purposeful spread of smallpox in the 18th century as a tactic against American Indians was its own kind of biological warfare.

The feeling that such poisons are not an appropriate or honorable tactic of warfare is also an old one. As Julian Perry Robinson has written in his history of the subject, the earliest example of that idea might possibly be found in ancient Indian epics. And in Greek mythology, the use of poison as a weapon of war was often considered cowardly, a tricky technique used by those who were not heroes. By 1675, according to the Organization for the Prohibition of Chemical Weapons, France and Germany had signed what was the first international treaty that limited such weapons (in this case, poisoned bullets).

So it should be no surprise that in 1899, during a conference at the Hague on the laws of war, it was decided by the signatory nations that it would be "especially" prohibited "to employ poison or poisoned arms." Though the convention they signed did not come with any enforcement mechanism, the moral imperative to avoid using poison during wartime had been established by that point.

But, during the 19th century, the technology that could be deployed in the use of chemical weapons underwent a shift. Pressurized canisters of noxious gas could replace the poisoned arrow tips of the past. As Robinson describes, Germany had an "industrial edge" in the development of such technology, and soon enough a reason to want to take advantage of that edge. The infamous trench-based stalemates that quickly set in after the 1914 beginning of World War I made the combatants eager to try something new — and that something included gas, even despite those centuries of history condemning such an idea.

The World Wars

On April 22, 1915, "German infantrymen gave the world its first whiff of poison-gas warfare," as TIME later recalled, "by sending a huge, grey-green cloud of noxious chlorine rolling over two French divisions in the trenches at Ypres, killing

5,000, incapacitating 10,000, and cutting a 31-mile swath in Allied lines." Chlorine, phosgene, chloropicrin and mustard gas were all used during the Great War, though all involved — both sides developed and used chemical weapons — discovered that gas could be a difficult tool to use well, as the wind had to cooperate to make it work and developments such as increased use of tanks mitigated some of the chemicals' impacts.

By TIME's later estimate, that war saw 124,000 tons of chemical weapons used, between both sides, and the resulting deaths of 91,000 soldiers. So it was that, in the wake of that conflict, the Treaty of Versailles included a ban on Germany manufacturing any poison gas. In addition, as members of League of Nations met in Geneva in 1925, delegates from 45 countries sought to find a out a way to come up with what TIME called back then "a protocol generally prohibiting chemical and bacteriological warfare."

"[The] use in war of asphyxiating, poisonous or other gases, and of all analogous liquids, materials or devices, has been justly condemned by the general opinion of the civilized world," the protocol proclaimed. The Geneva Protocol, however, did not end the history of chemical weapons. It had "no teeth," per TIME, and allowed nations to make and keep such agents as long as they promised not to use them. (The U.S., which had not actually ratified its membership in the League, did not sign the Geneva Protocol at the time.)

And, before the League of Nations participants would have hoped, the world had cause to put the Protocol to the test. The Great War turned out not to be, as had been hoped, the "war to end all wars." When World War II began, as TIME noted in 1944, "the horror and repugnance aroused by the use of gas in World War I [was] still alive," though some Americans argued that using chemical weapons would be a more modern and humane approach to warfare. Yet, though soldiers had gotten much better prepared to withstand a gas attack since the 1915 Ypres battle that was still so fresh in humanity's collective memory, chemical weapons still held the deadly threat of death for civilians. Nor was it necessary to use chemical weapons, one military official told the magazine: in order to really make a difference the gas must be used by a combatant with a superior air force, and having a superior air force meant there was no reason to use gas.

In 1943, President Franklin Roosevelt warned the Axis powers not to use poison gas during war, and promised that the U.S. would only do so in retaliation: Use of such weapons has been outlawed by the general opinion of civilized mankind. This country has not used them, and I hope that we never will be compelled to use them. I state categorically that we shall under no circumstances resort to the use of such weapons unless they are first used by our enemies.

As President of the United States and as Commander in Chief of the American armed forces, I want to make clear beyond all doubt to any of our enemies contemplating a resort to such desperate and barbarous methods that acts of this nature committed against any one of the United Nations will be regarded as having been committed against the United States itself and will be treated accordingly. We promise to any perpetrators of such crimes full and swift retaliation in kind and I feel obliged now to warn the Axis armies and the Axis peoples, in Europe and in Asia, that the terrible consequences of any use of these inhumane methods on their part will be brought down swiftly and surely upon their own heads. Any use of gas by any Axis power, therefore, will immediately be followed by the fullest possible retaliation upon munition centers, seaports, and other military objectives throughout the whole extent of the territory of such Axis country.

Even as Nazi scientists were experimenting with new and potent poison gases, including nerve agents like sarin, some of which were manufactured by concentration camp prisoners, Hitler chose not to endorse their use against Allied soldiers. ("Although many senior military officers encouraged Hitler to deploy their powerful new chemical weapon, he waffled, likely for two reasons," according to Sarah Everts' summary of the history for the Chemical Heritage Foundation. Those reasons were Hitler's own experience as a victim of battlefield gas in World War I and his worry that the Allies might have developed similar technology and would retaliate in kind.)

But despite what happened on the battlefield, deadly chemicals were widely used by the Nazi regime as part of their effort to wipe out the population of Jews and other minorities from the area they controlled. For example, in 1944, when TIME's Moscow Correspondent Richard Lauterbach visited the Majdanek concentration camp and reported on the tour he received from Dmitri Kudriavtsev, Secretary of the Soviet Atrocities Commission, he saw the bathhouses in which Nazis had used Zyklon B to kill as many as 250 people at a time. He was told that on Nov. 3, 1943, alone, "they annihilated 18,000 people — Poles, Jews, political prisoners and war prisoners" with the gas.

New Agreements, New Trespasses

After World War II, as proud as the world powers may have been to have avoided the use of chemical weapons during the battles, the Cold War arms race extended to chemical-weapons research competition, too. One rationalization for that research was helped along by the widespread Cold War idea that, as long as one didn't strike first, any weapon could be on the table. Plus, the Geneva Protocol only prevented the *use* of those weapons, not the creation or storage of them. So it should perhaps be no surprise that the late 20th century was a time of both new diplomatic advances and new uses of new weapons, despite those advances.

On the one hand, the U.S. — after decades of supporting the doctrine voiced by Roosevelt — signed agreements that barred the use of chemical weapons, as did other nations. On the other hand, research continued apace, and the prohibition on the use of chemical weapons did not completely stop them from being put into action.

Controversy over whether the U.S. was using gas in Vietnam raged during the 1960s — that the U.S. was using chemicals such as Agent Orange was clear, but whether that herbicide counted as a chemical weapon as governed by the Geneva Protocol was disputed — and by the end of that decade the U.S. was spending hundreds of millions of dollars a year on its chemical and biological weapons program, stockpiling the results. Then, in the wake of that controversy, President Nixon resubmitted the Geneva Convention to the U.S. Senate, shortly before the 1972 Biological Weapons Convention — which strengthened the biological-weapons portion of the Geneva protocol — was submitted, too. Both were approved by the Senate in late 1974 and ratified by President Ford in early 1975.

In 1988, Iraq used poison gas on Kurdish towns during the course of its war with Iran. "The bloated bodies of Kurdish residents littered the silent streets of the northern Iraqi town of Halabja. A dead turbaned man who had tried to shield a porcelain-faced infant in his arms from a cloud of poison gas lay frozen in time on a road. Families died together in their homes or in cars. The dead were among the hundreds and possibly thousands of victims of one of the worst chemical-warfare attacks since World War I," TIME reported. The weapons used were primarily mustard gas. The world's response was somewhat muted — perhaps due to a lack of desire to take the side of Iran among many of the Geneva Protocol signatories who might have otherwise spoken up — but President Ronald Reagan said in a speech that year that the use of those weapons "jeopardizes the moral and legal strictures that have held those weapons in check since World War I."

In 1993, after the fall of the Soviet Union, an even tougher U.N. Chemical Weapons Convention was created. This agreement prohibited stockpiling. At the time of the signing, both the U.S. and Russia had tens of thousands of metric tons of chemical weapons in store. Following through on the timely destruction of the chemical agents, as required by that agreement, has proveddifficult.

And yet one question, raised by Julian Perry Robinson, has remained unanswered through these many decades: if chemical weapons were more tactically useful, easier to control and harder for armies (if not civilians) to guard against, would those who make such decisions have come up with justifications for their use?

After all, as a TIME essay in 1969 began, "The dark side of progress is man's spectacular skill at devising better and better ways to kill other men."

5

Poison Gas and World War One

Poison gas was probably the most feared of all weapons in World War One. Poison gas was indiscriminate and could be used on the trenches even when no attack was going on. Whereas the machine gun killed more soldiers overall during the war, death was frequently instant or not drawn out and soldiers could find some shelter in bomb/shell craters from gunfire. A poison gas attack meant soldiers having to put on crude gas masks and if these were unsuccessful, an attack could leave a victim in agony for days and weeks before he finally succumbed to his injuries.

It is generally assumed that gas was first used by the Germans in World War One. This is not accurate. The first recorded gas attack was by the French. In August 1914, the French used tear gas grenades containing xylyl bromide on the Germans. This was more an irritant rather than a gas that would kill. It was used by the French to stop the seemingly unstoppable German army advancing throughout Belgium and north-eastern France. In one sense, it was an act of desperation as opposed to a premeditated act that all but went against the 'rules' of war. However, while the French were the first to use a gas against an enemy, the Germans had been giving a great deal of thought to the use of poison gas as a way of inflicting a major defeat on an enemy.

In October 1914, the Germans attacked Neuve Chapelle. Here they fired gas shells at the French that contained a chemical that caused violent sneezing fits. Once again, the gas was not designed to kill rather than to incapacitate an enemy so that they were incapable of defending their positions.

This took place against a background of a war in the west that was still mobile. Once trench warfare had literally dug in, all sides involved in the conflict looked for any way possible to bring movement back into their campaigns. One of the more obvious was to develop a weapon that was so appalling that it would destroy not only an enemy frontline but also the will to maintain troops on that frontline. Poison gas might even provoke a mass mutiny along a frontline thus causing it to collapse. In other words, poison gas was the answer for the war's lack of mobility.

Poison gas (chlorine) was used for the first time at the Second Battle of Ypres in April 1915. At around 17.00 hours on the 22nd April, French sentries in Ypres noticed a yellow-green cloud moving towards them – a gas delivered from pressurised cylinders dug into the German front line between Steenstraat and Langemarck. They thought that it was a smokescreen to disguise the movement forwards of German troops. As such, all troops in the area were ordered to the firing line of their trench – right in the path of the chlorine. Its impact was immediate and devastating. The French and their Algerian comrades fled in terror. Their understandable reaction created an opportunity for the Germans to advance unhindered into the strategically important Ypres salient. But even the Germans were unprepared and surprised by the impact of chlorine and they failed to follow up the success of the chlorine attack.

What did occur at Ypres was a deliberate use of a poison gas. Now, the gloves were off and other nations with the ability to manufacture poison gas could use it and blame it on the Germans as they had been the first to use it.

The first of the Allied nations to respond to the Ypres gas attack was Britain in September 1915. The newly formed Special

Gas Companies attacked German lines at Loos. In the Ypres attack, the German had delivered their chlorine by using pressurised cylinders. For the attack at Loos, the British also used gas cylinders. When the wind was in a favourable direction, chlorine gas was released from the British front line so that it could drift over to the German front line. This was then to be followed by an infantry attack. However, along parts of the British front line, the wind changed direction and the chlorine was blown back onto the British causing over 2,000 casualties with seven fatalities. The Special Gas Companies were not allowed to call their new weapon gas – it was referred to as an "accessory".

However, the risk of the wind blowing gas back onto you also affected the Germans and French in some of their gas attacks during late 1915. The development in the use of poison gases led to both phosgene and mustard gas being used. Phosgene was especially potent as its impact was frequently felt only 48 hours after it had been inhaled and by then it had already bedded itself in the respiratory organs of the body and little could be done to eradicate it. Also it was much less apparent that someone had inhaled phosgene as it did not cause as much violent coughing. By the time that phosgene had got into a person's bodily system, it was too late. Mustard gas was first used by the Germans against the Russians at Riga in September 1917. This gas caused both internal and external blisters on the victim within hours of being exposed to it. Such damage to the lungs and other internal organs were very painful and occasionally fatal. Many who did survive were blinded by the gas.

By the time the war ended, the main user of poison gas was Germany, followed by France and then Britain. Though poison gas was a terrifying weapon, its actual impact, rather like the tank, is open to debate. The number of fatalities was relatively few – even if the terror impact did not diminish for the duration of the war.

The British army (including the British Empire) had 188,000 gas casualties but only 8,100 fatalities amongst them. It is believed that the nation that suffered the most fatalities was Russia (over 50,000 men) while France had 8,000 fatalities. In total there were about 1,250,000 gas casualties in the war but only 91,000 fatalities (less than 10%) with over 50% of these fatalities being Russian. However, these figures do not take into account the number of men who died from poison gas related injuries years after the end of the war; nor do they take into account the number of men who survived but were so badly incapacitated by poison gas that they could hold down no job once they had been released by the army.

Armies quickly produced gas masks that gave protection as long as sufficient warning was given of a gas attack. Soldiers also used make-shift gas masks if they were caught in the open without a gas mask during a gas attack – cloth soaked in their own urine and placed over the mouth was said to give protection against a chlorine attack. By the end of the war, relatively sophisticated gas masks were available to soldiers in the trenches on the Western Front.

GERMANS INTRODUCE POISON GAS

On April 22, 1915, German forces shock Allied soldiers along the western front by firing more than 150 tons of lethal chlorine gas against two French colonial divisions at Ypres, Belgium. This was the first major gas attack by the Germans, and it devastated the Allied line.

Toxic smoke has been used occasionally in warfare since ancient times, and in 1912 the French used small amounts of tear gas in police operations. At the outbreak of World War I, the Germans began actively to develop chemical weapons. In October 1914, the Germans placed some small tear-gas canisters in shells that were fired at Neuve Chapelle, France, but Allied troops were not exposed. In January 1915, the Germans fired shells loaded with xylyl bromide, a more lethal gas, at Russian troops at Bolimov on the eastern front. Because of the wintry cold, most of the gas froze, but the Russians nonetheless reported more than 1,000 killed as a result of the new weapon.

On April 22, 1915, the Germans launched their first and only offensive of the year. Known as the Second Battle of Ypres, the offensive began with the usual artillery bombardment of the enemy's line. When the shelling died down, the Allied defenders waited for the first wave of German attack troops but instead were thrown into panic when chlorine gas wafted across no-man's land and down into their trenches. The Germans targeted four miles of the front with the wind-blown poison gas and decimated two divisions of French and Algerian colonial troops. The Allied line was breached, but the Germans, perhaps as shocked as the Allies by the devastating effects of the poison gas, failed to take full advantage, and the Allies held most of their positions.

A second gas attack, against a Canadian division, on April 24, pushed the Allies further back, and by May they had retreated to the town of Ypres. The Second Battle of Ypres ended on May 25, with insignificant gains for the Germans. The introduction of poison gas, however, would have great significance in World War I.

Immediately after the German gas attack at Ypres, France and Britain began developing their own chemical weapons and gas masks. With the Germans taking the lead, an extensive number of projectiles filled with deadly substances polluted the trenches of World War I. Mustard gas, introduced by the Germans in 1917, blistered the skin, eyes, and lungs, and killed thousands. Military strategists defended the use of poison gas by saying it reduced the enemy's ability to respond and thus saved lives in offensives. In reality, defenses against poison gas usually kept pace with offensive developments, and both sides employed sophisticated gas masks and protective clothing that essentially negated the strategic importance of chemical weapons.

The United States, which entered World War I in 1917, also developed and used chemical weapons. Future president Harry S. Truman was the captain of a U.S. field artillery unit that fired poison gas against the Germans in 1918. In all, more than 100,000 tons of chemical weapons agents were used in World

War I, some 500,000 troops were injured, and almost 30,000 died, including 2,000 Americans.

In the years following World War I, Britain, France, and Spain used chemical weapons in various colonial struggles, despite mounting international criticism of chemical warfare. In 1925, the Geneva Protocol of 1925 banned the use of chemical weapons in war but did not outlaw their development or stockpiling. Most major powers built up substantial chemical weapons reserves. In the 1930s, Italy employed chemical weapons against Ethiopia, and Japan used them against China. In World War II, chemical warfare did not occur, primarily because all the major belligerents possessed both chemical weapons and the defenses–such as gas masks, protective clothing, and detectors–that rendered them ineffectual. In addition, in a war characterized by lightning-fast military movement, strategists opposed the use of anything that would delay operations. Germany, however, did use poison gas to murder millions in its extermination camps.

Since World War II, chemical weapons have only been used in a handful of conflicts–the Yemeni conflict of 1966-67, the Iran-Iraq War of 1980-88–and always against forces that lacked gas masks or other simple defenses. In 1990, the United States and the Soviet Union signed an agreement to cut their chemical weapons arsenals by 80 percent in an effort to discourage smaller nations from stockpiling the weapons. In 1993, an international treaty was signed banning the production, stockpiling (after 2007), and use of chemical weapons. It took effect in 1997 and has been ratified by 128 nations.

WORLD WAR I AND THE LEGACY OF CHEMICAL WEAPONS

There are few weapons in war as nefarious as poison. One hundred years after the Germans first used chlorine gas during the Second Battle of Ypres, chemical weapons remain widely stigmatized and outlawed. Of all the technologies from World War I that went on to redefine combat in the 20th century, chemical weapons have the most sordid legacy.

Ultimately, however, the use of lethal and incapacitating gasses proved largely ineffective in conventional warfare. They were comparatively easy to counter, difficult to use and rarely achieved the desired or planned result. The impact of chemical weapons is less practical than it is psychological, which partly justifies the reluctance to use such measures but also explains why many countries still have chemical stockpiles.

At 5 p.m. on April 22, 1915, the Germans released around 168 tons of chlorine gas, using the prevailing wind to carry the toxic cloud toward the French 45th and 87th Divisions at Gravenstafel. The gas worked far better than anticipated, creating chaos among the French, Moroccan and Algerian troops and opening a 7-kilometer (4-mile) gap in the defensive line. The Germans failed to effectively capitalize on the break; surprised by the effectiveness of the gas, they were unprepared to exploit the situation. For military planners on all sides, however, the apparent usefulness of poison gas had been proved.

The main reason for the effectiveness of the first chlorine attack was that the troops on the receiving end did not know what they were facing. As the green-tinged cloud washed over them and the chemical began taking effect, panic struck, resulting in many soldiers either running away or dropping down into the trenches. Both options proved fatal for many. By withdrawing with the movement of the cloud, many prolonged their exposure to the gas. And for those who sought refuge in the trenches, the heavier-than-air gas sunk into the secluded spaces, creating a poisonous environment.

Yet for the remainder of the war, the Germans never saw a repeat of the rout at Gravenstafel, even with deadlier gasses and improved delivery methods. The chemical genie had been released from the bottle, and once the secret was out, all sides worked to perfect their own weapons while mitigating the risk of the enemy's. This is not to say that there were no casualties, but out of the approximately 16 million fatalities in World War I, chemical weapons caused less than 100,000. Instead, artillery was by far the greatest killer of the war, accounting for around

60 percent of all fatalities. But the use of poison gas is irrevocably burned into the collective memory of the nations that participated in the conflict. It is perhaps the psychological impact of chemical warfare that lingers more than its physical toll.

GERMAN GAS TACTICS

Probably the most important thing that was done as the result of the Somme Battle experience was to insist on there being at least one protected or gas-proof dugout at every headquarters, battery position, signal station, aid post, or wherever gas shell were particularly likely to drop. I have deferred describing these protected shelters until now, but as a matter of fact they had been devised and adopted nearly a year previously, though not many of them had got into actual use. The protection consists essentially of a damp blanket fitting closely over the entrance to the cellar or dugout or emplacement, whichever it may happen to be. The value of the blanket depends on the fact that if you prevent the movement of air you prevent the movement of gas. That is all there is to it. Stop any possible draft and you will keep out the gas. In practice the blankets are kept rolled up out of the way and are let down only when the alarm is sounded or when gas 'is about. In order to get an air~tight joint the blanket is made to rest on a sloping framework set into the entrance to the dugout. To make sure that the blanket really does remain stretched out over the frame and does not gap at all, two or three wooden battens are fastened across it at intervals.

Where space is available two, such sloping blankets are used, at least two feet apart and preferably far enough apart to allow a stretcher in between. This forms an "air lock" -you must go into the lock and close the outer blanket before going through the inner one - and not only makes protection of the interior doubly sure but makes it possible to enter the dugout even in the middle of an attack or bombardment. In the old days the blankets used to be sprayed with the Vermorel sprayer solution, but anything that will keep them damp and flexible will do. In the early days, too, the companies or batteries used to do all their own work on protecting dugouts, and it was always possible in cold weather to obtain an extra supply of blankets on the plea that they were required for making gas-proof shelters. Nowadays a close eye is kept on these supplies, which are doled out by the engineers, and it is seen that if blanket material is supplied for protected dugouts it is going to be used for protected dugouts, and for nothing else.

Gradually all dugouts, cellars and buildings within the gas-shell area - let us say up to three miles from the front line-are being provided with blanket protection, which means a big decrease in casualties, for once inside such shelters men can sleep in more or less comfort until they again have to don their respirators and face their tour of duty in the poisoned air outside.

It practically came then to this - that protection against the poison-gas shell was a question of gas-proof dugouts on the one band and rapidity of spreading the alarm and quickness of getting protected on the other. At the gas schools and in the regiments and batteries men are trained to be so quick in their movements that they can get on their masks in six seconds. They are also taught on the burst of a gas shell in their neighbourhood to hold their breath at once. It sounds easy enough to do this, but it must come to a man automatically in any circumstances he may happen to find himself - and you can find yourself in some queer circumstances in war-and to assure this a great deal of training is needed. Anybody, however, can hold his breath for thirty seconds, and with practice it is possible to go well over a minute. During this time it is possible to make a fool of oneself in half a dozen different ways in putting on a respirator, and yet get it on in time in the end. But drill sergeants will stand for nothing less than the standard time and the most meticulous accuracy. God bless these tyrants - they must have saved a lot of lives. One of the difficulties we began to encounter with regard to gas shell was the spreading of the alarm among men on the march or in communication trenches where no alarm devices are installed. In some battalions it was the custom to teach men to spread the glad tidings by taking off their steel helmets and beating them with their bayonets. This certainly makes a good old noise, but unfortunately it is just when gas shell are coming over that shrapnel is also likely to be. in the air, and to deprive a man of this tin hat at this time in order to provide him with a gas alarm is rather robbing Peter to pay Paul.

The best way undoubtedly, and the one now taught throughout the British and American forces, is to hold the breath, then put on the respirator, and finally spread the news to everyone else by shouting "Gas shell!" as loudly as possible with the mask on. In this way the information can be spread throughout a big working party or from front to rear of a column of infantry on the march in a remarkably short space of time. Even in the trenches it is well to give word-of-mouth warning as well as by means of the local alarm devices, for a second or two of absolutely invaluable time may be saved in this way. One soldier questioned by an officer going the rounds as to what he would do in the event of a gas shell bombardment replied nervously: "Put on my gas mask and shout 'Rattles!'

For the remainder of 1916 the boche treated us with gradually increasing numbers of Green Cross Shell. His tactics, too, got a bit better - I mean for him - for he began to make more concentrated bombardments on particular targets. Possibly this was because of special orders that were issued on the subject. One of these was by General von Buelow to the artillery of his army, in which he said: "There have been many instances of Green Cross Shell being fired in small quantities. This is a waste of ammunition, as with all gas shell good effects are only obtained by using them in large quantities. The firing of small quantities of gas shell has also the disadvantage that the enemy is practiced in the use of anti-gas appliances and attains a higher degree of gas preparedness. For this reason the effect produced by larger quantities will be reduced"

This shows the increasing interest in the use of gas shell taken by the German General Staff, and heavier and more concentrated bombardments based on the above orders became more frequent. One of these, brought off in unusual circumstances, occurred at Arras in December, 1916. 1 say "unusual" because the weather was so cold at the time that the Green Cross liquid did not evaporate so quickly as usual. but hung about in some places for long periods. The bombardment occurred at night and about three thousand shell must have been fired into one corner of the town-in fact, all round the old gateway through which the whole of the transport from the St-Pol road would have to pass. The surrounding houses and cellars got filled with gas, and in such billets, especially where shell had actually burst inside a room, the liquid soaked into the walls and floors and only evaporated the next morning.when the air grew warmer. A lot of men were gassed in this manner on the following day, as they naturally thought the gas had vanished, and were gradually overcome as things warmed up.

In the open, gas disappeared more at its usual rate, though it hung about all during the bombardment and for several hours after, thus forcing men in the neighbourhood to wear respirators for long periods. Some of these men, overcome by fatigue, actually slept in their respirators. I think this was the first time I had heard of its being done, though it has been done often enough since.

By this time the British Army had been fitted out with the celebrated box respirator - a respirator of particular interest to Americans, as it was the type adopted for and at present in use in the American Army. A short description of it will not be out of place. The principle of the respirator is to have a box filled with chemicals and attached by a flexible tube to a face piece or mask, which fits closely to the face. All air breathed by a man must therefore pass through the chemicals, and these are so chosen that they will absorb any and every poison that may be present in the atmosphere at the time. In order to keep the air pure in the mask and to have a double line of protection a man breathes through a special mouthpiece and has his nose clipped. So even if the face piece, which is made of rubber cloth, should be torn or damaged in any way the soldier is perfectly safe as long as he does not attempt to talk - that is, if he keeps his nose clipped and does not remove the mouthpiece from his mouth.

The respirator is not only active against a diversity of poisonous gases but it will keep out very high concentrations of gas for many hours.

One of the most misleading statements made about gas masks - sometimes by newspaper men and consequently given wide publicity-is that such and such a mask will stand up for so many hours against gas. It is a very natural thing to want to know or to state how long your respirator will last, but without stating what concentration of gas is being talked of it is impossible to give such definite information about any mask. It simply depends on the amount of gas there is in the air. But the box respirator if kept in good condition and properly used is guaranteed to keep out German gas continuously for many hours, even in concentrations which it is quite impossible for the boche to maintain in the field. In the American modification of the box respirator the absorptive power of the chemicals used is even greater than in the British box, and this makes it the best respirator in the world, which is very reassuring for those who have to make use of it.

The box respirator is contained in a haversack and is carried slung on the shoulder until such time as the soldier comes into the forward areas, where it must be carried tied up on the chest ready for instant adjustment in case of need. As I mentioned before, it can be put on in six seconds from the word "go," and once a man is practiced in wearing it he can walk, run, shoot, dig, speak or do anything but eat and smoke in it; and this for long stretches at a time. I know many cases where men have been forced to wear masks literally continuously for more than eight hours; and much longer periods than this, with perhaps short intervals of rest in protected dugouts or in unaffected areas, are common.

Of course the soldier has to be practiced in putting the mask on quickly. It is not quite so simple as the old "gas bag," about which a drill sergeant said to a squad: "You just whops it out and you whops it on". But it does not take long to make men proficient with the respirator, at any rate on the parade ground. It is making him proficient under conditions of war that counts and all his instruction is now aimed toward this end.

With the mask in position and a tin hat on top of his head a soldier has a peculiar beetlelike appearance, which is not very improving, though the following conversation .was. reported to have been overheard by an officer about to enter a dugout:

"Ere, mate, take yer gas mask off."

"It is off.",

"Then for Gawd's sake put it on!"

The Germans were much interested in our new respirators and their development, and apparently had great difficulty in obtaining specimens for examination. During the winter of 1916-17 German soldiers were being offered a reward of ten marks for every British box respirator that they brought in; but as we were doing most of the shooting at that time I can hardly think that Fritz made a fortune out of his chance.

But to return to the gas shell. During 1917, it became apparent that the Germans were placing. more and more reliance on the use of gas shell and were manufacturing them in enormous numbers. For a whole year after the introduction of the Green Cross there was only one modification of the chemicals used and that was the admixture with the diphosgene of a material which has been called "vomiting gas." This substance is a chemical named chloropicrin, and it certainly lives up to its pet name if you take a real good breath of it. The boche mixed it with his diphosgene in order to make the latter more potent if possible, or else because he was running short of diphosgene; but he still calls the mixture Green Cross and uses the gas for its killing. power.

The chief development, however, was rather in the tactics than in the chemicals used. Gas shell were no longer thrown away; each target or area was.apparently considered separately and was given enough shell to make certain of putting up a very high concentration of gas on it. At this time the boche divided his gas-shell shoots into two classes-those for "destructive" effect,. and those for "harassing" purposes.

The destructive fire was intended to take on big targets, which were not only definite but were known to contain living targets for example, concentration points where troops were bound to be gathered; billeting areas, well- known villages or towns; areas known to have a number of batteries collected in them, and so on; in the latter case the batteries themselves would be taken on individually if their positions were known.

Apart from a number of fairly big bombardments, like that at Arras, mentioned above, the destructive shoots were chiefly counter-battery ones, intended if possible to, "neutralise" our artillery while it should be actively engaged in putting down a barrage, either to prevent a German attack or in preparing the way for our own infantry when we were attacking, which, of course, was much more frequently the case in 1916 and the first half of 1917.

This neutralisation business wants a bit of explaining. It will have been realised that the Germans were and still are using two very distinct kinds of gas shell-those which kill, like the Green Cross, and those which only temporarily put a man out of action, like the lachrymators, and nowadays; the mustard gas. Of course, the idea underlying the use of gas shell in general - and the whole war for that matter-is to put men out of action. The most effective way of doing this is to kill, as that puts a man out of action for good and he doesn't return. But you can kill men with gas only by taking them by surprise, because of the excellence of the gas masks.

After the surprise has been effected the chief use of the gas shell is to force the opposing side to continue wearing their gas masks and in that way to hamper them and reduce their fighting efficiency for considerable lengths of time. This is where the lachrymators and mustard gas and similar stuffs come in, because they are very persistent, and a little goes a long way in forcing a man to keep his respirator on. The quick-killing gases, like phosgene and the Green Cross, are not very persistent, and it would be waste of material to continue shooting them when you could effect the same thing with another stuff, which would hang about for hours or perhaps for days.

Now see how this affected the German "fire for effect, " or destructive shooting, as applied to a battery, and why the gas shell are so particularly suited for taking on targets of this kind, which used to be engaged only by high-explosive shell. Imagine a battery of, let us say, field howitzers. Our men are making an attack. The howitzers are busy pounding the German trenches to bits, and then they are going to "lift" on to the support trenches when our men go in. The whole of the success of the infantry assault may rest on the guns' keeping up to the program with the requisite amount of fire. The boche business then is to try to put our guns out of action. If he can do this he has the infantry - I won't say at his mercy, but at any rate at such a serious disadvantage that their losses will be tremendous compared with what they would be under cover of a good barrage from the guns.

Now if the enemy uses high-explosive shell to take on our batteries he can put them out of action only by registering a direct hit. If the guns are well dug in in good emplacements with head cover it will be possible for high-explosive shell to drop within a dozen yards without doing anything but scare the gunners. Not so, however, with the gas shell. Drop enough gas shell within a dozen or twenty yards of the battery position and the gas will float down with the wind and penetrate every nook and cranny. If the gunners are not quick some of them may be gassed; and if, as is sometimes the case, the gun has been worked short-handed this alone may throw down the rate of fire to a .very considerable extent. Add to this the fact that the remainder of the crew will have to don their respirators in order to fight their gun at all, and it can be seen that the rate of fire may be reduced to such a low limit as to make it of little value for the time being; or the gun may even be put out of action completely.

Once the first surprise is over and no more immediate killing can be counted on, the bombardment may be continued with persistent gas shell, which are just as effective in making the men wear masks.

From our point of view it all comes down to the ability of the gunners to be quick enough at first in preventing themselves from being gassed; and then later of their being capable of carrying on with their firing while wearing masks. It means that gas training and discipline are, if possible, more important for the artillerymen even than for other branches of the service. This is realised to the full in all their training and practice, for if they are not able to respond to an S 0 S call from the infantry an otherwise abortive German attack may be turned into a disaster. It is like everything else in this war-a question of training and discipline.

The neutralisation of the infantry or the transport is conducted on similar lines, and though it rarely reaches the point of being complete a partial neutralisation of reserves which prevents their getting up in sufficient .numbers or in time, either for reinforcement or attack, may have most serious consequences in an operation. The partial neutralisation is attempted,Just as for the artillery, by killing as many as possible by heavy surprise bombardments with the lethal shell and then continuing with persistent gas in order to force the remainder to wear their gas masks.

Let me describe as an example a particular way in which the infantry may be partially neutralised if they they are not thoroughly steady, well-disciplined and trained up to the final dot in gas-defensive measures and the use of their respirators. Troops in the front line, whether they are in settled lines of trenches or merely in temporary positions, are absolutely dependent on their supplies. Supplies of ammunition, barbed wire and, above all, rations must be brought up to them constantly; otherwise they cannot continue to fight. All these things are brought up at night. The motor lorries of the Army Service Corps take the supplies up to selected points, where they are taken over by the first-line transport that is,. the regimental transport, which consists of horse or mule drawn general service or limber wagons.

As night approaches everything is loaded up and departure timed so that the trysting place with the infantry carrying parties is reached after dark. These meeting places are very frequently crossroads immediately below the lines, and in position warfare are usually situated close to the entrances of the communication trenches. Pass by such a place by day and you will find it deserted, but as soon as darkness has fallen it becomes a hive of activity - as busy a crossroads as you might find in the centre of a big city. There is a constant movement in and out of men, animals and vehicles. Unloading and taking over of the supplies alternate with checking off the goods and the moving off of the carrying parties. Military policemen direct the traffic and relieve the ever threatened congestion. Altogether it is one of the busiest and most important phases of the routine side of war, and anybody there without a special job is a nuisance and is not wanted.

Places like this of course are apt to be well known to the boche, and every now and again he will drop in some high-explosive shell or put over some shrapnel in the hope of catching the crossroads at its busy hour. But even if he is lucky and manages to get on to the spot it hardly holds up the work at all. I have seen a big shell drop into just such a place and make a huge hole in the road, killing men and horses and smashing up a wagon. Half an hour later there was hardly a sign that anything had happened. The hole had been filled in and the material debris cleared away. The wounded of course had been looked after first.

Now imagine instead of ordinary shell that a number of gas shell had been dropped into this busy centre. On a dark night, probably very muddy underfoot and with all the excitement of kicking mules, flares going up and anything from machine-gun bullets at long range to shell of every size dropping in or expected, things are difficult enough. But with the advent of the gas shell every man must. get himself protected. It is now that the "hold the breath, add mask on in six seconds" stunt is going to be of value. With well-trained troops the losses from the gas may be negligible, and it is equally true that they will be heavy if the discipline is poor. But whether one way or the other it means that all the frightened horses and mules must next be fixed with their respirators and the work in hand must be proceeded with by everybody while wearing gas masks. This is the real test.

If the men are well trained the carrying parties-perhaps with loads of barbed wire on their backs-will get away as before and proceed up the filthy communication trench to the front line; swearing probably, uncomfortable certainly, but safe. Similarly the drivers will be able to get their teams away from the gassed area as soon as they are unloaded, and the serving out of the supplies will go on as before, though at a reduced rate. But if the soldiers were not able to carry on in these terrific circumstances-could not wear masks for long periods and could not do anything in them, confusion would undoubtedly supervene and the work be brought to a standstill. If this happened the men in the front line next day would be short of rations, of ammunition, of wire. They would, in fact, be neutralised.

It is attempted neutralisation of artillery and infantry by methods such as these, carried out over large selected areas and generally as a preface to an attack - either their own or ours - which constitutes the German "fire for effect." The "harassing fire" is simply the same thing on a smaller scale and with no immediate tactical reason at the back of it except that of killing and general annoyance. As a rule a sudden burst of a few shell will be landed on some likely place, such as the entrance to a communication trench, a sunken road, a bridge or an observation post. These small shoots were always causing us a few casualties. There was no warning, or somebody was not quick enough, or did not get his respirator on, or took it off too soon. There would always be some reason-but in the end it would generally come down to something that the disciplinary thumbscrew could cure.

It is almost unbelievable nowadays that at one time one of the chief sources of these constantly occurring casualties was shamefacedness at being seen in a mask. Men would not protect themselves until absolutely forced to do so, for fear others would regard them as being too easily frightened. This was especially the case with new comers, who did not want to drop in the estimation of the older hands.

One case was reported where a corporal in charge of a small party of men in passing along a communication trench ran into some pockets of gas from a bombardment that had just stopped. He ordered his party to don their masks and proceeded up the trench. A few yards farther on they passed through the support line, which happened to be fairly free from gas, and here they were met by jeers from some of the supporting troops who shouted " Hello, got the wind up!" and in this way induced the corporal, really against his better judgment, to order masks off. Not more than twenty or thirty yards farther along the party ran into a particularly bad pocket of Green Cross and the corporal and several of his men were so badly gassed that they had to be sent to the rear.

The attitude of the officers is always reflected in the attitude of the men. At that time you would sometimes meet young officers who had either been on the outer fringe of a gas-shell shoot or had merely smelled tear gas thinking they knew all about it and refusing to believe in the extreme deadliness of the poison gas and the need for enhanced discipline. They would damn the gas and the need for taking precautions, and their men would consequently damn the gas and the need for taking precautions. This of course would mean another batch of casualties when Fritz did treat them to the real article.

Just to show how a small matter of indiscipline may result in disaster I would instance the case of two men who took off their respirators in a front-line trench. Their battalion was going to be relieved that night and they took off their webbing equipment for the purpose of fastening on the haversack and pack. Absolutely against orders they also removed their box respirators, and of course it was just that moment that the boche chose for dropping in half a dozen small trench-mortar bombs filled with phosgene. These vicious little guns are very accurate and most of the shell landed on or near the parapet and filled the fire bay with gas. Both men dived at once for their respirators and in so doing upset three other men in the bay. All five were gassed and three of them died later.

THE CHEMIST'S WAR

The principles of chemical (and biological) warfare have been around for thousands of years, but it was not until the industrial age that harmful agents were successfully manufactured, bottled and shipped in vast quantities. Going into the war, Germany had an expansive chemical industry. As a byproduct of the development of industrial compounds, dyes and agricultural products, German chemists unlocked the door to noxious vapors and liquids that could be easily weaponized.

The world's first industrial war was rapidly driven to stalemate on the Western Front between opposing forces unable to outmaneuver or break the defenses of the other. It was inevitable that creative and scientific minds would consider unorthodox ways to gain advantage. The Spartans used chemical weapons during the Peloponnesian War to displace sentries, burning sulfur to form a harmful gas. It was hoped the same effect could be achieved by modern means. In the era of the professional soldier, however, there were many traditionalists that considered chemical weapons to be dishonorable, even cowardly. There were even Hague conventions prohibiting their use. But as the stalemate dragged on and the death count continued to rise, the stubborn practicality of warfare eroded the desire for caution or restraint.

The French and Germans used fairly benign tear gas in the first year of the war, but the effects were almost unnoticeable. What had become a very symmetric war led almost inevitably to asymmetric thinking, fueled by an age of technical innovation. The quest was for a decisive weapon, one that could break the line and bestow a battle-winning advantage on the first side that used it. It was hoped that poison gas would be that panacea, but the success of April 22 was never to be repeated.

Despite the rigorous methods that went into developing and weaponizing chemicals for the battlefield, the deployment was far less scientific. Success was largely dependent on the prevailing wind, as the British learned with mounting horror at the Battle of Loos. When the taps were opened on the "white star" containers (denoting chlorine in the English nomenclature), a change in the wind blew the released gas back toward friendly troops, resulting in catastrophe.

The best use of chemical weapons was for area saturation and denial. The more prolonged the exposure, the more lethal the effect. The problem with gas — even the more deadly types, such as phosgene — was that it was not persistent. Gas masks were rapidly developed and delivered to soldiers on the front line with instructions on how best to survive a gas attack: mask up, stay on the parapet and wait for the cloud to pass.

Gas shells later obviated some of the random effects of wind, but while gas rounds could be delivered on target and at range, the required level of saturation was often lacking and equally at the mercy of a stiff breeze. The only exception was mustard gas, which landed in the desired concentration, survived as a persistent liquid and provided suitably appalling effects. But mustard gas, as horrible as it was, killed only a fraction of those exposed.

Chemists were very good at explaining the properties and compositions of the weapons they produced. Doctors, through treating those exposed to chemical weapons, became adept at describing the specific physiological effects on the body. Psychologists, nicely insulated from the front lines, were still wrapping their heads around the concept of "battle shock" but could recognize the fear response that poison gas instilled. But the most graphic accounts of what chemical weapons could do to the body and mind came from the soldiers themselves — and the nurses that treated them at the dressing stations. Chemical weapons instilled fear like almost nothing else.

Of all the ways to die in World War I, death by gas was among the most dreaded. As well as infecting the minds of young soldiers with fear, reports soon filtered back to the civilian population, affecting the public consciousness and further diminishing popular support for the war effort. The thought of young men taking weeks to die, blinded and in constant agony was almost too much to bear. Conditions in the trenches were already appalling, and ingenious modern weapons, such as phosgene and mustard gas, were only exacerbating the situation. To understand the acute effect chemical weapons had on the psyche of the World War I soldier, it is perhaps the war poets — Wilfred Owen, John McCrae, Robert Graves and Siegfried Sassoon, to name a few — and writers such as Erich Maria Remarque that explain it most profoundly.

Though chemical weapons killed a comparatively small number of people in World War I, as many as a million soldiers and civilians were exposed, many of whom would carry debilitating symptoms for the rest of their lives. Following the armistice, the horrors of war returned with the surviving soldiers and gas was at the forefront. The psychological effect of poison gas far outweighed its usefulness as a casualty-causing weapon, and continues to do so.

THE LEGACY

While the 1925 Geneva Protocol officially banned chemical weapons in war, countries continued development and stockpiling. The changing nature of battle meant that chemical weapons had little play in World War II combat, though large arsenals were amassed. The limitations of chemical weapons had been writ large in the Great War, and saturating wide swathes of land with noxious vapors for short periods did not necessarily fit into the concept of Blitzkrieg. Also, training, knowledge and protective equipment effectively mitigated the effects and utility of chemical weapons. However, German scientists still maintained an edge, developing the first nerve agents, including tabun, sarin and soman. These were never used, although consideration was given to installing chemical warheads in V-2 rockets. But the Germans realized that chemical weapons had a very specific utility, when employed in confined spaces for the purposes of mass murder.

Although huge amounts of chemical weapons were produced and stockpiled during the Cold War, they have been used only a handful of times in the latter half of the 20th and early 21st centuries, most notably during the Iran-Iraq War in the 1980s and most recently in Syria. On each occasion, the public outcry and international condemnation was fierce. Chemical weapons continue to be heavily stigmatized, fairly ineffective and largely indiscriminate. They also remain difficult and expensive to store, because of their corrosive nature and susceptibility to temperature and moisture, as well as to dispose of. The United States has already neutralized the bulk of its chemical weapons stockpile, at a cost of around $1 billion per 1,000 tons. Washington has also assisted with the disposal of post-Cold War chemical weapon arsenals, most recently addressing the estimated 1,000 tons possessed by Syria. It will take decades to destroy or neutralize the remaining stockpiles in existence. While ineffective, chemical weapons maintain their poisonous legacy, both in the mind and hopefully sealed in the last remaining storage facilities.

6

Classification and Methods of War Gases

CLASSIFICATION BY PHYSIOLOGICAL ACTION

The gases used against American troops by the Central Powers may be classified according to their physiological action, as lacrymators (eye irritants and "tear gases"), sternutators (nasal irritants, "sneeze gases," "vomiting gases"), lung irritants (suffocants, respiratory irritants), and vesicants (skin irritants, escharotics).

As follows: (1) Acute lung irritants; (2) lacrymators; (3) direct poisons of the nervous system or paralysants; (4) sensory irritants of the eyes, nose, and upper respiratory passages (sternutators); vesicants. The paralysant group (hydrocyanic acid and sulphuretted hydrogen) is not included in the classification followed in the present volume, since our troops were not subjected to these gases.] THE LACRYMATORS produced temporary blindness. Liberation of small quantities of a gas of this type made it impossible to carry on without wearing a mask. These gases, while not responsible for many evacuations to the rear, harassed troops engaged in close fighting or in manipulating guns. Practically all of the long list of lacrymators had a bromine base.

THE STERNUTATOR gases or nasopharyngeal irritants were nonlethal. They were capable, however, of producing extreme irritation of the nose, throat, and eyes, caused severe headache and nausea. The symptoms were comparatively short in duration, and the gases were not effective when the mask was worn. The inhalation of these gases before the application of the mask made mask wearing very uncomfortable and was apt to cause its premature removal and thus to subject the wearer to the effects of more important gases which usually accompanied or immediately followed the use of the sternutators. This type of gas usually arrived in the nature of a surprise, since it was used in high explosive shells. Because of this it was difficult for the troops to recognize immediately the presence of the gas. A good example of this type of gas is diphenylchlorarsine, which was long and extensively used at the front.

THE SUFFOCATING gases were used to kill and contained the most deadly substances employed in chemical warfare. Severe edema of the lungs quickly followed their inhalation, and death from asphyxiation frequently resulted within a few hours. Gases of this character were rather quickly dissipated, however, and it was difficult for the enemy to maintain an effective concentration over a long period of time. Good mask discipline robbed these gases of most of their terror and placed heavy expense on the enemy when they were extensively used. The two gases of this group most widely employed along our front were phosgene and chloropicrin.

Many combinations were made from these gases with other substances intended to assist them in their action.

PHOSGENE, a gas of high density, with an odor much like that of decaying hay or grain, is little, if at all, irritating to the eyes and has no irritant action on the skin. Its presence, therefore, was perceived with difficulty and men were gassed before they were aware of exposure.

CHLOROPICRIN requires a higher degree of concentration to cause a suffocative action than could readily be obtained in field use. It was frequently used in conjunction with phosgene the enemy hoping that the prompt irritant effect of the chloropicrin would prevent the wearing of the gas mask, thus rendering the soldier an easy prey to the accompanying phosgene.

THE VESICANT TYPE of gas made its appearance later than the others mentioned, but soon became the most important in gas warfare. It first came into prominence at Ypres on July 12, 1917, dichlorethylsulphide being the chemical used. It was called by the French soldiers "yperite," by the Italians "yprite," and by the British, "mustard gas." Gas-mask discipline offered ample protection to the eyes and lungs, but very important military results were obtained from skin burns which caused the evacuation of enormous numbers of casualties. The Central Powers considered dichlorethylsulphide their most pernicious gas, and the experience of the Allies certainly confirmed the opinion that it had won this place in military importance. This gas had many features which rendered it especially suitable. It was toxic in concentrations which could not be detected by the sense of smell; the person affected suffered no discomfort at the time of the exposure, and symptoms were not evident until man hours later. Mustard gas penetrated all clothing and was remarkably persistent on the earth or on foliage over which it had been scattered. These factors tended to increase its effectiveness; in addition to the physical action of the gas on the men themselves, the morale of troops was impaired.

Truly speaking, dichlorethylsulphide is not a gas, but a liquid, which slowly vaporizes, and is effective in either state. It volatilizes slowly at ordinary temperatures and dissociates only at high temperatures. This latter fact was taken advantage of in the treatment of contaminated clothing. Furthermore, it is readily oxidized by such substances as chlorine or bleaching powder, and these chemicals were used in purifying dugouts, trenches, and ground or foliage saturated with the gas.

The following toxic substances were most frequently used by the Germans in their chemical warfare: (1) Lacrymators: Benzylbromide. (2) Sternutators: Diphenylchlorarsine. (3) Lung irritants: Chlorine, phosgene, carbon oxychloride, chlormethylchlorformate, bromacetone, chloropicrin. (4)

Vesicants: Dichlorethylsulphide, chlorarsines, bromoarsines.

This classification, while eminently practical and convenient, does not imply that some of the gases have no physiological action other than that of their group. This is not true. For instance, bromacetone and chloropicrin, when employed in concentrations too low to affect the lungs, are lacrymators.

In addition to the four groups mentioned, gas officers occasionally reported the use of substances which possessed some of the properties of both the suffocative and vesicant gases. The usual shell filling which produced this result was made of equal parts of ethyldichlorarsine and dichlormethylether. This combination caused a vesicant action of an important nature, if kept in contact with the skin, with the air excluded; under ordinary battle conditions, however, this seldom happened. These gases possessed the properties of the: suffocative type to a greater degree though not so effective as phosgene and chloropicrin. Innumerable combinations of gases were encountered occasionally.

A complete list, in so far as is known, of the gases used by the enemy, includes the following: Acrolein, allylisothiocyanate, arsenic trichloride, arsine, bromacetone, bromacetic ether, bromethylmethylketone, bromide of benzyl, bromide of xylyl, bromide of toluyl, bromine, carbon monoxide, carbonyl chloride (phosgene), chloracetone, chlorine, chloropicrin, cyanogen, dichlorethylsulphide (mustard gas), dichlormethylether, dimethylsulphate, diphenylchlorarsine, diphenylfluorarsine, ethyldichlorarsine, formaldehyde, hydrocyanic acid, hydrosulphuric acid, iodacetic ether, iodacetone, methylchlorsulphonic acid, monochlormethylchloroformate (palite), nitrogen peroxide, phenylcarbylamine chloride, phosphine, phosphorus trichloride, sulphur dioxide, sulphur trioxides and trichlormethylchloroformate (diphosgene or superpalite).

METHODS OF USE

The first gases used by Germany during the war were liberated from charged cylinders secretly installed in their trenches, the success of such a gas attack depending upon a favorable wind which would carry the gas in high concentration slowly over the trenches of the unprotected allied troops. There is no record of the American Army having been exposed to any of the original types of cloud gas attacks from such cylinders.

This method was superseded by the projector attack and trench-mortar firing of gas projectiles. Projectors, during most of the war, were large. smooth-bore cylinders. They were built to receive large drums or bombs of about 18 c. m. diameter. Charges of explosives were put in the bottom of these cylinders and the bomb placed on top. The cylinders were placed in batteries of from six to nine and operated at an angle of 45 degrees in a trench or in some special area that offered protection. Such a plant usually contained from 200 to 800 projectiles, and the batteries were fired by electricity. This permitted the simultaneous discharge of a vast amount of gas on a relatively small target at a range of from 1,000 to 1,500 meters. The gases so used were of the lung irritant type. A successful projector attack produced very serious results, and it could be carried out without much regard to wind direction and velocity. These bombs contained 50 per cent of their total weight in gas, as against 10 per cent in a gas shell. The great advantages were the cheap guns for the delivery of the gas and the enormous sudden concentration of the gas in a small area. Nevertheless, this method of using gas at a relatively short range necessitated great secrecy in installing the projector during the night and in getting off the attack before the allied air service located the line of projectors, else allied artillery would destroy the plant and liberate the gas among the enemy's own troops. Furthermore, the flash and noise produced usually gave the troops sufficient warning to put on masks. This method, at best, was limited to local uses and, although continued throughout the war, it became less and less frequent. During the late months of the war the enemy made an eflort to improve this method by building rifled cylinders and giving the bomb more of a shell contour. This gave a slightly increased range, but did not greatly enlarge the scope of its usefulness.

Hand grenades were employed for delivering gas under certain conditions; but their use was so limited for this purpose that they did not account for many casualties.

These methods all proved of relatively little importance, however, as soon as the enemy discovered that gas could be better distributed by shells.

The innovation which placed gas warfare on a very important military plane was the building of the gas shell and the distribution of these shells by the use of artillery.#5 When first employed by the enemy the shells- carried only lacrymator substances. Lethal gases made their appearance in shell about the time of the first battle of the Somme, and this method of gas warfare rapidly developed until, at the close of the war, all types of gases were being used in gas shells, with many of them as a part of the filling in high-explosive shells. Distribution of gas in this manner on a given target was limited only by the number of guns available and the rapidity of their fire. This method of delivering gas was in very small degree limited by weather conditions and had the advantage of long range. It sometimes aflfected the territory even beyond the actual range of the artillery, since with a favorable wind a harmful concentration of gas would float with the air currents well beyond the point of shell burst. Definite tactics were evolved with this use of gas, placing its employment on as definite a plane as were the tactical methods of other arms of the service. After the use of gas shells had been instituted, it was difficult for the troops attacked to determine during a bombardment whether only high explosives were being used or whether a gas attack as well had been launched. For this reason it compelled the wearing of gas masks by the troops as soon as they were subjected to an artillery attack, and this in itself greatly lessened their fighting efficiency.

Their shell were classified by the enemy as pure gas shell and high-explosive gas shell. The pure gas projectile was employed for its lethal and casualty-producing effect by gas alone, since the effect of detonation and fragmentation was very slight. Such shell, when filled with a lung-irritant gas, were marked with a green cross. Various combinations of these fillings were marked green cross 1, green cross 2, or green cross 3, according to the nature of the particular mixture in use. Commonly the suffocative types of shell fillings were referred to as green cross ammunition.

Pure gas shells containing dichlorethylsulphide were marked with a yellow cross, and sometimes less important vesicant types received a further mark of identification such as yellow cross 1. This was later changed to green cross 3, the filling then being ethyldichlorarsine and dichlormethylether, the mixture previously described. Gas shell containing lacrymators were indicated by lettering such as " T-Stoff," " K-Stoff," "C-Stoff," and " B-Stoff."

High-explosive gas shell usually contained the nasal irritants such as diphenylchlorarsine and were marked with a blue cross.#6 There is reason to believe that very late in the war some mustard gas may have been fired in high-explosive shell. The blue cross shell not only produced a gas effect but also detonation and fragmentation to a marked degree. The amount of gas filling in such a shell was necessarily small, the enemy entertaining the hope that the accompanying high explosive would assist in propelling, vaporizing, and concealing the gas. The burst of this shell, unlike the pure gas shell, could not easily be differentiated from the ordinary high-explosive shell burst.

The enemy found the markings mentioned necessary to make it easy for the storage and for artillery troops which handled such ammunition and served the guns. Fortunately, the relationship of these marks to the shell contents soon became known to the Allies. This proved of great value in quickly identifying the nature of gases employed in an attack, since unexploded shell or fragments of shell bearing these marks were found.

Among the tactical programs adopted by the enemy for the use of war gases under different conditions the following are examples:

I. Counter battery fire and long-range fire (calibers, 77 mm.,105 mm., 150 mm., howitzers, 10 cm. guns):

	Per cent
Explosive shell	20
Blue cross gas shell	70
Green cross gas shell	10

The 15 cm. guns constituting part of the long-range group were provided with high explosive shell only. The rate of fire during the preparation for the attack for the 77 mm. guns was found to be one shot per minute per gun.

II. Fire against infantry-creeping barrage (calibers, 77 mm., 105 mm., 150 mm., howitzers):

	Per cent
Explosive shell	60
Blue cross gas shell	30
Green cross gas shell	10

210 mm. howitzers were provided with high-explosive shell only.

III. Fire against infantry-box barrage (calibers, 77 mm., 105 mm., and 10 cm. guns):

	Per cent
Explosive shell	30
Blue cross gas shell	60
Green cross gas shell	10

Yellow cross gas does not appear in these orders, since the enemy never attacked immediately through an area that they had shelled with mustard gas.

Allied troops at points selected for attack by the enemy and the artillery supporting such allied troops were subjected, before the enemy infantry advance, to a gas attack with high-explosive shell containing blue cross substances, and this fire was immediately followed by green cross shell. Late in the war it very frequently happened that all areas lateral to the point of attack were neutralized by a saturating fire of yellow cross shell. Reserve troop concentrations in the rear of such points of attack, villages near the scene, roads, wooded areas, ravines, reverse slopes, and other strong points. not intended to be occupied by the enemy were also shelled with mustard gas. In some instances, when an enemy attack failed and an orderly retreat could be made, he used mustard gas to assist in covering the retreat.

Thus it can be seen to what extent gas could be used in open warfare and how extremely difficult it was for the medical officer to determine whether one gas or a combination of gases produced the casualties he was called upon to care for. The individual patient might have been exposed to all the gases used in such an operation, or, on the other hand, he might have been in a spot where there was a significant concentration of only one of the gases.

The persistent and insidious character of mustard gas made it effective for several days after the burst of the shell. It made a good weapon, therefore, against wooded areas, billeting spaces, roads, artillery and machine-gun positions, as well as all points of cover.

According to the needs of the situation, yellow cross shell could be used for surprise burst of fire, for saturation shoots, or for the area shoot. The last method, when used against inexperienced troops, was apt to cause them to minimize the danger of such concentration.

This method of fire consisted in maintaining a low concentration of mustard vapor in a given locality by slow intermittent shooting directed at that area. Such regions would be fired on frequently enough to keep up a low vapor concentration for days and weeks at a time. The inconspicuous way in which these areas were planted and kept planted with mustard gas resulted in many casualties. Directions for such area shooting are known in one instance to have been as follows:

Seventy-seven millimeter guns; 100 rounds per hectare (approximately 2M2 acres):

Target at 1,000 meters, 100 rounds. Target at 5,000 meters, 125 rounds.

Target at 6,000 meters, 125 rounds.

Target at 7,000 meters, 150 rounds.

GAS AS A RAT EXTERMINATOR-CAUSES OF ALLIED CASUALTIES

The great time for the German gas troops was undoubtedly 1916, and from April to August of that year they carried out five big cloud gas attacks on the British alone, not counting several on the French Front and a number against the Russians.

During the interval from the December attack of the previous year they had obviously been thinking hard and preparing lots of gas, for the new attacks showed several fresh features both as regards extent and tactics. Along the lines of making the gas more poisonous, using greater quantities and higher concentration and the springing of surprises, everything was done to make the gas cloud an even more deadly aflair than it had been in previous shows. That our own casualties were much less than before, and that the boche in at least one case had a lot more killed by his own gas than we had, were very satisfactory results of all the labour and research as far as we were concerned.

For the same reason that the December attack had been reduced in duration to half an hour, the new clouds lasted only ten to fifteen minutes; thus once more multiplying the concentration by two or three. On top of this the amount of phosgene was increased up to at least twenty-five per cent and probably to about fifty per cent, so that in this way also the cloud became much more deadly than before. It is interesting to note that pure phosgene cannot be used, otherwise the Germans would undoubtedly have employed it. Straight phosgene does not come out of the cylinders satisfaetorily-it must have a big proportion of something like chlorine mixed with it to force it out and get it into the air as quickly as may be.

All of this made the gas cloud a nasty thing to face. As it became progressively more deadly it required less and less to kill. A couple of breaths of the poisoned air became enough to kill a man; but as our protection was good enough, it meant that the most important thing for the enemy to do was to take us unawares by getting his gas over so quickly or deceiving us in some other way that we should be down and out almost before we knew it. This is where his surprise tactics came in.

These tactics consisted in attempting a great secrecy in the preparations, in the use of smoke clouds to put us off the real track of the gas, and the putting over of a number of different waves of gas at varying intervals. The value of the last two will be more apparent from the accounts of the individual attacks, but the importance of the first-mentioned method must be emphasised a bit.

It must be remembered that the carrying in of the gas cylinders is the work of the infantry and, as we discovered ourselves when we started retaliation, is a very unpopular job owing to the difficulties of the carry. Any carelessness in allowing the cylinders to clank by bumping against each other or against any other metal objects lin the trenches, or metallic sounds made by

rather bored pioneers in unscrewing the domes or attacking the pipes, are going to give away the fact to the opposing side that something unusual is going on. And something unusual going on or suspected generally spells g-a-s in the trenches.

In some cases, too, the opposing trenches can be seen from observation posts - O.P.'s or O.Pips, as they are called in British Army parlance - and in such cases if the carrying is started or the installation of the cylinders is continued during the day there is a good chance of the whole show being blown on by some watchful observer with a telescope to his eye a mile or so away. All this the boche realised and made his arrangements accordingly. But in at least one case, in April, in his anxiety to get the cloud over without diminution of strength and so that we should have little time for protecting ourselves and spreading the alarm, he chose as his venue for the attack a big portion of the line where the trenches were very close together -seldom, in fact, more than fifty yards apart. Of course it is just in such circumstances that secrecy of preparation is of the greatest importance - but at the same time it is of the greatest difficulty to maintain. As a matter of fact the Germans overreached themselves by this choice of position, and little indications spotted by our watchful sentries and patrols made us pretty certain that a gas attack was impending, and our watchfulness and preparedness were correspondingly increased and a constant state of "Gas Alert" kept up.

The first two attacks of the year were made against the 16th - the Irish Division. This was the division in which Willie Redmond was a captain, and it was composed of some of the best fighting material in the world-all Nationalist Irishmen and anxious to get one over at Fritz. Whether the Irishmen were chosen as a target with the foolish idea of "putting the wind up," or whether it was out of revenge for their appearance in the British ranks after all the labour that had been expended in trying to spread sedition in Ireland, we do not know. Whatever the idea was it terminated in most abject failure, for the Irishmen came through both attacks wonderfully well and absolutely smashed up the German infantry advances which were attempted after the passage of the cloud. Both attacks were made on that part of the line near, Hulluch running for about two miles south from Cité St. Elie.

The Germans opened the ball by letting. ,our support and reserve lines have a heavy bombardment of tear shells. Almost immediately after, in the dim light of the early dawn, the first gas cloud floated over. It was very thick and had been largely mixed with smoke in the hope of leading our fellows to believe that it was terribly strong. It was not. But the cloud was so dense that even at brigade headquarters, three miles behind the front line, it was impossible to see across the road. There was enough gas, in this mixed cloud to make it very dangerous and uncomfortable to unprotected men, but there were very few casualties. The alarm was quickly spread, the men remained cool, and an attempted attack by the enemy infantry to follow up the cloud was smashed up without being able to get closer than our barbed wire.

After this first wave there was a tendency among the men to regard the danger as over. and to congratulate themselves on the apparent and obvious boche failure. As they were prepared to go through with any-thing the boche could put over, there was a natural tendency to underrate the effects of gas, seeing it had caused them no losses. It is undoubtedly true that a number of helmets were discarded entirely - some of the soldiers thought they were useless after being through an attack, and threw them away, depending entirely on their reserve helmets. These they omitted to place in the "Alert" position, pinned up on their chests ready for immediate use. In one or two cases which came to my notice officers and men went off to the latrines or to headquarters without helmets at all. This of course, was not general, but it shows how some of our men fell for the boche ruse, which consisted of putting over a second wave two hours 1ater on exactly the same Front.

The second cloud was a frightfully strong one, composed entirely of gas in the highest possible concentration. It was this wave which caused all our losses on April twenty-seventh, as it took a number of men completely by surprise. But even so, the Irishmen were not a bit dismayed, and when the Germans again attempted to advance - parties of their bombers in some cases appearing immediately behind the gas cloud - they were met by such a stout resistance that those who were not shot down retired in disorder to their own trenches.

The intensity of the second wave can be gathered from the fact that buttons and ammunition were quickly corroded and turned a villainous green colour. In a few cases rifles stuck and Lewis guns jammed, owing to the effects of the gas on the ammunition and the breach mechanism. One good thing about the attack was that most of the rats in the trenches were killed. In some parts of the line the trench rats are an absolute plague. They eat any food or candles left lying about or kept in cardboard boxes. They swarm in the dugouts and appear in all sorts of odd corners. They disturb the little rest one does get; and I have had them run all over me, even over my face, while lying in my dugout. All attempts to clear them out were useless. But what ferrets and terriers and virus could not accomplish the boche gas did. Mister Rat cannot stand up to a strong mixture of chlorine and phosgene without a gas mask, and so in this attack, as in others we experienced, he died by hundreds; and nobody mourned him.

Curiously enough two kittens, which inhabited the dug-out of the commanding officer of one of the battalions of the Scottish Borderers, who were in reserve, came through alive. The kittens were badly gassed and lay breathing rapidly, suffering from spasms and with profuse salivation. Possibly their fur helped to absorb some of the gas, for five hours later the little victims were almost themselves again, though they continued to cough occasionally and drank water continually. The water they took in preference to milk.

The effects of the poison on the soldiers who were gassed were pretty much the same as has been so frequently described in the press before. In the lighter cases it was mostly severe and painful coughing and bronchitis, with occasional retching and vomiting. The severe cases had the frothing at the mouth, the painful fight for 'breath and the blue face with staring eyes which are typical of severe gassing with chlorine and phosgene. I was told that there were not many delayed cases-that is, men being taken seriously ill hours after the attack, though apparently unscathed before.

The casualties were really remarkably small in the circumstances, and even despite the surprise tactics, were not - as numerous as those of the December attack. Apart from the men who were caught without their respirators, most of the casualties were the result of some special circumstances. The helmets themselves when properly inspected and adjusted gave good protection. In connection with the laying aside of the respirators after the first cloud a sergeant told me that when the second wave came over he had seen two soldiers trying to get into the same helmet. The humorous side of this had apparently appealed to him even in the middle. of the attack.

Of course with the trenches so close together a lot of men had difficulty in getting protection in time. Parties of men in advanced saps and listening posts had the greatest difficulty, and numbers of these men were killed. One pioneer of a tunnelling company came out of a mine gallery knowing nothing about what had been happening aboveground, and walked straight into the middle of the gas cloud.

A man in one of the companies of the Irish Rifles was wounded in the head by shrapnel through both his steel and gas helmets. In spite of the wound and the hole in his gas helmet he held the latter close round his mouth and nose and was not gassed at all, a clear case of presence of mind saving his life.

One thing which impressed every one with the need for thorough gas training at home, and which should be taken to heart by all men in training at the camps or likely to go there, was the way in which reinforcements and men who had recently joined up suffered. Their casualties were out of all proportion to their numbers and were due entirely to the fact that insufficient attention was given at that time to the gas-defence training of the recruits. Many of them had never put on a helmet before, and none of them had ever smelled gas.

In one particular instance a batch of twenty men had come straight over from England and were in the gas attack the day after their arrival in the trenches. The only training they had had was a lecture from their own regimental officers, and consequently they knew little or nothing about the use of their helmets. Every one of these ,,men was gassed. It is true that they had scrambled into their helmets somehow, and none of them died; but the fact remains that absence of training at home cost the fighting line twenty men in one company. In this company they were the only men gassed. Largely as a consequence of this, gasdefence training was taken up very seriously in the early training of recruits, and big gas schools were established at all the camps both in England and at the bases in France, so as to catch the young soldier early.

The boche made another gas attack on the Irish Division on the same Front two days later. Once again he let off two waves-this time with an interval of only a quarter of an hour. But despite his idea of "mixing them up " he could not bring off that particular surprise again.

The second attack was one of the most interesting on record, for it was here, near Hulluch, that the gas blew back on the Germans and killed many more of them than our total gas casualties. The thing happened in this way: The first gas wave was loosed off at three-fifty A. M., opposite the celebrated Chalk Pit Wood. Fifteen minutes later a heavy cloud was discharged on the Hulluch front. But. the wind was too light and variable. The cloud came over our line and then the gentle wind first dropped altogether and then gradually veered round. The gas hung on No Man's Land and over both sets of trenches for a short time, and then with increasing pace drifted back right over the German position, just where Fritz had been seen massing for an attack on the Hulluch sector. We did not see the confusion which reigned, but almost simultaneously with the arrival of his own gas our barrage came down and the German attack dispersed.

All that day our observers reported the carrying out 'of German casualties from the trenches on stretchers and a constant stream of ambulances coming up and then returning along the roads to the rear. We surmised that the boche had swallowed some of his own poison, but it was not until several months later, from some documents captured during the Battle of the Somme, that we were able to appreciate his disaster to the full.

The first of these documents was the diary of a soldier who had been in the neighbouring trenches. It ran.. ". . . We went along the trenches to find the headquarters of the —th. It was awful. Everywhere lay dead bodies or men gasping for breath and dying from the gas.. Somebody must be to blame. At first I could not go on. One almost had to step on them to get through. I asked an officer of the —th what had happened. They were going to be relieved.

But the other documents were more explicit, as they happened to be the official report on the matter from the war office in Berlin. It appears that the Germans had eleven hundred deaths from their own gas. A most rigid enquiry was held and it was found that many of the men were not carrying respirators, either in the trenches or in the area immediately behind the line. But this did not explain the extent of the disaster, so eight hundred of the respirators collected from casualties were sent to Berlin for examination and report. Even allowing for those which might have been injured in transit, there were still thirty-three per cent of the masks so defective that their owners were certain to be gassed. To see whether this applied only to the area affected a large number of respirators were collected from up and down the whole Western Front, and it was found that even among those as many as eleven and a half per cent were similarly at fault. It would seem that there had been very poor inspection of the respirators both in manufacture and after issue to the troops. Apart from the joy of seeing the boche hoist with his own petard it was rather a relief to find that the efficient German Army was not so frightfully efficient after all.

This matter of inspection is taken very seriously in the British Army. Besides the rigorous factory inspection all respirators are inspected thoroughly every day even the trenches, and Tommy is expected to look after his respirator just as he looks after his rifle. As an official statement issued after he April attack said: "A defective helmet frequently leads to the death of the wearer. Inspection of respirators must be frequent and thorough." A sergeant who was notorious for his thorough dealing with recruits got away with it in even better terms when addressing a squad on parade. In thundering tones he said: "If you don't look for the 'oles in your 'elmet, they'll soon be looking for a 'ole for you."

Another thing that resulted from the attacks just described, and from another similar attack shortly afterward in the salient, was the putting on the screw with regard to the carrying of respirators continuously by every one in the trenches. A very good and well-known story on the British Army in this connection is that of a brigadier general who was proceeding to the line for his daily inspection when he discovered that he was minus a gas bag. He stopped the first orderly he saw, borrowed the man's helmet and serenely went his way with a clear conscience. Arrived in the trenches, one of the first sights that met his horrified gaze was a soldier without a gas mask. In virtuous tones he demanded the reason for its absence, and then, waving aside the halting explanation, went on loudly to assert his belief that the soldier would not know how to use a respirator even if he had one.

"Here," he said, "take mine and show me whether you can put it on in quick time." The awe-stricken Tommy slung the satchel over his shoulder, and on the word "Gas!" from the general thrust his hand into the haversack and pulled out - a very dirty pair of army socks.

The fourth German attack of 1916 was made on June seventeenth in Flanders, near Messines; in fact, just north of the Wulverghem-Messines road. Like those of April, it was intensely strong, very short, and sent over in successive waves at intervals of about twenty minutes. There were really no fresh features about the show, but the cloud seems to have been even stronger than before. 1 had no personal experience of this attack, but the cloud must have been very strong, for it killed animals at "Plugstreet" - the only name we used in the British Army for Ploegsteert - three and half miles away, and was quite distinctly perceptible even at Be'thune. At the "Piggeries" - the remains of a model farm in rear of Plugstreet Wood belonging to a notable French sportsman, a place well known to so many British soldiers - a calf was found dead, after the passage of the cloud, with the body very much blown out. Dead rats lay in close proximity.

Even farther back than this animals were seriously affected. The army mules in the line of the gas were seized with fits of coughing and kicked violently, making them even more difficult to handle than usual. It is probably not realised that horse masks are now issued on a scale sufficient to provide protection for all horses and mules, such as those of the first-line transport and the artillery, which have to approach anywhere near the lines. The present form of these respirators is that of a big bag soaked in chemicals which fits over the animal's nostrils, leaving its mouth free so that the use of the bit is not interfered with. When not in use the horse respirator folds up very nicely and neatly into a canvas case which can be carried on the breastband of the harness or any place from which it can be quickly adjusted. Some of the animals take to these masks" Horspirators, some wag called them - quite quickly, but others are strenuous objectors; some of those hardened sinners, the mules, transforming themselves into masses of teeth and hoofs whenever an attempt is made to fix on the gas bags.

In one case where a horse and a mule in the same supply column were fitted with their masks at the same time the difference was most marked. The horse was dressed up without much trouble, though he did not like it. He whinnied and sneezed, breathed hard and perspired and looked rather pitiable, but stuck it out. The mule, on the other hand, had to be roped to get the mask on at all. Then he danced about, heels in the air and head down, and tried to rub off the objectionable appendage against the rope, and then against a tree. This did not effect its removal, and for a minute the cunning animal stood still with his ears cocked at different angles. Then suddenly he put his head to the ground and before anything could be done to prevent it put his foot on the respirator, pulled his head up smartly and left the respirator under his hoof.

These masks have proved of the greatest value and have saved any number of horses' lives. The cavalry are not provided with them, as it is not anticipated that they will be near enough to be affected by gas-cloud attacks, and when the cavalry are mounted and in action it is unlikely that they will meet even poison-gas shells in large numbers. Added to this is the fact that a horse can stand more gas than a man without being distressed.

The casualties in the June attack were lower than in any one previously. Indeed, it was a satisfactory feature of the whole gas business that despite the increasing deadliness of the German clouds the losses they caused became less and less. Of course the proportion of severe cases in those gassed became greater, for with such strong clouds it had become a case of hit or miss. Either a man was protected completely or he was caught out badly; and this spoke well for the protection supplied, for otherwise there would have been a much bigger proportion of light cases.

Of the minor effects of these boche gas clouds, that on vegetation is the most marked and gives a good idea of the strength of the gas. For miles in the track of the cloud all green stuff is burned up or wilted. Grass i's turned yellow, the leaves of trees go brown and fall off, and the garden crops are entirely destroyed. I have seen root crops in the fields and garden crops of onions, beans and lettuce quite destroyed. But curiously enough, farther back, in places where this still happens to the garden crops, the cereals and the hedges seem to escape serious injury.

Of course over a wide area all metal work is thickly tarnished, and this might be a danger in the case of telephone instruments and other delicate appliances, except that the exposed parts are always kept slightly oiled and then cleaned thoroughly after the attack. The same thing is done with rifles and machine guns and their ammunition, and with the clinometres, fuses and breech mechanism of guns and trench mortars. Since this war started very little difficulty has occurred through corrosion, but the chief thing is to clean off the grease and re-oil all metal parts exposed to the gas immediately after the attack is finished, otherwise the greasy surface seems to hold the gas or the acid it engenders, and allows it to eat in at its leisure.

During the attacks of 1916 the alarm arrangements worked very well, and the Strombos Horns in particular justified their use. Even above the noise of machine-gun fire and the bursting of shells their shrill, Unmistakable note could be heard for long distances, giving warning to all troops on the flanks and in the rear. There were very few instances where they were not let off in time and the sentries posted over them apparently knew their jobs better, for instance, than one man who was questioned on the subject. This particular sentry was asked by a noncommissioned officer going the rounds in the trenches what he would do in the event of a gas attack being made. "Oh," replied the bright boy, "that's easy. If any gas comes over it blows the horn and I call the platoon sergeant and tell him about it."

A much more conscientious sentry over a Strombos Horn had been told to be particularly on the lookout for a gas attack, as one was expected at any time. The officer on duty, going round about midnight, heard a suspiciously regular sound coming from one of the fire bays, and thinking that one of the sentries was indulging in a stolen forty winks he cautiously rounded the traverse. Here he found the sentry lying on the top of the parapet staring into the darkness and going sniff, sniff, sniff with his nose.

Being asked more forcibly than politely what was the matter with him the man replied: "I'm sniffing for gas." Sniff, sniff, sniff. 'Can you smell any?" "No, sir; but I want to smell it if it does come, as I'm a gas sentry and the leftenant told me always to keep smelling for gas." Sniff, sniff, sniff. The job of seeing that the air cylinders of the Strombos Horns are kept at their full pressure is intrusted to the divisional gas noncommissioned officers, who go round periodically with pressure gauges and test them out. If they fall below a certain pressure they are replaced at once by fresh ones from the divisional store. Some Austrahans going up the line one night were carrying a number of such cylinders for replacement, when one of them got turned on accidentally and they didn't seem able to stop it.

PHYSIOLOGICAL ACTION OF WAR GASES

Toxicity

The first outstanding feature of the war gases is their very high toxicity. They kill where substances measuring up to our former ideas of high toxicity fail to injure. Thus prussic or hydrocyanic acid, which has usually stood at the head of toxic gases in the minds of scientists and laymen alike, is no more toxic, as a matter of fact, than a dozen other gases which were investigated or tried out in the war. In the field it proved practically harmless. The toxicity figure for chlorine is about 2.5 mg. per liter; that of phosgene 0.35; for mustard gas, hydrocyanic acid, and a considerable number of others, 0.2 or less.

The peculiar requirements for field use, as contrasted with controlled laboratory administration, was responsible, of course, for the fact that hydrocyanic acid was found almost useless as a war gas, while the commonly handled chlorine, produced industrially in such large amounts every day without accident, proved so very potent in war and the insidious phosgene ten times more so.

Experience showed that, to be valuable as a war gas, a poison must meet certain requirements. It should be a liquid or be easily liquefied, or it might be a solid, though the solids did not prove as effective as liquids. It must be readily volatilized at ordinary temperatures, and the vapor must have sufficient density to remain near the ground and to maintain its concentration for some time. It must be fairly stable in the presence of moisture and under the molecular shock of the detonating charge of the shell. In addition, it must compare favorably with the most toxic compounds known to science. Hydrocyanic acid fails as a war gas because of the low density of its vapor and the fact that the human organism can withstand the gas below certain concentrations without apparent injury. To kill, then, it requires a concentration which it is not practicable to obtain in the field. Gases like chlorine or phosgene injure in proportion to the amount encountered, so that, while a lethal concentration may not be attained at a given point, nevertheless they will cause casualties of greater or lesser extent, depending upon the concentration and time of exposure.

Organic Halogen Derivatives

The second outstanding feature of the war gases is the fact that they are practically all organic halogen derivatives. With the exception of hydrocyanic acid, acrolein, and a very few others, all of the gases which appeared to be of even possible value in the field contain chlorine, bromine, iodine, or fluorine in organic combination. The organic groupings impart the necessary volatility; the halogens give added weight to the molecule, increasing the vapor density, in many eases giving an instability in the presence of water sufficient to account for the final toxicity. The organic groups also give to a large number of the war gases their characteristic lipoid solubility. Of the three or four most effective compounds used, all are soluble in alcohol, acetone, fats, and oils, and so are able to penetrate the cells of the body with the facility of the anesthetics and for the same reason.

SPECIFICITY

The third outstanding feature of the war gases is their specificity. This is more apparent than real, perhaps, but it is sufficiently striking to allow of a rough classification based on the physiological attack. All the gases are irritating to all tissues with whi(h they come in sufficient contact, but under field conditions certain tissues and organs are more quickly or obviously injured by a given gas than are others.

Eye irritants:

1. Brombenzyl cyanide.
2. Benzyl bromide.
3. Bromacetone.
4. Chloracetophenone.

5. Chloropicrin.
6. Xylyl bromide.
7. Dichloretllylsulphide (mustard gas):

Lung irritants:

1. Chlorine, bromine.
2. Phosgene.
3. Trichlormethylchlorformate.
4. Chloropicrin.
5. Mustard.

Nasal irritants:

1. Diphenylchlorarsine.
2. Mustard.

Eye Irritant

Taking up the groups in their order, the lacrymators, are characterized by their instantaneous effect on the corneas nerves. Sudden contact with a very moderate concentration of a good lacrymator is as painful as a sharp blow on the eyes, and, indeed, feels very much like it. Such a concentration is immediately unbearable, the eyes are kept shut and the lacrymatory glands are stimulated to a copious secretion of tears. At very low concentrations the lacrymators are felt as a slight irritation of the eye, causing frequent winking and increased flow of tears. Such concentrations are not detectable by the nerves of taste or smell, and do not produce irritation of the respiratory tract except after exceedingly long exposure. Some substances, even with prolonged exposures, fail to show injury to the respiratory mechanism, while they are distinctly and immediately felt in the eye. For example, a concentration of chloropicrin which is perceptible to the eye in time will injure the lung epithelium, but several days of continuous exposure are required before there is evidence of the development of lung edema. The effect on the eyes, however is instantaneous, suggests a physical or a molecular effect, and is a striking example of specificity. The time element precludes the possibility of hydrolysis or other decomposition, and suggests that this compound is itself a protoplasmic poison with a particular chemical relation to the compounds of the corneal nerve filaments, so that these are stimulated long before other nerve endings or other types of tissue cells are affected. After prolonged exposure, recognizable only in the eye, the respiratory mucosa shows definite injury, and rhinitis, bronchitis, pneumonia, and lung edema develop. At a still later period the kidney also shows injury. Chloropicrin is evidently toxic, therefore, to many tissues. As is well known, it is quite stable chemically, and hydrolyzes only very slowly in water. It is soluble in the fat solvents and the fats. Like chloroform, it is picked up by the blood stream from the lungs, and because of a certain degree of tissue specificity it reaches and damages the kidney more perceptibly than the liver, muscles, nerve cells, or other types of tissues. In this it resembles its chemical relative, chloroform, whose specific action on the liver is well known.

Mustard gas, on the other hand, produces no instantaneous effect on the eye. The individual is usually entirely unaware of its presence unless he detects its odor and recognizes it. Hours after exposure the typical injury to the exposed corneal area appears, with conjunctivitis. There is nothing resembling the instantaneous action of the true lacrymators. It may be concluded that mustard gas has no special affinity for the corneal nerve filaments, and that it is not, itself, in the same sense or degree as are chlorine and chloropicrin, a protoplasmic poison.

Lung Irritants

A large number of casualties and some the most severe injuries produced by the war gases are to be credited to the lung irritants. Chlorine is interesting chiefly because of its historic position as the first war gas used, and because of the dramatic sufferings of the first, unprotected, victims. It is a highly reactive element, combining with protoplasm in a very great variety of ways, irritating and killing tissues, therefore, wherever it comes in contact with it. Chlorine gives evidence of instantaneous reactivity along the respiratory tract and in the eyes. Its effect on the nerve endings of the upper respiratory tract is so intense that in high concentrations it causes immediate spasms of the glottis or violent coughing and vomiting. The lungs later develop the usual reaction to injury of the lining epithelium, namely, edema and necrosis.

Chlorine may replace hydrogen in its organic combinations, incidentally producing hydrochloric acid; it may add directly on to unsaturated molecules or form more stable compounds; it may remove hydrogen from water, causing destructive oxidations, with the formation of hydrochloric acid; it may remove metallic ions from protein combination and thus alter the distribution of electric charges and so change the physical properties of the protoplasm; it may combine with the basic organic groups. These are some of the more obvious ways in which chlorine reacts with and alters protoplasm. These alterations are probably irreversible, chemically or physically, and any such change is assumed to be injurious or, if extensive enough, fatal.

The action of chloropicrin on the respiratory tract has already been touched upon. At moderate concentrations it produces lung edema, intense irritation of the whole tract, violent coughing, and retching. The edema comes on with considerable delay after exposure. Chloropicrin hydrolyzes very slowly in water, so that its effect on the respiratory mucosa can hardly be attributed to a production of hydrochloric acid within the cells, though this factor may contribute in the delayed action. A very general injury to the whole organism is suggested in the fact that men exposed to this gas are described as aging quickly, though the kidney lesions may account for part of this general deterioration. Nothing at all definite is known concerning the chemical action of this gas on protoplasm.

Phosgene and its relative, superpalite, are the most effective of the lung irritant group. Phosgene is quite reactive chemically. It dissolves and quickly hydrolyzes in water thus it is readily soluble in oils and fats and the fat solvents. While phosgene may react in a large number of ways, its lipoid solubility and its production of acid in contact with water would appear to be sufficient to account for its great toxicity. The former carries it into the cells like an anesthetic, the latter breaks it up when inside them, with the production of acidity. There is no strong evidence that it is immediately toxic. It produces no striking irritation of the corneal nerves nor, at medium concentrations, of those in the respiratory tract. Diluted, it may be inhaled without discomfort and has, at such times, a rather pleasant odor reminiscent of muscat grapes or of fermenting corn stalks. In more concentrated form the gas produces a sense of shock and a gripping of the chest, but even this immediate sensation passes off and leaves no well defined sense of injury. Some time later the developing injury to the lung tissues and the resulting edema become sufficient to make the patient aware of his condition, and the feeling of malaise rapidly intensifies. Phosgene itself probably gets as far as the lung capillaries. The packing of the corpuscles in these capillaries during the early stages of phosgene gassing has been established and is probably due to the production of acid in the corpuscle membranes. There is no evidence of action to a greater distance, and from the rate of hydrolysis of phosgene it is improbable on theoretical grounds.

Superpalite behaves like phosgene but is still more toxic. Mustard gas must be classed as a lung irritant. It has no immediate effect but, like phosgene, is absorbed and hydrolyzes within the cell to produce an acid. It produces, however, a type of reaction in the respiratory tract quite different from that of phosgene, with the formation of a tenacious membrane in the upper portion of the trachea and bronchial tree instead of the excessive edema of the alveoli.

Nasal Irritants

The nasal irritants, as a rule, are not, strictly speaking, gases. They are solids which are highly dispersed in the form of smokes, and which are therefore more apt to collect in the upper respiratory passages rather than in the alveoli. Sufficient concentration or deep breathing incident to heavy work, however, will carry the particles into the deeper portions of the respiratory tract. The phenylchlorarsines are the typical examples of this group. These compounds irritate the nerve endings in the nose and throat, producing violent sneezing or vomiting and coughing. The mode of action of these smokes is not known definitely, though they are probably protoplasmic poisons per se, and on decomposition yield phenyl and arsenic groups as well as acid. The fact that they are not gaseous prevents their affecting tissues to any large extent and so limits their field of importance. They ean be rather easily removed from the inspired air by a filtering device attached to the mask.

Skin Irritants

Next to the lung irritants the skin irritants have proved most effective and Mustard gas was the substance most commonly used. It acts on all the tissues with which it comes in contact-eyes, respiratory tract, and skin. It is a heavy, oily liquid, volatilizing slowly. It dissolves in the ordinary fat solvents, fats, and lipids, but only to a very small extent in water. It penetrates the cells with considerable rapidity and by virtue of its lipoid solubility, tends to collect in the fat droplets and lipids of the cell. In the watery phase of the cell it hydrolyzes to produce hydrochloric acid. The passage from oil solution to water solution, and finally to hydrochloric acid, is slow and may continue for several days in the cells of a tissue exposed to mustard gas. This leads to a slowly developing injury to skin, eye, and respiratory tract, which increases in intensity, at times, for a period of two to three days and is then followed by the removal of the necrotic tissue and the very slow process of repair. There is very little evidence that mustard gas owes its tremendous toxicity to anything more than its ability to penetrate cells and there to produce acidity. Mustard gas has no immediate irritating action on nerve endings or tissues. Its toxicity develops slowly and is presumably the result of its decomposition products. One of these is hydrochloric acid, and while it is quite possible that other toxic fragments are developed in its breakdown, the acid alone can easily account for much of the injury. One of its hydrolytic products, dihydroxethyl sulphide, has been shown by Marshall to be practically nontoxic.

In concluding this chapter it seems appropriate to emphasize again the injury which results from the development of acidity within cells. Aside from the well-known action of phosphorus and perhaps chloroform on the liver cells, few clean-cut examples of this type of reaction had been described prior to the war. It may prove, however, that many types of cell intoxicants owe their action to an indirect development of acidity, which becomes the immediate cause of the injury.

There is considerable evidence to show that acid outside of the cell does very little harm. For example, very large amounts of hydrochloric acid may be injected into the veins of an animal without producing noticeable physiological effects. In this case the acidity is immediately taken care of by the effective buffer system of the circulating medium and the injected acid never reaches the interior of the tissue cells. The mucosa of the stomach is regularly bathed with 0.2 to 0.4 per cent hydrochloric acid, with a hydrogen ion concentration sufficient to indicate with Congo Red, but without damage to the mucosa cells. The neutrality of the cell interior is maintained by the impermeability of its membranes to acid. In the same way the skin resists damage from dilute acids for long periods.

On the other hand, the appearance of acidity within the cell instantly sets in motion the autolytic machinery of the cell, and in direct proportion to the amount of acid developed. Cell proteins are not digested by the cell proteases in the normal reaction of its fluids. When this reaction shifts toward the acid side these proteins become digestible by the enzymes always present. The more acid produced the more protein is rendered available for digestion. These available proteins liquefy and digest away, the structure of the cell is obliterated, the products diffuse out and are transported elsewhere by the blood and lymph, and the cell shrinks or dies and is completely autolyzed. All tissues which have been studied behave in this way toward acidity, but they differ very markedly in the extent of the reaction. Muscle and connective tissues are only slightly digested by their own enzymes, even under the most favorable conditions. They contain relatively large proportions of stroma or skeletal proteins which are not rendered digestible by a physiological or pathological rise in the hydrogen ion concentration. The epithelial tissues, on the other hand, are exceedingly sensitive to increased hydrogen ion concentration. They respond by very rapid and complete autolysis to the optimum increase of acidity. Anything, therefore, which can reach and penetrate epithelial structures and produce acidity within these tissue cells will do the maximum amount of tissue injury. If injury is done to a particularly vital gland or structure, the conditions are right for the maximum disablement of the organism as a whole. Phosgene, superpalite, and " mustard " combine the properties of the anesthetics with rapid hydrolysis to acids. By the strategy of the war they were applied directly to epithelial tissues. With phosgene and superpalite contact is made with the alveolar epithelium, a vital link in the fundamental functions of tissue respiration. Injury to it is like injury to the heart or blood vessels or the blood. It makes precarious the maintenance of the proper oxygen supply to the body as a whole. With mustard gas the skin epithelium is injured, or the upper respiratory tract. While the former injury is not necessarily fatal unless of large extent, it effectually eliminates the man from active service until the wounds are healed.

When such a combination is effected of a penetrating, acid-forming substance coming in contact with epithelial organs-there is a lethal toxicity quite equal to that of hydrocyanic acid and, in addition, injuries grading all the way down to zero, in proportion to the amount of gas received by the epithelium. In spite of its chemical reactivity, chlorine has only a tenth the toxic power of these gases (phosgene, superpalite, and "mustard") because it penetrates only slightly, and in the many combinations which it makes with protoplasm only a few lead to the production of acid.

7

War in Syria: Geopolitics of Gas and Conflict

What is happening in Syria is no longer about a democratic movement against a dictatorship, nor is it simply a civil war between two camps. Syria has become the theater of a proxy war which is spilling over to its neighbors. Consequently, to focus only on the departure of President Bashar al-Assad is a strategy doomed to failure because it will not solve the conflict. The crisis is spreading far beyond the person of Bashar al Assad. As a result, demanding the departure of the dictator will not achieve a lasting ceasefire to stop the bloodshed and a transition to a brighter political future for the Syrian people.

Though the humanitarian stakes are high, the European Union (France at the forefront) and the U.S. have chosen their allies and continue to defend geostrategic and economic interests by pushing for the fall of the Syrian regime. To pursue this objective, the political discourse is idealistic and focuses on the massacres and humanitarian issues while national interests are real, but not mentioned.

However, from a realistic point of view, the conflict can be viewed as a broader struggle between mainly Russia and Western countries which attempt to advance their national interests. For the West these interests are isolating Iran and bolstering the strategic and economic alliance with Arab allies like Qatar, which invests in Europe and offers an alternative to Russian gas.

Isolating Iran

One of the pillars of the U.S. and the E.U. foreign policy is to isolate Iran because of its nuclear program. The fall of a strategic ally of Tehran such as Bashar al-Assad would be a blow to the Islamic Republic in its showdown against Europe, the United States and Israel. Indeed, the strategic alliance with Damascus allows Iran to maintain its Shia "axis of resistance" (Iraq-Syria-Lebanon with the Hezbollah).

On the one hand, these partnerships allow Tehran to counter the isolation imposed by the E.U. and U.S. sanctions. On the other hand, they allow Tehran to maintain proxies that serve as a leverage utilized for negotiations on the nuclear issue with world powers. These proxies also help Iran to counter the threats of Israeli attacks. With this in mind, Bashar al-Assad replaced by an authority that would agree to isolate Iran would favor the interests of the E.U. and Washington, but also the rival Arab countries in the Persian Gulf (mainly Saudi Arabia, Qatar and the United Arab Emirates), and to another extent Israel (depending on the nature of post-Assad government).

Maintaining the strategic and economic alliance with the Persian Gulf allies

France enjoys a privileged partnership with one of Iran's main competitors, namely Qatar. Under Nicolas Sarkozy's presidency, Emir Hamad Ben Khalifa al-Thani was the first Arab State leader to be received at the Elysées Palace in 2007. It is now François Hollande who continues this special relationship. Since his election, Qatar is the country which was received the most at the Elysées with a visit of the Emir on August 22 and two more discreet visits of Prime Minister Hamad bin Jasem al-Thani.

This economic power invests billions in real estate, in the capital of CAC 40 companies (such as Total, Vivendi, Veolia, Lagardère, Suez, LVMH or even Bouygues and Vinci for the different sites of the world to the Qatar 2022 and also the construction of the Friendship Bridge between Qatar and

Bahrain), sport (with the purchase of the Parisian club PSG — soccer and handball), the media (Al Jazeera acquired French Champions League rights) and most recently in projects in the Parisian suburbs.

With the European economic crisis, Qatar's partnership with France gives the small Emirate the ability to sway the French decision-making, something Qatar denies. Same investments in Germany where Qatar holds 17 percent of the capital of Volkswagen, 10 percent of Porsche, 9 percent of the Hochtief construction giant or even more recently 3 percent of Siemens.

The Qatari investments are also important in Great Britain. With 20 percent of the shares of the London Stock Exchange, Qatar is the main shareholder of Barclays. The Emirate has also invested massively in the Olympic Games, it has financed 95 percent of the highest building in London (the Shard) and British homes are supplied by up to 59.3 percent by Qatar's Liquefied Natural Gas (LNG).

As a result, Qatar advances its long-term interest by investing and signing important contracts with the European governments in crisis. Therefore, Qatar — the first Arab country to propose Arab military intervention — has more leverage to increase pressure against Damascus and through the U.N. Security Council (leverage Qatar also has in the Arab world through al Jazeera).

Geopolitics of gas

However, there is a major actor that does not allow the U.N. to intervene militarily: Russia (along with China). Europe has significant gas energy needs and a quarter of it comes from Russia.

Qatar shares the largest gas field in the world with Iran, the South Pars (Iranian appellation) / North Dome (Qatari appellation). Tensions exist between the two countries because Iran is unable to extract its gas as fast as Qatar, mainly because of the sanctions imposed on Iran (Tehran frowns upon the Qatari extraction which is "emptying" the common gas field).

Meanwhile, Qatar transports its gas through the Strait of Hormuz and is therefore dependent on Iran for its exports (with LNG tankers which then need to pass through the Suez Canal). The Emirate had plans to build a gas pipeline through Saudi Arabia, Jordan and Syria. But, Bashar al-Assad blocked this project, preferring to sign an agreement with his Iranian ally, but above all, to preserve its long-term energy deals with Russia.

As a result, Europe — which is largely dependent on the Russian giant Gazprom for its energy needs — has an interest in seeking a competitor to lower its growing gas bill. We understand that a Sunni power could protect a Qatar-Saudi Arabia-Jordan-Syria pipeline to diversify its sources. Besides, this path would allow Europe to further isolate Iran by preventing it getting supplies from a "Shia pipeline" Iran-Iraq-Syria.

Consequently, the centerpiece is Syria and geostrategic realities explain why the Syrian people have become the victims of this bloody proxy war. The different geostrategic interests in Syria explain the positions of the permanent members of the UN Security Council, and the deadlock. It also explains the difference in the framing by world powers that are competing and advancing their own national interest on the Syrian theater.

"SIEGE, STARVE, AND SURRENDER": INSIDE THE NEXT PHASE OF THE SYRIAN CIVIL WAR

This is what the nearly 400,000 people in Eastern Ghouta, a suburb of the Syrian capital of Damascus, have faced over the past two weeks. Syrian forces have dramatically escalated their attacks on the area, which is mostly controlled by rebel forces who for five years have opposed President Bashar al-Assad's rule. Human rights observers say thousands are injured and more than 500 people — including around 120 children — have died during the uptick in fighting, marking this as one of the bloodiest stretches of the eight-year Syrian civil war.

The offensive highlights a grim reality about the current

state of the war: Assad is winning and has now turned his attention to retaking parts of the country he lost. Recapturing Eastern Ghouta — an area that lies only 6 miles away from Damascus — is an important part of his push to force the rebels holding the area to surrender once and for all.

The fighting seems certain to intensify. Last Saturday, the United Nations Security Council passed a resolution calling for a 30-day ceasefire in Syria. Two days later, Russian President Vladimir Putin — whose forces back the Assad regime and are the main reason the Syrian ruler is winning the conflict — requested a daily five-hour "humanitarian pause" in the fighting so civilians in Eastern Ghouta could escape the targeted area.

Syrian planes have continued bombing, however. The US has harshly condemned the onslaught — "The regime claims it is fighting terrorists, but is instead terrorizing hundreds of thousands of civilians," State Department spokesperson Heather Nauert tweeted on Monday — but Syrian leaders say the fighting will continue.

"We practice a sovereign right of self-defense," Bashar Jaafari, Syria's UN ambassador, saidafter the ceasefire vote on Saturday.

More than anything, the attacks show how Eastern Ghouta is the next battlefield in one of the world's worst civil wars — and just how stunningly bloody the fight will be. "The Syrian people are just going to suffer as this continues to be a huge humanitarian disaster," Mara Karlin, who spent years on Middle East security issues at the Pentagon, told me.

"Siege, starve, surrender"

Jennifer Cafarella, a Syria expert at the Institute for the Study of War, says that Assad is trying to "recapture every square inch of Syrian territory." He's done so by leading a brutal campaign across the country — one that Eastern Ghouta now faces.

"The regime has been leading a 'siege, starve, and surrender' campaign for years," she said in an interview.

In practice, that means the Assad government purposely overwhelms opposition-held areas with attacks to make life for the civilian population unlivable. Assad's forces destroy hospitals, schools, markets, and even mosques, so it's nearly impossible for noncombatants to eat regular meals, receive medical attention, or pray where they want.

Assad followed this playbook most notably in the city of Aleppo. With Russian and Iranian help, Assad retook control of the city in December 2016 after months of brutal fighting. The tide turned in the regime's favor after it imposed a blockade around the city, once one of Syria's biggest and most vibrant, which cut off food and medical supplies to some 320,000 people. Assad also launched a campaign to systematically destroy the medical facilities in rebel-held parts of the city, killing or wounding many of its remaining doctors and nurses.

"I PROMISE I WILL TEACH THEM A LESSON, IN COMBAT AND IN FIRE"

Assad continues to use this strategy today because it works: Rebels who don't have food or medical provisions quickly lose the will or the ability to fight, and civilians in besieged areas often start cooperating with the government just to make it stop. There's no reason to think Assad will change course in Eastern Ghouta.

"Clearly, the government made a judgment that they wanted to stay in power all costs," Shanna Kirschner, a Syria expert at Allegheny College, told me. "Once you go down that road, it's very unlikely a government reverses that decision."

Assad can now focus on Eastern Ghouta

It's worth reiterating that the regime has tried for years to bring Eastern Ghouta back under its fold — and has allegedly committed war crimes to do so.

On August 21, 2013, for example, regime forces launched a chemical weapons attack on Eastern Ghouta, killing hundreds of men, women, and children. At the time, it was one of the biggest and most horrific attacks in the civil war. Since then,

Assad has slowly, and under the radar, continued to lay siege to the area.

But he hasn't been able to overtake Eastern Ghouta yet because he's short on troops, Cafarella told me. Many of Assad's forces have died during years of fighting, she continued, which is why the regime hasn't yet mustered the ground troops needed to force Eastern Ghouta's myriad rebel groups to surrender.

Circumstances have since changed. "Now Assad has the luxury of getting to focus more on various rebel groups," Karlin, who's now at Johns Hopkins University, told me, because "ISIS is now less of a military problem for the regime." Recall that in 2015, ISIS took and governedmuch of northern and eastern Syria. But two years later, the US-led anti-ISIS coalition effectively defeated the terrorist group's so-called caliphate in Syria (and Iraq).

ISIS's physical demise gave pro-regime forces the time and space to focus on Eastern Ghouta — and they've been explicitly threatening the area's civilian population ever since.

"I promise I will teach them a lesson, in combat and in fire," Gen. Suheil al-Hassan, commander of the elite, Assad-backed Tiger Forces, said in a February 19 video. "You won't find a rescuer. And if you do, you will be rescued with water like boiling oil. You'll be rescued with blood."

It's hard to know the true extent of the devastation since the fighting started because the conditions make it hard to report there, but the early indications suggest it's significant, and getting worse.

"THE FUTURE IS VERY BLEAK FOR SYRIA"

For example, Syrian warplanes have targeteddozens of hospitals, leading Doctors Without Borders to grimly state on Saturday that the region's ability to provide health care is "in its final throes." Some aid convoys can't even enter the area to provide assistance because of the danger.

Anti-Assad activists also claimed the regime has used chemical weapons, primarily chlorine gas, in recent attacks that on Sunday killed a child. The Organization for the Prohibition of Chemical Weapons, the world's chemical weapons watchdog, immediately opened an investigation into the attack.

But the Syrian American Medical Society claimed in a February 25 tweet that some of its patients are "suffering from symptoms indicative to exposure to chemical compounds."

That, in part, is why international leaders are calling for the bloodshed to end. "Eastern Ghouta cannot wait, it is high time to stop this hell on earth," UN Secretary General Antonio Guterres told the UN Human Rights Council in Geneva on Sunday.

The problem is it's not clear that the hellish conditions will ease anytime soon.

This is only likely to get worse

Last weekend showed why diplomacy has failed to even make a dent in Syria's carnage. It took three days for the United Nations to approve a resolution for a month-long ceasefire in Eastern Ghouta due to Russian objections. Moscow's representative initially vetoed the resolution on February 22, saying that reports of widespread civilian casualties were nothing more than "mass psychosis." Instead, Russia proposed amendments that would allow it and Syrian forces to continue targeting anti-Assad groups.

But the UN Security Council resolution passedrelatively unchanged on February 25. It "demands that all parties cease hostilities without delay" and allows for the provision of emergency aid and evacuations of the wounded.

It seems the resolution is nothing more than words at this point. Mere hours after the vote, Syrian warplanes resumed bombing Eastern Ghouta, according to human rights groups, even though some on the ground say the resolution *slightly* improved conditions. "Shelling is calmer than before, it's true, but there is still shelling," Mohammad Adel, a young man in the area, toldthe New York Times on Tuesday. Some experts I spoke to raised the possibility of America carrying out a limited strike on Syria to punish Assad for the attacks. The US did something similar in April 2017, launching 59 Tomahawk missiles at Syria in response to Assad's chemical weapons attack that killedaround 85 people.

Seeing photos of dead children could compel President Donald Trump to choose to strike now, experts noted. US Ambassador to the UN Nikki Haley recalled those images after the UN resolution vote as a way to criticize Syria and Russia for their actions. "How many mothers lost their kids to the bombing and shelling?" she said. "How many more images did we need to see of fathers holding their dead children?

There's currently no public indication that Trump is considering the use of force. The White House and Pentagon didn't respond to my questions about potential strikes against Syrian targets. And it's not clear what other options, if any, are on the table to help stop the bloodshed. "There's really no will for any robust measures to stop the fighting," Kirschner told me. "The future is very bleak for Syria."

GAS HAS BEEN USED 86 TIMES IN THE SYRIAN WAR AS A WEAPON

In the early hours of Friday, April 13, U.S. President Donald Trump, in coordination with French and U.K. armed forces, ordered a series of strikes against targets in Syria in apparent retaliation against the Syrian regime's alleged use of chlorine gas on civilians in Eastern Ghouta. The strikes were aimed against chemical weapons and logistics facilities throughout Syria, and were condemned by much of the world. Hours later, Syrians were seen dancing on the streets, elated by how light and ineffectual Trump's strikes were. For his part, Trump tweeted "Mission accomplished!"

This bizarre episode of the Syrian war—a gas attack followed by a series of Trump strikes, gives the impression that gas attacks are rare in the country, and receive an international response with a frenzy of media attention. Tragically for Syrians, the truth is almost the exact opposite. Gas attacks are common;

they go unpunished and rarely receive any attention. Counter-strikes aimed at deterrence have failed, and Trump quietly already learned when he struck a Syrian airbase in April of last year after hearing that Assad used gas to maime civilians.

Gas Attacks are Common in Syria

The recent use of chemical weapons in Eastern Ghouta and Trump's counter-attack on Syrian chemical facilities has given much of the world the impression that chemical weapon use is often a one-off strategy that receives a strong response. This is simply false. The Syrian regime routinely uses chlorine gas as a weapon despite its international ban, and has used sarin gas as well, which is much more lethal than chlorine. Sarin is also banned by Chemical Weapons Convention, which Syria acceded to in September 2013. This has not stopped Assad from using it.

The Human Rights Watch (HRW) released a report on April 4, counting the total number of times chemical weapons were verified by independent inquiries to have been used in Syria. The report found that chlorine, mustard and sarin gas were used 85 times since the start of the Syrian war.

The report was released before the latest gas attack in Douma, making the total verified count 86. It also admits that, "the total number of actual chemical attacks is likely higher," because it only lists instances of gas that were verified by independent investigative bodies that have limited access to the warzone in Syria.

International response to the use of chemical weapons has been weak and ineffectual, according to the report. Last year in April, Trump responded to an regime gas attack in Khan Shaykhun by launching 59 missiles on a Syrian airbase. The move failed at neutralizing the airbase and evidently did not deter Assad from continuing to launch gas attacks.

Rather than ordering insular military interventions into Syria, the HRW report recommends to wield the power invested in the official body designated to investigate instances of chemical weapons use (OPCW) and apply collective action and sanctions to Syria to pressure it diplomatically.

"The OPCW should suspend and sanction the Syrian government for its failure to comply with the Convention," HRW said. It is legally empowered by Article XII of its charter to apply "necessary measures to ensure compliance with this Convention and to redress and remedy any situation which contravenes it." In other words, the OPCW is allowed to take collective actions such as sanctions to ensure compliance with international laws on banned weapons, like weaponized gas.

The Mistake of Misunderstanding Gas Attacks in Syria

Gas attacks in Syria are deployed as a tool by the regime and opposition forces. ISIS also used mustard gas several times throughout the war. The danger of mis-representing the frequency of chemical attacks, to misportray them as rare and highly specialized episodes, is that it downplays just how cruel and illegal the war in Syria has been so far. With almost 100 reported and verified gas attacks in Syria, and over 50 at the hands of Assad, the war has been consistently catastrophic for Syrians.

To the myriad gas attacks and resulting investigations, substantive measures to prevent their future use have failed. In fact, the overall violence and terror deployed by the sides involved has been so devastating that Nadim Houry, terrorism and counterrorism director at HRW stated in an interview with Al Bawaba, "There's no morality in the Middle East right now... I don't think any these countries have been moral."

Trying to understand precisely why Trump ordered the series of strikes on April 13 has been a perplexing task. On April 11, two days before his attack on Syria, Trump tweeted: "Russia vows to shoot down any and all missiles fired at Syria. Get ready Russia, because they will be coming, nice and new and 'smart!' You shouldn't be partners with a Gas Killing Animal who kills his people and enjoys it!"

The next day on April 12, the Washington Post published a story that contained a hint at how the current administration's foreign policy functions. "A decision or statement is made by the president, and then the principals — Mattis or Pompeo or Kelly — come in and tell him we can't do it," one senior administration official told the Washington Post. "When that fails, we reverse-engineer a policy process to match whatever the president said." Reverse-engineering a response in Syria may well have happened, given that there appears to be no follow-up, and Trump declared victory shortly after the missiles hit their targets.

In other words, there does not appear to be a long-term strategy from the U.S. to militarily ensure compliance to international conventions banning chemical weapons usage. This is especially true when it comes ensuring opposition forces do not use chemical weapons.

They have been found to be responsible for a substantial chunk of the total gas attacks in Syria, and the U.S. has not responded to them with the same hostility it has to the Assad regime's deployment of the same tactic. If the goal is ensuring compliance to international conventions and human rights, selective and isolated strikes have done little.

SYRIAN GAS ATTACK: LITTLE-KNOWN EASTERN GHOUTA HAS BECOME THE FOCAL POINT OF ONGOING CONFLICT

These attacks have killed almost 2,000 people — the majority civilians, including 371 children — according to the Syrian Observatory for Human Rights (SOHR). As the US threatens retaliatory strikes against Syrian president Bashar al-Assad, key European nations have weighed in to condemn the chemical attack and offer a "strong and joint response" alongside the US.

With Syrian ally Russia warning of repercussions if the US acts, the impact of the strike on Eastern Ghouta could ripple well beyond Syrian borders. So what is it about Eastern Ghouta that has made its population the victims of such frequent and vicious attacks?

Why Eastern Ghouta?

Ghouta is a semi-rural outer district of Syria's capital. It lies just 10 kilometres east of central Damascus. After the Syrian conflict began as a revolution in 2011, rebels took control of a large section in the east of Ghouta in November 2012.

While other parts of Ghouta have fallen in and out of rebel hands, Eastern Ghouta has remained the rebels' major stronghold within striking distance of the capital. The Syrian Government has frequently claimed rebels have launched shells and missiles into suburban areas of Damascus, making reclaiming the area crucial for the security of the city.

In February 2013, the Government began a siege on the area, blocking major supplies of food and medicine while frequently bombarding it from land and air. Fighters and civilians alike living in Ghouta have since suffered starvation, epidemics, death and destruction.

The Ghouta region was previously home to about 2 million people, but thousands have been killed since the conflict began and hundreds of thousands have fled to other areas of Syria or internationally.

When the latest wave of attacks began in February 2018, the population of Eastern Ghouta was estimated to be just 400,000. Local activists said this number included about 20,000 rebel fighters.

Not the first or worst chemical attack on Ghouta

In August 2012, then US President Barack Obama said in a press conference at the White House that the use of chemical weapons in Syria would be "a red line". "That would change my calculus. That would change my equation," said Mr Obama who until then had stayed clear of direct involvement in the Syrian crisis.

One year later, rebel held areas of Ghouta were attacked by rockets containing sarin gas. A US Government report put the death toll at 1,429, including 426 children.

International medical group Doctors Without Borders said a further 3,500 patients were treated for neurotoxic symptoms following the attack. The Syrian Government and Russia at first denied the attack, but later claimed it was a false flag attempt by rebel forces to initiate an international strike against the regime.

Both a UN investigation team and the US Government concluded this scenario was extremely unlikely as rebel forces were not believed to have access to chemical weapons or the missiles used to launch them into Ghouta at this early stage of the conflict. The red line was crossed, but Mr Obama refrained from action.

Instead a deal was brokered by Russia in which the Syrian Government were to hand over their chemical weapon stockpiles for destruction and join the Chemical Weapons Convention (CWC).

Aren't chemical weapon attacks in Syria common?

Various groups have used chemical warfare in Syria on many occasions. Reports of the use of phosphorus and chlorine gas as well as other unidentified chemical agents by the Syrian army against opposition forces have been frequent and often verified.

The Government has also claimed similar attacks by rebels and even some attacks have been reportedly launched during in-fighting between rebel groups. But not all chemical agents fall under the CWC, which was created in 1993 in an effort to eliminate the production, stockpiling, and use of deadly chemical warfare.

Non-fatal chemicals such as teargas are frequently used for crowd control. Phosphorus and chlorine, while often deadly, have largescale industrial uses and are therefore not regulated or monitored by the CWC.

But sarin gas is banned internationally which makes this particular attack on Eastern Ghouta — while nowhere near as deadly as the daily attacks by barrel bombs and missiles — a violation of the chemical weapons agreement brokered following the first attack on Ghouta. When Mr Obama was weighing a response to the 2013 attack, Syria was not a signatory of the CWC.

Although the number of casualties of this recent attack pale in comparison to the first, Syria may now be in violation of a treaty they are signatories too and the agreement to destroy their chemical stockpiles. The Syrian conflict has claimed more than 465,000 lives and displaced over 12 million Syrians.

The SOHR reported 40 deaths as a result of sarin gas in Eastern Ghouta last week. While this single attack does seem insignificant in comparison to the average daily death toll, the consequences may be very significant for both the outcome of the Syrian conflict and international relations extending well beyond the Middle East.

Who are the rebels controlling Ghouta?

Various Syrian rebel groups have controlled parts of Ghouta over the years. The main groups in control in recent months were Faylaq al-Rahman, belonging to the more moderate Free Syrian Army coalition, and extremist groups Ahrar al-Sham and Jaysh al-Islam — previously an Al Qaeda affiliate.

Following 10 days of bombardment that claimed about 600 lives with thousands more injured in February, civilians were offered a chance to flee Eastern Ghouta through a "humanitarian corridor", during a daily five-hour pause announced by Syrian ally Russia. But no-one left. Russia claimed rebel groups were stopping civilians from fleeing, even shelling the corridor.

Civilians inside Ghouta said they were afraid to flee as there were no guarantees for their safety if they walked out into government-controlled areas. Activist Osama Nassar, speaking to ABC by telephone from Eastern Ghouta at the time of the evacuation plan, said people did not trust the regime and feared arrest or forced military service if they fled into Government hands.

He described the impossible choice civilians like himself were facing. A new deal was brokered that would allow rebel fighters and civilians to travel by bus to rebel controlled Idlib province. Most groups took the deal and much of the rebel enclave was shipped out in a convoy of buses.

But Jaysh al-Islam — an extremist group the Syrian regime and others have labelled as terrorists — still held Douma, the largest city in Eastern Ghouta. While reportedly engaged in negotiations, they had not agreed to the final terms. With the rebels on the brink of defeat, the alleged chemical attack seemingly handed the Government total victory in Ghouta.

Jaysh al-Islam released their regime prisoners and boarded buses for what civilians described as a harrowing 30-hour journey to rebel territory just 400 kilometres away. Russia and the Syrian Government continue to deny there was a chemical attack at all.

IS THE FIGHT OVER A GAS PIPELINE FUELLING THE WORLD'S BLOODIEST CONFLICT?

THE Syrian war often seems like a big confusing mess but one factor that is not often mentioned could be the key to unlocking the conflict. Some experts have pointed out that many of the key players have one thing in common: a billion-dollar gas pipeline. Factor in this detail and suddenly the war begins to make more sense, here's how it works:

IT'S THE GAS, STUPID

Many have questioned why Russia became involved in the Syrian war but often overlook the fight over natural gas. As Harvard Professor Mitchell A Orenstein and George Romer wrote last month in*Foreign Affairs,* Russia currently supplies Europe with a quarter of the gas it uses for heating, cooking, fuel and other activities.

In fact 80 per cent of the gas that Russian state-controlled company Gazprom produces is sold to Europe, so maintaining this crucial market is very important. But Europe doesn't like being so reliant on Russia for fuel and has been trying to reduce its dependence. It's a move that is supported by the United States as it would weaken Russian influence over Europe.

This has not gone down well with Russia, which uses its power over gas as political leverage and has a history of cutting off supply to countries during conflicts. It has even gone to war in Georgia and Ukraine to disrupt plans to export gas from other parts of the Middle East. As David Dalton, the editor of the *Economist Intelligence Unit*, told *The New York Times*: "Russia has always used gas as an instrument of influence. The more you owe Gazprom, the more they think they can turn the screws."

Much of Russia's power comes from established pipelines used to transport gas to Europe cheaply. But other countries are now trying to get around Russia and provide new sources of gas to Europe. Last year US President Barack Obama spoke openly about the need for Europe to reduce its reliance on Russian gas following the conflict in Ukraine.

The US also wants to use its own natural gas supply, recently developed through fracking, to undercut Russian supply. But it will be years before the US will be in a position to ship this overseas. The US is not the only country trying to outmanoeuvre Russia, and this is where the role of Syria becomes more important.

TWO NEW PIPELINES

Before the civil war, two competing pipelines put forward by Qatar and Iran aimed to transport gas to Europe through Syria. Qatar's plans were first put forward in 2009 and involved building a pipeline from the Persian Gulf via Saudi Arabia, Jordan, Syria and Turkey.

The gas field located 3000 metres below the floor of the Persian Gulf is the largest natural gas field in the world. Qatar owns about two-thirds of the resource but can't capitalise on it fully because it relies on tankers to deliver it to other countries and this makes its gas more expensive than Russia's. It was hoped the pipeline would provide cheaper access to Europe but Syrian President Bashar al Assad refused to give permission for the pipeline to go through his territory. Some believe Russia pressured him to reject the pipeline to safeguard its own business.

In the meantime Iran, which owns the other smaller, share of the Persian Gulf gas field, decided to lodge its own rival plan for a $10 billion pipeline to Europe via Iraq and Syria and then under the Mediterranean Sea. These plans apparently had Russia's blessing, possibly because it could exert more influence over Iran, which, unlike Qatar, did not host a US air base.

Assad signed off on the Iran plan in 2012 and it was due to be completed in 2016 but it was ultimately delayed because of the Arab Spring and the civil war. Many countries supporting or opposing the war against Assad have links to these pipeline plans. Failed pipeline bidder Qatar is believed to have funded anti-Assad rebel groups by $3 billion between 2011 and 2013. Saudi Arabia has also been accused of funding the terrorist group.

In contrast Orenstein and Romer noted the successful pipeline bidder, Iran, was believed to be helping Assad by running the Syrian army, supplying it with weapons and even troops. Major Rob Taylor, an instructor at the US Army's Command and General Staff College wrote in the Armed Forces Journal last year that the rival pipelines could be influencing the conflict in Syria.

"Viewed through a geopolitical and economic lens, the conflict in Syria is not a civil war, but the result of larger international players positioning themselves on the geopolitical chessboard in preparation for the opening of the pipeline," he noted. Just as the 2003 Iraq War has been linked to oil in the Persian Gulf, Syria may turn out to be all about gas.

WHY DOES TURKEY CARE?

One of the countries that has a lot to gain from getting rid of Assad is Turkey. Turkish President Recep Tayyip Erdogan has been vocal in calling for the Syrian President to step down and has also been accused of helping Islamic State, something it has rejected.

While Turkey could have other reasons for supporting the rebels in Syria, such as Assad's support for the Kurds, Harvard University Professor Orenstein told news.com.au that gas would definitely be one reason it was opposing the regime. Turkey, which stands at the crossroads of Asia and Europe, is an aspiring member of the European Union, and some consider it to be the best option for facilitating the movement of gas supplies from the Middle East to Europe.

As a hub, Turkey would benefit from transit fees and other energy-generated revenues. It could also insure, with US support, that all gas suppliers in the Middle East could freely export their product. Qatar's plans put Turkey at the centre of its plan.

As one of the countries relying on Russia for gas, freeing it from this dependence would be an added bonus. But none of this can be realised if the pipeline bypasses Turkey and if Assad becomes instrumental in approving an alternative that does not involve it.

Now that Russia is stepping in to help the Assad regime in Syria — possibly to protect its own dominance in the gas market — Turkey is facing a formidable barrier to its aspirations. When Turkey downed a Russian plane earlier this month, some speculated it may want to weaken any potential co-operation between Russia and the US which could see Assad continue his leadership.

Russia's motives for its air strikes have also been questioned. CNN military analyst Cedric Leighton, a retired air force colonel, noting that its bombing of Islamic State extremists seemed to have hit Turkmen in northern Syria, who had strong ties to the Turkish government. Prof Orenstein said the competition over natural gas could ultimately prevent co-operation between the two world powers on fighting Islamic State.

"I doubt there is much basis for US-Russia co-operation due to opposite interests in gas issues and Iran," he told news.com.au But despite fears that the world is facing a new Cold War, Prof Orenstein believes it's more of a "free for all", with the fight over natural gas acting as just another fuel.

NATURAL GAS A NEW CAUSE FOR CONFLICT IN THE MIDDLE EAST

In recent weeks, two wars of words have erupted — one between Israel and Lebanon, the other involving Egypt and Turkey — as a result of disputes over natural gas fields in the Eastern Mediterranean. Competition over energy sources has played a central part in shaping Middle Eastern history since the turn of the 20th century: This was the case in the Gulf, Iraq and Libya, while Syria had limited hydrocarbon sources and Egypt and Lebanon enjoyed none. But new discoveries have shown that the Eastern Mediterranean is home to one of the world's largest natural gas reserves — if not the largest ever.

Historically, the Eastern Mediterranean has never been a geopolitical backwater. Its key position on the road to the east had European powers competing for dominance over it. The Russian and Ottoman empires fought countless wars for the right to access its waters through the Turkish Straits. But, in the second half of the 20th century, and despite Cold War tensions reaching that area, the Eastern Mediterranean was never at the center of great power politics.

And, apart from the Turkish invasion and occupation of northern Cyprus in 1974, there were no regional conflicts either. Despite the many wars Arabs had fought with Israel, no major naval engagements were recorded. The United States had no permanent bases there and the Soviet Union only had a support base for its Mediterranean "squadron" in Syria's Tartus.

Optimistic observers once argued that, with energy sources spanning different territorial waters, the European interest in developing Mediterranean natural gas as a counterweight to Russian gas imports, and the need for a stable environment in order to attract investors and for production to take place, regional players might be induced to resolve their disputes peacefully. Unfortunately, a combination of unsettled borders, diplomatic machinations and vital economic stakes might engulf the Eastern Mediterranean in conflicts no less serious than elsewhere in the Middle East.

The US and Russia, the world's largest and second-largest producers of natural gas respectively, are both poised to play a vital role in brokering (and benefiting) from the coming crises. European powers will, despite being the primary beneficiary of these riches, take a back seat in the coming "Eastern Mediterranean game."

Owing to its air and naval bases in Syria, Russia is currently the dominant power in the area of the Mediterranean between Turkey, Cyprus and Syria. Moscow has already secured a pre-eminent role in the Syrian oil and gas sectors for years to come, including offshore gas reserves. Turkey is aggressively asserting its rights to benefit from the gas fields off its shores and those of the Republic of Northern Cyprus — which no one in the world recognizes except for Turkey. UN peace efforts in Cyprus have not come to fruition and the EU, of which Cyprus is a member, does not seem to have any workable initiatives. Russia, however, enjoys good relations with Cyprus, which does not recognize any Turkish rights in its northern waters.

The Russian-Turkish rapprochement is moving forward, as political and economic cooperation is strengthening between the two countries — including a Russian pipeline to transport natural gas through Turkey. This web of relations and Russia's preponderant military presence will make Moscow the prime arbiter in any crisis in the area.

If President Vladimir Putin could bring Turkey to the negotiating table in Syria, he could do the same in Cyprus. This would enable Russia to keep a close eye on the development of Eastern Mediterranean gas riches, which the Europeans desperately need in order to decrease their dependence on Russian imports.

The largest of the gas fields discovered, Zohr, is in Egyptian territorial waters. Extraction of natural gas from this 850 billion cubic meter behemoth has already begun. This is a much-needed boost to the Egyptian economy and could help solve many of its chronic problems. Egypt has no disputes with Israel over these gas reserves, but Egyptian-Turkish tensions are escalating over Cyprus. Egypt has settled its maritime borders with the latter, and is supporting Cypriot claims against Turkey. Egyptian foreign minister Sameh Shoukry met with his Greek counterpart during the Munich Security Conference last weekend to coordinate action against Turkey.

This row has broadened the existing gulf between the two countries. The US, whose relationship with Turkey is also heading south, has done little to resolve their differences, while Europe has no hand to play.

Here too, Russia is a possible broker. Russian-Egyptian relations have surged under President Abdel Fattah El-Sisi, as well as Russian arms sales to Egypt. There is even talk of Russia deploying forces to bases there. This will only strengthen Russia's position as the arbiter of the Eastern Mediterranean.

In December, Putin visited Ankara and Cairo in one day — the same day he announced victory over Daesh from the Russian air base in Syria's Latakia. Good relations with both Egypt and Turkey will enable Russia to broker reconciliation talks between the two key regional powers. It is also worth mentioning that Putin enjoys a special relationship with Greek Prime Minister Alexis Tsipras, who has broken Europe's anti-Russia consensus on numerous occasions.

Lebanon and Israel, meanwhile, are looking forward to benefiting from offshore natural gas, but an American initiative failed to resolve disputes over the unsettled maritime border, which runs through some of the gas fields. Israel has threatened Lebanon, and both Hezbollah and the Lebanese government have responded. Yet, for the time being, it is unclear whether Russia, the US or the EU will mediate this looming crisis.

The discovery of such enormous riches has already transformed the Eastern Mediterranean into a geopolitical hotspot. Conflicts seem inevitable, but the ability of Russia and the US to contain them is yet to be tested. Yet, given their disagreements, the two great powers may very well use this space as an additional battleground in their ever-growing competition in the Middle East, and the world over.

THE NATURAL GAS WAR BURNING UNDER SYRIA

In 2009, Qatar, a leading natural gas producer, approached Syria about routing its planned 1,500 mile pipeline to the gas markets of Europe through Syria's Aleppo province. Qatar wanted a pipeline straight to Europe as its current gas transport modes were limited to Liquefied Natural Gas (LNG) tanker, mostly to Asia with limited spot shipments to Europe or the Dolphin pipeline to the United Arab Emirates and Oman. The pipeline would head north and end in Turkey after crossing Saudi Arabia, Jordan, and Syria. Syria declined Qatar's offer, which would have cut the European market share of its partner, Russia, and instead agreed to participate in the "Friendship Pipeline"between Iran and Iraq that was considered a "Shia Pipeline" to some and a target for the Sunni monarchies of the Gulf. Not understood, or ignored, was Syria's longstanding support of the Iranian regime, especially during the 1980-1988 Iran-Iraq War, and its long relationship with Russia, dating from 1944, which should have been a warning of who might appear if things hotted up.

In 2010, Israel and Syria held back-channel talks that reportedly included Israel's return of the Golan Heights to Syria in exchange for security guarantees. The talks lagged due to mutual suspicions about the other side's ability to deliver and, by early 2011, the Arab Spring had erupted across the region and leaders' attentions turned to more immediate concerns.

At this point, America had the opportunity to strike a blow against the Islamic Republic's ally, the Assad regime. In 2011, Turkey provided a home for the opposition Syrian National Council and, in August 2011, the U.S., its allies, and the UN were calling on Bashar Assad to step down.

In 2011, Syria, Iran, and Iraq agreed to build a pipeline to connect Iran's South Pars gas field to Europe. The pipeline would run from Assalouyeh, Iran to Europe via Iraq, Syria, and Lebanon, with Syria as the center of assembly and production.

What remains unclear is why, when Syria turned down its original pipeline proposal, it didn't pursue its second option for the pipeline route: Saudi Arabia – Kuwait – Iraq. Aside from the challenging terrain in Iraq, the mostly likely reasons are the discovery of vast gas reserves in the eastern Mediterranean, and Saudi opposition to a pipeline through Kuwait. If a more Qatar-friendly regime were to gain control of Syria, Qatar would be able to garner more profit and have influence over the state, something it is unable to do with Saudi Arabia, which vehemently opposes Qatar's historic support of the Muslim Brotherhood, Jordan, a U.S. ally, or Iraq, an Iranian ally. At that point it was nothing personal, just business, and the Assads had to go.Related: Why Oil Markets Should Brace For OPEC Disappointment

This was Qatar's best chance to influence the affairs of the region. It has a tiny native population – guest workers make up almost 90 percent of Qatar's population of 2.2 million – and an unhealthy one, so some options are limited as it has a very small military. It does, however, have a healthy check book and was able to use it to help finance the Syrian opposition forces.

To better understand the war in Syria, remember the surge in natural gas discoveries in the Eastern Mediterranean starting in 2009. Israel, Cyprus, and Egypt have found large gas deposits, and offshore Lebanon has the potential for significant gas resources. Israel has the potential to export gas to Egypt, Jordan, the Palestinian Authority, and Turkey. (Israel and Turkey have discussed a pipeline to Turkey, but Cyprus has objected as it does not have diplomatic relations with Turkey.)

If the pipeline from Iran to Syria it could create an energy hub in Syria, and could block Qatar gas sales to Europe at a time when Qatar's gas exports to the U.S. have dropped to zero, largely due to increasing U.S. domestic production of natural gas. Thus Qatar would be limited to the Asian LNG market as it scrapped for the EU market with Iran, Iraq, Syria, and Russia. And the only thing that could make it worse is happening: Europe is forecast to take more than half of U.S. LNG exports by 2020.

Qatar, Saudi Arabia, and their confederates are in it to win it, and the fighting in Syria has focused on the pipeline routes. Aleppo province, which would host the Qatari pipeline, is where Turkey wants to establish a buffer zone to support "moderate" rebel forces. If Turkey can control this territory, it will bolster the Qatari pipeline and ensure its own preeminence as the energy hub in southern Europe, where it would gather oil and natural gas from Russia, Central Asia, the Caspian, the Eastern Mediterranean, and the Middle East, and become less reliant on Russian gas, which accounted for over 50 percent of its imports in 2014. But Russia hasn't been standing still: it has surrounded Turkey on three sides by occupying Crimea, sending more troops to Armenia, and deploying the S-400 air defense system to Syria, creating a no-fly zone, and maybe a "no-buy" zone for potential customers of Qatari gas.

The Pasha's increasingly autocratic behavior may spur hedging behavior in Europe, such as balancing the Pasha with the Tsar and completing Russia's Nord Stream pipeline, negotiating better deals with key suppliers Norway and Algeria, importing LNG from the U.S., and getting serious about fracking for shale gas. Turkey turned the flow of refugees to Europe on and off to get what it wanted, and the possibility remains that it will one day do the same with energy.

And Qatar may have to write some more checks in addition to the ones it has sent to Assad's opposition. Turkey has some serious policy and infrastructure shortfalls that work against it becoming a serious energy hub soon: weak domestic gas regulation, state subsidies, monopoly control of the gas transmission network, only two LNG terminals, and a lack of storage capacity. Syria may be too wrecked to be a hub and Turkey lacks the infrastructure for the role. Russia may be interested in investing in increasing Turkey's hub capacity and Turkey, which is making amends with Russia, may take the money over Qatar's for a pipeline that may never be built. Russia's good relations with Cyprus and Israel could propel movement towards a resolution of the Cyprus dispute so the gas pipeline from Israel to Turkey becomes a reality, having the knock-on effect of attracting more outside investment to Turkey.

To succeed in its pipeline goals, Qatar will have to make serious investments in the Turkish end of its project as well as resisting political pressure from Russia. Until then, it will be limited to making LNG shipments to Europe by tanker. In the meantime, these pipeline geopolitics have contributed to serious consequences for the Middle East.

THE GEOPOLITICS OF GAS AND THE SYRIAN CRISIS

What has one of the most democratic countries of the Middle East, Syria, done to tick off some of its neighbors in the West, the fierce fighters for democracy? The irrationality and unscrupulousness of the approaches Western countries have taken to the Syrian crisis, when the same people who in Europe are considered terrorists are declared «freedom fighters» when it comes to Syria, becomes clearer in light of the economic dimension of the Syrian tragedy. There is every reason to think that by helping destroy its own cultural and historical roots in Syria, Europe is first and foremost fighting for energy resources. And a special role is played by natural gas, which is emerging as the main fuel of the 21st century. The geopolitical problems connected with its production, transportation and use are perhaps more than any other topic on the radar of Western strategists.

In the apt expression of F. William Engdahl, «Natural gas is the flammable ingredient that is fueling this insane scramble for energy in the region.» A battle is raging over whether pipelines will go toward Europe from east to west, from Iran and Iraq to the Mediterranean coast of Syria, or take a more northbound route from Qatar and Saudi Arabia via Syria and Turkey. Having realized that the stalled Nabucco pipeline, and indeed the entire Southern Corridor, are backed up only by Azerbaijan's reserves and can never equal Russian supplies to Europe or thwart the construction of the South Stream, the

West is in a hurry to replace them with resources from the Persian Gulf. Syria ends up being a key link in this chain, and it leans in favor of Iran and Russia; thus it was decided in the Western capitals that its regime needs to change. The fight for «democracy» is a false flag thrown out to cover up totally different aims.

It is not difficult to notice that the rebellion in Syria began to grow two years ago, almost at the same time as the signing of a memorandum in Bushehr on June 25, 2011 regarding the construction of a new Iran-Iraq-Syria gas pipeline... It is to stretch 1500 km from Asaluyeh on the largest gas field in the world, North Dome/South Pars (shared between Qatar and Iran) to Damascus. The length of pipeline on the territory of Iran will be 225 km, in Iraq 500 km, and in Syria 500-700 km. Later it may be extended along the bottom of the Mediterranean Sea to Greece. The possibility of supplying liquefied gas to Europe via Syria's Mediterranean ports is also under consideration. Investments in this project equal 10 billion dollars. (1)

This pipeline, dubbed the «Islamic pipeline», was supposed to start operation in the period from 2014 to 2016. Its projected capacity is 110 million cubic meters of gas per day (40 billion cubic meters a year). Iraq, Syria and Lebanon have already declared their need for Iranian gas (25-30 million cubic meters per day for Iraq, 20-25 million cubic meters for Syria, and 5-7 million cubic meters until 2020 for Lebanon). Some of the gas will be supplied via the Arab gas transportation system to Jordan. Experts believe that this project could be an alternative to the Nabucco gas pipeline being promoted by the European Union (with a planned capacity of 30 billion cubic meters of gas per year), which doesn't have sufficient reserves. It was planned to run the Nabucco pipeline from Iraq, Azerbaijan and Turkmenistan through the territory of Turkey. At first Iran was also considered as a resource base, but later it was excluded from the project. After the signing of the memorandum on the Islamic Pipeline, the head of the National Iranian Gas Company (NIGC), Javad Oji, stated that South Pars, with recoverable reserves of 16 trillion cubic meters of gas, is a «reliable source of gas, which is a prerequisite for the building of a pipeline which Nabucco does not have».It is easy to observe that about 20 billion cubic meters per year will remain from this pipeline for Europe, which would be able to compete with Nabucco's 30 billion, but not the 63 billion from the South Stream.

A gas pipeline from Iran would be highly profitable for Syria. Europe would gain from it as well, but clearly someone in the West didn't like it. The West's gas-supplying allies in the Persian Gulf weren't happy with it either, nor was would-be no. 1 gas transporter Turkey, as it would then be out of the game. The new «unholy alliance» which formed between them shamelessly declared its goal to be «protecting democratic values» in the Middle East, although logically speaking the U.S. and its allies ought to begin this with their own partners in the coalition against Syria from among the monarchies of the Persian Gulf, which are questionable in this regard.

The Sunnite countries also see the Islamic Pipeline from the viewpoint of interconfessional contradictions, considering it a «Shiite pipeline from Shiite Iran through the territory of Iraq with its Shiite majority and into the territory of Shiite-friendly Alawite Asad». As renowned researcher on energy issues F. William Engdahl writes, this geopolitical drama is intensified by the fact that the South Pars field lies in the Persian Gulf directly on the border between Shiite Iran and Sunnite Qatar. But tiny Qatar, which is no match for Iran in power, makes active use of its connections with the military presence of the U.S. and NATO in the Persian Gulf. On the territory of Qatar are a command node of the Pentagon's Central Command of the U.S. Armed Forces, the headquarters of the Head Command of the U.S. Air Force, the No. 83 Expeditionary Air Group of the British Air Force and the 379th Air Expeditionary Wing of the U.S. Air Force. Qatar, in Engdahl's opinion, has other plans for its share in the South Pars gas field and is not eager to join efforts with Iran, Syria and Iraq. It is not at all interested in the success of an Iran-Iraq-Syria pipeline, which would be completely independent of the transit routes of Qatar or Turkey leading to Europe. In fact, Qatar is doing all it can to thwart the construction of the pipeline, including arming the «opposition» fighters in Syria, many of whom come from Saudi Arabia, Pakistan and Libya.

Qatar's resolve is fed by the discovery by Syrian geological exploration companies in 2011 of Syria's own large gas-producing area near the Lebanese border, not far from the Mediterranean port of Tartus which Russia leases, and the detection of a significant gas field near Homs. According to preliminary estimates, these discoveries should substantially increase the country's gas reserves, which previously amounted to 284 billion cubic meters. The fact that the export of Syrian or Iranian gas to the European Union could take place through the port of Tartus, which has ties to Russia, is unsatisfactory to Qatar and its Western patrons as well.

The Arabic newspaper Al-Akhbar cites information according to which there is a plan approved by the U.S. government to create a new pipeline for transporting gas from Qatar to Europe involving Turkey and Israel. The capacity of such a pipeline is not mentioned, but considering the resources of the Persian Gulf and Eastern Mediterranean region, it could exceed that of both the Islamic Pipeline and Nabucco, directly challenging Russia's South Stream. The main developer of this project is Frederick Hoff, who is «in charge of gas issues in the Levant» and a member of the U.S. «Syrian Crisis Committee». This new pipeline is to begin in Qatar, cross Saudi territory and then the territory of Jordan, thus bypassing Shiite Iraq, and reach Syria. Near Homs the pipeline is to branch in three directions: to Latakia, Tripoli in northern Lebanon, and Turkey. Homs, where there are also hydrocarbon reserves, is the «project's main crossroads», and it is not surprising that it is in the vicinity of this city and its «key», Al-Qusayr, that the fiercest fighting is taking place. Here the fate of Syria is being decided. The parts of Syrian territory where detachments of rebels are operating with the support of the U.S., Qatar and Turkey, that is, the north, Homs and the environs of Damascus, coincide with the route that the pipeline is to follow to Turkey and Tripoli, Lebanon. A comparison of a map of armed hostilities and a map of the Qatar pipeline route indicates a link between armed activities and the desire to control these Syrian territories. Qatar's allies are trying to accomplish three goals: «to break Russia's gas monopoly in Europe; to free Turkey from its dependence on Iranian gas; and to give Israel the chance to export its gas to Europe by land at less cost».

As Asia Times analyst Pepe Escobar indicated, the Emir of Qatar apparently made a deal with the «Muslim Brotherhood» according to which it will support their international expansion in exchange for a pact of peace within Qatar. A «Muslim Brotherhood» regime in Jordan and in Syria, supported by Qatar, would abruptly change the entire geopolitical world gas market - decidedly in favor of Qatar and to the detriment of Russia, Syria, Iran and Iraq. It would also be a crushing blow to China.

The war against Syria is aimed at pushing this project through, as well as at the breakdown of the agreement between Tehran, Baghdad and Damascus. Its implementation has been halted several times due to military action, but in February 2013 Iraq declared its readiness to sign a framework agreement which would enable the construction of the pipeline.

It is worth noting that after this, more and more new groups of Iraqi Shiites have risen up in support of Asad; as The Washington Post admits, they have «no little battle experience» in confronting Americans in their country. Along with fighters from Lebanon's Hezbollah, they make an ever more formidable force.

The stakes in the «elimination game» started in Syria by the West over the gas pipeline continue to grow. The end of the European Union's embargo on supplying weapons to the Syrian opposition, which according to the BBC the majority of EU member countries were against (democracy, where are you?), might not be able to help the rebels.

As for civilization and justice, when profit is at stake, sentiment doesn't matter. The main thing is not to play the wrong card in this unfair game that smells of blood and gas.

THE 'PIPELINEISTAN' CONSPIRACY: THE WAR IN SYRIA HAS NEVER BEEN ABOUT GAS

Six years into a conflict that has killed at least 400,000 people, there is a widely held belief that the bloodshed in Syria is simply another war over Middle Eastern energy resources. The bloodshed, so the theory goes, is a proxy battle about two proposed pipelines which would run across the country and on to Turkey and Europe.

While neither pipeline has left the drawing board, or indeed was ever realistic, this has not dampened the theory's popularity as a core reason for the Syria conflict. The first pipeline is allegedly backed by the US and runs from Qatar through Saudi Arabia and Jordan to Syria. The second is a supposedly Russia-backed pipeline that goes from Iran, via Iraq, to Syria.

Syrian President Bashar al-Assad, it is claimed, rejected the Qatari pipeline in 2009, at the request of Moscow, to ensure that European reliance on Russian gas would not be undermined. As a result, some commentators claim, the US and its European and Gulf allies, including Qatar, decided to orchestrate a rebellion against Assad to ensure that their pipe dreams became a reality rather than the Iranian option. Russia, in turn, backed Syria to ensure its own energy interests prevailed. Iran is also an ally of the current regime in Damascus.

These claims have been promoted in several quarters: the Qatari-based Al Jazeera first floated the concept of a "Pipelineistan war" in 2012. Even US establishment journal Foreign Affairs and the Guardian newspaper picked up on the theory, which gained further traction in 2016 in an article by Robert Kennedy Jr, and was flagged by, among others, Jill Stein of the Green Party, a former US presidential candidate.

The idea was floated again after the US bombing of Syria in April. This, it was claimed, was further "proof" of Washington's desire to oust Assad and enable Europe to diversify its gas dependency away from Russia. While the US has been covertly working with Gulf allies against the Assad regime, controlling

Syria's energy resources and pipeline networks was not a primary concern. If so, it would be a very low priority for regime change.

Why? Firstly, the timeline is wrong. Covert action against Syria started under the George W Bush administration, in 2005, well before the alleged Qatari offer to Damascus in 2009. "We can see US action against the Syrian regime well before the notion of this pipeline came into existence," says Justin Dargin, an energy scholar at Oxford University.

Secondly, the pipeline hypotheses do not stand up to the realities of how energy is transported through the Middle East and the obstacles faced by pipeline proposals, many of which fail to come to fruition. Even the Arab Gas Pipeline, whose second phase came online in 2005, has been mired in problems. Robin Yassin-Kassab, author of *Burning Country: Syrians in Revolution and War*, says the Pipelineistan theory also ignores how the conflict started and the early months of the revolution. "Like all conspiracy theories, it thrives on the absence of content and in-depth knowledge of the country," he says.

Domestic demand

In 2009, Syria announced a policy that attracted minimal attention beyond its borders at the time. Called the "Four Seas Strategy," it aimed to turn the country into a transit hub for gas between the Gulf, the Black Sea, the Caucus and the Mediterranean by expanding the 6,300 kilometres of gas and oil pipelines that criss-cross the country and by making use of the Euro-Arab Mashreq Gas Pipeline (AGP).

The AGP is not a core feature in the Pipelineistan narrative, but it does indicate the problems faced when it comes down to laying down pipelines in the region.

On the drawing board for nearly 20 years, construction of the AGP started in 2003. It was slated to cost $1.2 billion and run 1,200 km from Egypt to Jordan and Syria, before reaching Turkey. There, it would connect with the planned Nabucco pipeline, which would export gas to Europe. One key element of the AGP plan was that Egypt would pump gas to Syria and Jordan. Syria would use the Egyptian gas and then top up the pipeline with gas from its own northern fields before it was sent north.

When war broke out in Syria in 2011, the last leg of the AGP – the stretch from Aleppo to Kilis in Turkey – was being constructed, never to be completed. But there were problems with the pipeline, which cost $1.5 million per kilometre, even before the conflict erupted. Jim Deacons is a Scottish energy consultant who worked on the AGP in Syria, including designing the final phase of the project.

"When I left [Damascus in 2010] there wasn't enough gas being fed up through Jordan," he says. "The Egyptians were gas trapped. They didn't have enough gas to export, despite signing contracts left, right and centre, so they couldn't meet their obligations."

Egypt's gas production dropped from 220 million cubic feet (mcf) per day in 2010 to 80 mcf in 2011. The AGP was shut down in 2012 after terrorist attacks on the pipeline in Sinai and Egypt's increasing need for gas for home consumption, and has not resumed operations.

The same issues that plagued the AGP would also apply to any planned Iranian pipeline to Syria, namely a lack of gas. "Iran has been attempting to develop its South Pars field [in the Persian Gulf] for a long time," says Dargin, "but there are big obstacles, not least within Iran, where there are competing theories on which development plans should have priority. One idea is for gas to be used domestically as they've quite a lot of issues meeting their own needs."

Indeed, Iran could not meet its own gas needs before an agreement was even signed with Damascus in 2011. Deacons explains: "The whole point is that while Syria was actively talking about gas from Iran, Tehran was importing gas from Azerbaijan during the winter months.

"That really blows the theory of a gas grab out of the window. That Iran would supply gas to Syria was complete nonsense, and I told the Syrian [energy] minister that [at the time]."

The missing jigsaw piece

The AGP's viability beyond Syria was also dependent on Nabucco, another pipeline proposal intended to diversify Europe's gas imports. That idea, floated by a consortium of European and Turkish energy companies in 2002, was slated to cost more than $10 billion.

The project would pipe 31 billion cubic meters of natural gas a year some 3,000 km from Central Asia, via Turkey, to Baumgarten in Austria. But by 2009 Nabucco had still not started, and projected construction costs ballooned to more than $25 billion.

Eight years later, Nabucco has still not progressed due to the extraordinary cost and the politics at play. Dargin says: "At energy conferences, Nabucco is still brought up. But it's like, 'Where's Waldo?' It is phenomenal."

The Nabucco pipeline would be essential for both of the contending pipelines, which would need to piggyback off it if they want gas to reach Europe. But while Russia was opposed to Nabucco and the idea of a Qatari pipeline, it was not enough of a reason for conflict, says Dargin. "You have a motive, a victim, but not a murder weapon. There is no evidence." Furthermore, Russia had managed to axe Nabucco in 2007 by announcing its South Stream pipeline project, which was to cut out Turkey altogether by crossing the Black Sea to Bulgaria and onto Europe.

The project was cancelled in 2014 due to political issues with the European Union. Then Moscow proposed the Turkstream project in 2014, which was again to cut across the Black Sea but then on to the European side of Turkey. It was cancelled after a Russian jet fighter was shot down by Turkey in November 2015. While both projects are back on the cards, especially Turkstream, neither could transport Iranian or Qatari gas across Turkey.

No Qatari offer to Damascus

The pipeline narrative, from 2013 onwards, also makes much mention of Damascus rebuffing an alleged Qatari offer in 2009 to build a pipeline. This part of the story hinges around statements by unnamed diplomats in a 2013 Agence France-Presse articleabout a meeting between Russia's President Vladimir Putin and Saudi Arabia's Bandar bin Sultan.

The report says: "In 2009, Assad refused to sign an agreement with Qatar for an overland pipeline running from the Gulf to Europe via Syria to protect the interests of its Russian ally, which is Europe's top supplier of natural gas." But Dargin says: "There are no credible sources that show that Qatar even approached Syria in 2009 and was rebuffed in the process. I am not saying it definitely did not occur, rather there is no evidence supporting this claim."

Syrian experts also support Dargin's rebuttal, highlighting the burgeoning economic and political ties between Doha and Damascus. Yassin-Kassab says: "The absurdity is that relations between the Assad regime and the Qataris were excellent until summer 2011. Assad and his wife and the Qatari royal couple were also being portrayed as personal friends."

Although Assad may have repeatedly criticized Qatar since late 2011 onwards for supporting "terrorists," he has never publicly stated that Qatari support for the rebels was over a future pipeline. Jihad Yazigi, editor of economy website Syria Report, says: "An important aspect that we don't talk about is the Syrian government never said the Qataris were fighting for a pipeline; that is telling in itself, that Assad never mentioned it."

The Moscow-Tehran connection

Then there's the other part of the Pipelineistan puzzle – the Iran-Syria pipeline, also known as the Islamic Pipeline. Yazigi explains: "The Islamic pipeline has been talked about for years. There were pre-contract memorandums of understanding, but until July 2011, there was no formal signing [between Syria and Iran]. You can't argue this is a serious reason to destroy the whole country."

While the project was politically expedient, it ignored economic and energy realities. First, the project was estimated to cost $10 billion, but it was unclear who would foot the bill, particularly as Tehran was – and still is – under US and international sanctions, as is Syria, since 2011.

Second, Iran lacks the capabilities to export significant amounts of gas. Sanctions mean it cannot access the advanced US technology that would allow it to exploit gas from the South Pars field that borders Qatar. "Competition for gas access in the region is not between Qatar and Iran, but Russia and Iran," says Yazigi.

"The ones with the biggest share of the European market are the Russians, and they want to secure that. They are the ones to fear the Iranians." Despite talk of how pipeline wars would enable Europe to diversify away from Russian gas, Russian gas exports to Europe hit a record high in January 2017.

In December 2016, commodities trader Glencore and the Qatar Investment Authority, the country's sovereign wealth fund, acquired a 19.5 percent stake in Rosneft, Russia's state-owned oil company, for $11 billion. Result: Qatar has achieved easier access to the European market than any pipeline through Syria ever could offer.

Politics makes plan a pipedream

The Iranian pipeline would have to cross Iraq. Aside from the problems of building infrastructure in a conflict zone, plans to pipe gas just a short distance from Iraq to Syria were not viable even in 2009.

Deacons says that the Iraqis were observers of the AGP project and that he also discussed bringing gas in from Iraq over the Euphrates with the EU ambassador to Iraq.

"But it all got bogged down in politics. And the Iraqi infrastructure was so badly maintained and destroyed that they would have had to rebuild, not just fix, it. "Huge infrastructure investment was needed before even bringing in pipelines." Likewise, politics would also impact any Qatari plans.

Dargin explains: "Such a pipeline would have had to pass through Saudi territory, which perhaps would have been an even larger obstacle than Syria, as Riyadh has blocked and obstructed numerous proposals for regional pipelines." Indeed, Saudi obstruction caused planners in the mid-2000s to redraw routes for the Dolphin pipeline, which pipes gas from Qatar to the UAE. All three are members of the Gulf Cooperation Council.

"Saudi Arabia placed numerous hurdles in the undersea passage of the Dolphin pipeline as it would pass through its maritime boundaries," says Dargin. "Saudi opposition was the principle reason we do not see a Qatari pipeline to Bahrain or Kuwait."

As a result, Doha has become the world's largest LNG exporter during the past 15 years. It has invested more than $11bn on an LNG cargo shipping fleet that is independent of fixed pipeline infrastructure and can take LNG anywhere. The fastest-growing gas markets are in Asia, especially Japan, China, South Korea and India. LNG is also a more competitive option than piping dry gas to Europe, where gas demand is flat and forecasts depressed compared to Asia and within the Middle East itself.

Naser Tamimi, an independent Qatari energy expert, says: "With the existing infrastructure, Qatar doesn't have enough gas to sell to Europe through a pipeline, as most contracts currently are to Asia and long-term, while demand within Qatar is rising." "A pipeline has to be economically justifiable and secure demand from buyers in the long-term to recover pipeline costs."

Such factors all coalesce to make both the Qatari and Iranian suggestions nigh impossible. As Tamimi explains: "If Syria and Iraq stabilise, and political relations with Saudi Arabia and Iraq improve ... after all of that, then you could think of a pipeline. "But at the end of the day it's a pipe dream."

CHEMICAL ATTACKS IN SYRIA

Since 2013, thousands of Syrians have been injured and hundreds killed by chemical warfare. The first chemical attack on record in Syria was in March 2013 near Aleppo. Since then, 17 locations have been attacked with chemical weapons.

One year ago, sarin gas (or a sarin-like substance) was used to attack the town of Khan Sheikhoun. On the anniversary of that attack, Al Jazeera looks at the various chemical weapons used to attack rebel-held areas since 2013:

Sarin

Sarin gas is odourless and tasteless and works immediately to inhibit natural processes that control neurotransmitters in the body. The nerves are overstimulated uncontrollably, and the afflicted person's nose starts running, eyes crying, and they vomit continuously as their bowel and bladder evacuate themselves. Depending on the level of exposure, sarin gas can cause death within 10 minutes.

White phosphorus

White phosphorus has been used in conflicts since World War I. It is highly efficient at creating smoke and is used to cover troop movements or positions in conflicts. Exposure to white phosphorus causes severe burns as the gas sticks to the skin and causes severe burns that can result in the absorption of phosphorus into the organs of the body. In addition, inhalation of phosphorus smoke or fumes, as well as the oral ingestion of as little as 15mg can affect the body's organs and bones, sometimes causing death.

Chlorine gas

Used as a chemical weapon in World War I, chlorine gas is dispersed when pressurised chlorine is delivered via any explosive device. An everyday chemical with many peace-time uses, chlorine is readily available and exists in a grey area as a chemical weapon. Exposure to chlorine gas causes respiratory distress, severe irritation to the respiratory tract and eyes, and, depending on the level of exposure, can cause lasting damage to both.

Mustard gas

Mustard gas, or sulfur mustard, is a yellowish brown gas that has an odour resembling mustard, garlic or horseradish. It is a blistering agent, causing severe blisters on the skin and in the lungs. The effects of mustard gas are not immediate, and victims can start showing symptoms up to 24 hours after exposure, with chemical burn blisters appearing all over the body and, in some cases, damage to eye tissue and lungs. Severe mustard gas burns (on more than 50 percent of the body) can be fatal, and mustard gas victims are said to be more likely to develop cancer later in life. It was used towards the end of World War I and during the Iraq-Iran war between 1979-1988.

RUSSIA'S SYRIA INTERVENTION IS NOT ALL ABOUT GAS

Questions regarding the possible role of natural gas in the Syrian conflict have come up once more since direct Russian military intervention began at the end of September. It has been erroneously contended that Russia perceives a need to control Syria to protect its dominance of the European gas market, in particular from a proposed Qatari pipeline that would cross Syrian territory. Although the Russian state and its gas export monopoly, Gazprom, have a vital strategic interest in maintaining their 30 percent share of the European gas market and keeping an eye on potential competition, the actual or potential role of Syria in this is irrelevant to Russia's involvement in the Syrian conflict.

The theory that Syria is significant to Russia's gas exports rests on three possible scenarios: one would involve the construction of a pipeline from Qatar, through Saudi Arabia, Jordan, and Syria to Turkey, and onwards to Europe; another entails a pipeline from Iran through Iraq to Syria and onwards; and the third would arise from the discovery and development of offshore gas fields in Syrian waters of the Mediterranean.

The Qatari pipeline scenario has been given some credence in light of Qatar–Turkey discussions in 2009 and 2010, which floated the idea that the Gulf Arab state could contribute gas to the proposed Nabucco pipeline. However, grandiose pronouncements about pipeline deals are the common currency of high-level diplomacy, and it is rare for such projects to progress beyond the stage of the joint communiqué. Turkey may have had an interest in using the *possibility* of getting Qatari gas as a bargaining chip in its price negotiations with Gazprom, while Qatar at that time was grasping every opportunity it could get to advertise its global importance.

It has been claimed that the Qatar–Turkey pipeline plan failed because President Bashar al-Assad rejected it in order to protect the interests of Syria's ally, Russia, in preserving its dominant position in Europe. There are more prosaic explanations. In 2005, Qatar had declared a moratorium on the development of new export-oriented gas projects, following a decade of rapid growth in output from the North Field, most of which was dedicated to sales of liquefied natural gas (LNG). Its only pipeline export deal was the Dolphin Gas Project to the UAE and Oman.

Qatar has refused to expand Dolphin until its neighbors agree to higher prices, and a proposal in 2005 to build another pipeline to Kuwait came to nothing as a result of Saudi objections. Qatar already has a presence in the European gas market through sales of LNG. In 2014, almost one quarter of Qatar's total LNG exports went to Europe. About half of this was accounted for by the United Kingdom, where Qatar holds a majority stake in the South Hook LNG import plant. Other European cargoes went to Italy, Spain, and Belgium. Exporting LNG gives Qatar more flexibility of market access than a pipeline that would have to cross more than a dozen countries before it could reach the large northern European markets.

And the notion that Iran's gas export ambitions are a factor in the Syrian crisis is, if anything, more absurd. Iran is the largest gas producer in the Middle East, but it is also the largest gas consumer. It exports up to 10 billion cubic meters (353 billion cubic feet) of "dry" natural gas a year to Turkey, but it imports a similar amount from Turkmenistan. Plans to liquefy their gas and begin LNG exports have been on the drawing board for 20 years and are no nearer to coming to fruition, as is a plan to build a gas pipeline to Pakistan and India. Iran is now looking to entice international oil companies to invest in a major expansion of its oil and gas production capacity, but this will take time to achieve, particularly given the constraints on the companies' capital spending budgets. Even if Iran had enough surplus gas to export to Europe, the simplest options would be to boost the capacity of the existing line through Turkey or to build LNG plants. Sending gas through Iraq and Syria would make no sense, as it would either have to loop back into Turkey or be exported from an LNG plant on the Syrian coast, which would be an odd choice of location when Iran could build such plants in its own territory.

The third supposed threat to Russian gas interests are the possible natural gas reserves in Syria itself. Syria's onshore gas reserves have been developed over the past 30 years, producing enough by 2010 to meet domestic electricity generation needs. Ultimately, Syria could benefit from building a domestic gas distribution system so households would become less reliant on *mazut* and *butagaz* (fuel oil and liquefied petroleum gas) for cooking and heating. Russian companies such as Stroytransgaz have built processing plants and pipelines for Syria's gas sector, some of which have been financed by swaps included in Russia's write-off of about $12 billion of Syrian debts in 2005.

In the mid-2000s, the Syrian government commissioned seismic surveys of its territorial waters to assess their oil and gas prospects. Interest in the potential of this zone grew following the major gas discoveries made in Israeli waters and off the coast of Cyprus. Syria offered four offshore blocks in two exploration bid rounds, but received only a limited response.

At the end of 2013, an agreement was reached with Russia's Soyuzneftegaz to explore one of the blocks. In addition, the company held Syria's onshore exploration concession (Block 12) and briefly had a 50 percent stake in Block 26, operated by Gulfsands Petroleum. On September 29, 2015, one day before the start of Russian air strikes in Syria, the company announced that it was withdrawing from Syria for security reasons. It is possible that Syria's maritime territory contains natural gas reserves, but as yet there is no proof. The process of turning such reserves into a profitable source of exports is complex and expensive, as can be gauged from the difficulty that the operators of the Leviathan field in Israel are facing in developing the 450 billion cubic meters (16 trillion cubic feet) of reserves that they have identified. In light of this it is simply not credible to cite the potential of Syrian gas to infringe on Russia's commanding position in the European gas market as a factor influencing Russia's military intervention.

Furthermore, due to the expansion of production in the United States and elsewhere, there is currently a large surplus in the global gas market. Much of the growth in recent demand has come from China, but the rate of increase in Chinese gas consumption has started to slow down as economic growth eases and services start to play a more prominent role. In China, India, and Europe, the efforts to phase out coal for power generation have not led to a surge in natural gas use, because of the rapid growth and falling costs of renewable energy, in particular solar power. European gas consumption has fallen sharply in the past two years, and in 2014 was at about the same level as it was in 2002. There is huge overcapacity in the pipeline network connecting Europe to Russian gas supply, and Russia has recently signaled its determination to hold on to its share of the northern European gas market by launching the Nord Stream 2 pipeline project, which aims to carry 55 billion cubic meters (1.9 trillion cubic feet) per year across the Baltic to northern Germany. The fate of Russia's planned Turk Stream pipeline across the Black Sea hangs in the balance, mainly because of the weak demand projections from southern Europe and Turkey's wish for lower prices.

Identifying Russia's major strategic interests in Syria can help to make sense of a conflict so brutal when explaining it in terms of naked power politics, state dysfunction, and warped ideology seem inadequate. However, the contention that Russia's involvement in Syria is influenced by natural gas interests is farfetched.

PIPELINE POLITICS IN SYRIA

Much of the media coverage suggests that the conflict in Syria is a civil war, in which the Alawite (Shia) Bashar al Assad regime is defending itself (and committing atrocities) against Sunni rebel factions (who are also committing atrocities). The real explanation is simpler: it is about money.

In 2009, Qatar proposed to run a natural gas pipeline through Syria and Turkey to Europe. Instead, Assad forged a pact with Iraq and Iran to run a pipeline eastward, allowing those Shia-dominated countries access to the European natural gas market while denying access to Sunni Saudi Arabia and Qatar. The latter states, it appears, are now attempting to remove Assad so they can control Syria and run their own pipeline through Turkey.

The standard Shia-Sunni conflict is little different from many other socio-ethnic-economic-political-religious (SEEPR) conflicts that originate in competition for resources, but in Syria it has a lucrative twist. The pattern of SEEPR control in Syria is similar to that in many other Middle Eastern and sub-Saharan Africa countries (and is arguably common in every country, but more so in traditional societies): Who controls the government controls the state's resources, and by extension, the wealth derived from them. In Syria, the Sunnis have tried to unseat the Alawites ever since France installed them during the French mandate that ended in 1943. But now the stakes are higher, thanks to natural gas.

Any review of the current conflict in Syria that neglects the geopolitical economics of the region is incomplete. (Nearly all media reports fit this description.) Take "The Geopolitics of the

Syrian Civil War," published in January by STRATFOR's Reva Bhalla, which provides an effective Syria-specific revision of Robert Kaplan's "Geography Strikes Back," complete with historical acuity, but without mentioning the pipeline. Reports such as these shed little light on current geopolitical economic developments that are at the heart of the issue. Oil and natural gas pipelines bring large amounts of wealth to states which control them, thus attracting international attention, intrigue, and in many instances, terrorist activity.

It is helpful to look at a similar situation: the GAAT region (Georgia, Armenia, Azerbaijan, and Turkey), also known as the Caucasus. As proposals for an oil pipeline from the Caspian Sea to Europe took form, every power broker in the region struggled to influence the route, seeking the wealth that would flow to any country involved in the deal.

Conflict between Azerbaijan and Armenia, a key Russian ally in the region, prevented the shortest pipeline route, through Armenia. The pipeline ultimately went west through Tbilisi and Ceyhan, but only after Moscow demanded and received a partial diversion pipeline that transports Azerbaijani oil north into Russia. In 2005, oil first flowed through the BTC Pipeline, so named because of its route from Baku, the capital of Azerbaijan, through Tbilisi, Georgia, and on to Ceyhan, Turkey.

But the pipeline's completion hardly settled questions in the conflict-ridden Caucasus. Potential malcontents include factions from Armenia's Nagorno-Karabakh region (backed by Armenia's sponsors Russia and China), separatists in Abkhazia and South Ossetia, Chechnya, Dagestan, and Turkey. In October 2012, an explosion damaged the pipeline in Turkey; although it remains unclear whether the blast was an accident, the PKK separatist group was quick to claim responsibility.

The potential for conflict in the Caucasus is so great that the U.S. Army uses it as the setting for capstone exercises at several of its service schools. Conducting several iterations each year at various locations, officers from all branches of the U.S. military, interagency community, and several international partners study coalition warfare using the Caucasus and its pipeline as a theater of operations. These field-grade officers study the general regional strategic implications of the pipeline's development, including the controversy involved in its formation.

If the BTC pipeline is destabilizing enough to convince the world's superpower military to plan key developmental exercises around it, the planned pipeline in Syria must have similar implications.

Viewed through a geopolitical and economic lens, the conflict in Syria is not a civil war, but the result of larger international players positioning themselves on the geopolitical chessboard in preparation for the opening of the pipeline in 2016. Assad's pipeline decision, which could seal the natural gas advantage for the three Shia states, also demonstrates Russia's links to Syrian petroleum and the region through Assad. Saudi Arabia and Qatar, as well as al Qaeda and other groups, are maneuvering to depose Assad and capitalize on their hoped-for Sunni conquest in Damascus. By doing this, they hope to gain a share of control over the "new" Syrian government, and a share in the pipeline wealth.

The main point for decisionmakers is that the upcoming pipeline increases the geopolitical stakes surrounding the Syrian conflict. The tremendous wealth from the natural gas flow, enough to transform regional economies, has drawn in competing regional players from both ideologies. Analyses that include the pipeline make Syria look a lot like the Caucasus scenario playing out in real time, and they provide reliable information on which to base international decisions. Reports that disregard the pipeline and its geopolitical implications ignore the elephant in the room.

8

Twenty-first Century Energy Wars: Oil and Gas Fuelling Global Conflicts

Iraq, Syria, Nigeria, South Sudan, Ukraine, the East and South China Seas: wherever you look, the world is aflame with new or intensifying conflicts. At first glance, these upheavals appear to be independent events, driven by their own unique and idiosyncratic circumstances. But look more closely and they share several key characteristics – notably, a witch's brew of ethnic, religious, and national antagonisms that have been stirred to the boiling point by a fixation on energy.

In each of these conflicts, the fighting is driven in large part by the eruption of long-standing historic antagonisms among neighboring (often intermingled) tribes, sects, and peoples. In Iraq and Syria, it is a clash among Sunnis, Shiites, Kurds, Turkmen, and others; in Nigeria, among Muslims, Christians, and assorted tribal groupings; in South Sudan, between the Dinka and Nuer; in Ukraine, between Ukrainian loyalists and Russian-speakers aligned with Moscow; in the East and South China Sea, among the Chinese, Japanese, Vietnamese, Filipinos, and others.

It would be easy to attribute all this to age-old hatreds, as suggested by many analysts; but while such hostilities do help drive these conflicts, they are fueled by a most modern impulse as well: the desire to control valuable oil and natural gas assets. Make no mistake about it: these are twenty-first-century energy wars.

It should surprise no one that energy plays such a significant role in these conflicts. Oil and gas are, after all, the world's most important and valuable commodities and constitute a major source of income for the governments and corporations that control their production and distribution. Indeed, the governments of Iraq, Nigeria, Russia, South Sudan, and Syria derive the great bulk of their revenues from oil sales, while the major energy firms (many state-owned) exercise immense power in these and the other countries involved. Whoever controls these states, or the oil- and gas-producing areas within them, also controls the collection and allocation of crucial revenues. Despite the patina of historical enmities, many of these conflicts, then, are really struggles for control over the principal source of national income.

Moreover, we live in an energy-centric world where control over oil and gas resources (and their means of delivery) translates into geopolitical clout for some and economic vulnerability for others. Because so many countries are dependent on energy imports, nations with surpluses to export – including Iraq, Nigeria, Russia, and South Sudan – often exercise disproportionate influence on the world stage. What happens in these countries sometimes matters as much to the rest of us as to the people living in them, and so the risk of external involvement in their conflicts – whether in the form of direct intervention, arms transfers, the sending in of military advisers, or economic assistance – is greater than almost anywhere else.

The struggle over energy resources has been a conspicuous factor in many recent conflicts, including the Iran-Iraq War of 1980-1988, the Gulf War of 1990-1991, and the Sudanese Civil War of 1983-2005. On first glance, the fossil-fuel factor in the most recent outbreaks of tension and fighting may seem less evident. But look more closely and you'll see that each of these conflicts is, at heart, an energy war.

Iraq, Syria, and ISIS

The Islamic State of Iraq and Syria (ISIS), the Sunni extremist group that controls large chunks of western Syria and northern Iraq, is a well-armed militia intent on creating an Islamic caliphate in the areas it controls. In some respects, it is a fanatical, sectarian religious organization, seeking to reproduce the pure, uncorrupted piety of the early Islamic era. At the same time, it is engaged in a conventional nation-building project, seeking to create a fully functioning state with all its attributes.

As the United States learned to its dismay in Iraq and Afghanistan, nation-building is expensive: institutions must be created and financed, armies recruited and paid, weapons and fuel procured, and infrastructure maintained. Without oil (or some other lucrative source of income), ISIS could never hope to accomplish its ambitious goals. However, as it now occupies key oil-producing areas of Syria and oil-refining facilities in Iraq, it is in a unique position to do so. Oil, then, is absolutely essential to the organization's grand strategy.

Without oil, ISIS could never hope to accomplish its ambitious goals.

Syria was never a major oil producer, but its pre-war production of some 400,000 barrels per day did provide the regime of Bashar al-Assad with a major source of income. Now, most of the country's oil fields are under the control of rebel groups, including ISIS, the al-Qaeda-linked Nusra Front, and local Kurdish militias. Although production from the fields has dropped significantly, enough is being extracted and sold through various clandestine channels to provide the rebels with income and operating funds. "Syria is an oil country and has resources, but in the past they were all stolen by the regime," said Abu Nizar, an anti-government activist. "Now they are being stolen by those who are profiting from the revolution."

At first, many rebel groups were involved in these extractive activities, but since January, when it assumed control of Raqqa, the capital of the province of that name, ISIS has been the dominant player in the oil fields. In addition, it has seized fields in neighboring Deir al-Zour Province along the Iraq border. Indeed, many of the U.S.-supplied weapons it acquired from the fleeing Iraqi army after its recent drive into Mosul and other northern Iraqi cities have been moved into Deir al-Zour to help in the organization's campaign to take full control of the region. In Iraq, ISIS is fighting to gain control over Iraq's largest refinery at Baiji in the central part of the country.

It appears that ISIS sells oil from the fields it controls to shadowy middlemen who in turn arrange for its transport – mostly by tanker trucks – to buyers in Iraq, Syria, and Turkey. These sales are said to provide the organization with the funds needed to pay its troops and acquire its vast stockpiles of arms and ammunition. Many observers also claim that ISIS is selling oil to the Assad regime in return for immunity from government air strikes of the sort being launched against other rebel groups. "Many locals in Raqqa accuse ISIS of collaborating with the Syrian regime," a Kurdish journalist, Sirwan Kajjo, reported in early June. "Locals say that while other rebel groups in Raqqa have been under attack by regime air strikes on a regular basis, ISIS headquarters have not once been attacked."

However the present fighting in northern Iraq plays out, it is obvious that there, too, oil is a central factor. ISIS seeks both to deny petroleum supplies and oil revenue to the Baghdad government and to bolster its own coffers, enhancing its capacity for nation-building and further military advances. At the same time, the Kurds and various Sunni tribes — some allied with ISIS — want control over oil fields located in the areas under their control and a greater share of the nation's oil wealth.

Ukraine, the Crimea, and Russia

The present crisis in Ukraine began in November 2013 when President Viktor Yanukovych repudiated an agreement for closer economic and political ties with the European Union (EU), opting instead for closer ties with Russia. That act touched off fierce anti-government protests in Kiev and eventually led to Yanukovych's flight from the capital. With Moscow's principal ally pushed from the scene and pro-EU forces in control of the capital, Russian President Vladimir Putin moved to seize control of the Crimea and foment a separatist drive in eastern Ukraine. For both sides, the resulting struggle has been about political legitimacy and national identity – but as in other recent conflicts, it has also been about energy.

By annexing the Crimea, Russia virtually doubled the offshore territory it controls in the Black Sea, which is thought to house billions of barrels of oil and vast reserves of natural gas.

Ukraine is not itself a significant energy producer. It is, however, a major transit route for the delivery of Russian natural gas to Europe. According to the U.S. Energy Information Administration (EIA), Europe obtained 30% of its gas from Russia in 2013 – most of it from the state-controlled gas giant Gazprom – and approximately half of this was transported by pipelines crossing Ukraine. As a result, that country plays a critical role in the complex energy relationship between Europe and Russia, one that has proved incredibly lucrative for the shadowy elites and oligarchs who control the flow of gas, while at the same time provoking intense controversy. Disputes over the price Ukraine pays for its own imports of Russian gas twice provoked a cut-off in deliveries by Gazprom, leading to diminished supplies in Europe as well.

Given this background, it is not surprising that a key objective of the "association agreement" between the EU and Ukraine that was repudiated by Yanukovych (and has now been signed by the new Ukrainian government) calls for the extension of EU energy rules to Ukraine's energy system – essentially eliminating the cozy deals between Ukrainian elites and Gazprom. By entering into the agreement, EU officials claim, Ukraine will begin "a process of approximating its energy legislation to the EU norms and standards, thus facilitating internal market reforms."

Russian leaders have many reasons to despise the association agreement. For one thing, it will move Ukraine, a country on its border, into a closer political and economic embrace with the West. Of special concern, however, are the provisions about energy, given Russia's economic reliance on gas sales to Europe – not to mention the threat they pose to the personal fortunes of well-connected Russian elites. In late 2013 Yanukovych came under immense pressure from Vladimir Putin to turn his back on the EU and agree instead to an economic union with Russia and Belarus, an arrangement that would have protected the privileged status of elites in both countries. However, by moving in this direction, Yanukovych put a bright spotlight on the crony politics that had long plagued Ukraine's energy system, thereby triggering protests in Kiev's Independence Square (the Maidan) – that led to his downfall.

Once the protests began, a cascade of events led to the current standoff, with the Crimea in Russian hands, large parts of the east under the control of pro-Russian separatists, and the rump western areas moving ever closer to the EU. In this ongoing struggle, identity politics has come to play a prominent role, with leaders on all sides appealing to national and ethnic loyalties. Energy, nevertheless, remains a major factor in the equation. Gazprom has repeatedly raised the price it charges Ukraine for its imports of natural gas, and on June 16th cut off its supply entirely, claiming non-payment for past deliveries. A day later, an explosion damaged one of the main pipelines carrying Russian gas to Ukraine – an event still being investigated. Negotiations over the gas price remain a major issue in the ongoing negotiations between Ukraine's newly elected president, Petro Poroshenko, and Vladimir Putin.

Energy also played a key role in Russia's determination to take the Crimea by military means. By annexing that region, Russia virtually doubled the offshore territory it controls in the Black Sea, which is thought to house billions of barrels of oil and vast reserves of natural gas. Prior to the crisis, several Western oil firms, including ExxonMobil, were negotiating with Ukraine for access to those reserves. Now, they will be negotiating with Moscow. "It's a big deal," said Carol Saivetz, a Eurasian expert at MIT. "It deprives Ukraine of the possibility of developing these resources and gives them to Russia."

Nigeria and South Sudan

The conflicts in South Sudan and Nigeria are distinctive in many respects, yet both share a key common factor: widespread anger and distrust towards government officials who have become wealthy, corrupt, and autocratic thanks to access to abundant oil revenues.

With oil selling at around $100 per barrel, this represents a potentially staggering source of wealth for Nigeria [...] Were these revenues – estimated in the tens of billions of dollars per year – used to spur development [...] Nigeria could be a great beacon of hope for Africa.

In Nigeria, the insurgent group Boko Haram is fighting to overthrow the existing political system and establish a puritanical, Muslim-ruled state. Although most Nigerians decry the group's violent methods (including the kidnapping of hundreds of teenage girls from a state-run school), it has drawn strength from disgust in the poverty-stricken northern part of the country with the corruption-riddled central government in distant Abuja, the capital.

Nigeria is the largest oil producer in Africa, pumping out some 2.5 million barrels per day. With oil selling at around $100 per barrel, this represents a potentially staggering source of wealth for the nation, even after the private companies involved in the day-to-day extractive operations take their share. Were these revenues – estimated in the tens of billions of dollars per year – used to spur development and improve the lot of the population, Nigeria could be a great beacon of hope for Africa. Instead, much of the money disappears into the pockets (and foreign bank accounts) of Nigeria's well-connected elites.

In February, the governor of the Central Bank of Nigeria, Lamido Sanusi, told a parliamentary investigating committee that the state-owned Nigerian National Petroleum Corporation (NNPC) had failed to transfer some $20 billion in proceeds from oil sales to the national treasury, as required by law. It had all evidently been diverted to private accounts. "A substantial amount of money has gone," he toldthe New York Times. "I wasn't just talking about numbers. I showed it was a scam."

For many Nigerians – a majority of whom subsist on less than $2 per day – the corruption in Abuja, when combined with the wanton brutality of the government's security forces, is a source of abiding anger and resentment, generating recruits for insurgent groups like Boko Haram and winning them begrudging admiration.

"They know well the frustration that would drive someone to take up arms against the state," said National Geographic reporter James Verini of people he interviewed in battle-scarred areas of northern Nigeria. At this stage, the government has displayed zero capacity to overcome the insurgency, while its ineptitude and heavy-handed military tactics have only further alienated ordinary Nigerians.

The conflict in South Sudan has different roots, but shares a common link to energy. Indeed, the very formation of South Sudan is a product of oil politics. A civil war in Sudan that lasted from 1955 to 1972 only ended when the Muslim-dominated government in the north agreed to grant more autonomy to the peoples of the southern part of the country, largely practitioners of traditional African religions or Christianity. However, when oil was discovered in the south, the rulers of northern Sudan repudiated many of their earlier promises and sought to gain control over the oil fields, sparking a second civil war, which lasted from 1983 to 2005. An estimated two million people lost their lives in this round of fighting. In the end, the south was grantedfull autonomy and the right to vote on secession. Following a January 2011 referendum in which 98.8% of southerners voted to secede, the country became independent on that July 9th.

The very formation of South Sudan is a product of oil politics. The new state had barely been established, however, when conflict with the north over its oil resumed. While South Sudan has a plethora of oil, the only pipeline allowing the country to export its energy stretches across North Sudan to the Red Sea. This ensured that the south would be dependent on the north for the major source of government revenues. Furious at the loss of the fields, the northerners charged excessively high rates for transporting the oil, precipitating a cut-off in oil deliveries by the south and sporadic violence along the two countries' still-disputed border. Finally, in August 2012, the two sides agreed to a formula for sharing the wealth and the flow of oil resumed. Fighting has, however, continued in certain border areas controlled by the north but populated by groups linked to the south.

With the flow of oil income assured, the leader of South Sudan, President Salva Kiir, sought to consolidate his control over the country and all those oil revenues. Claiming an imminent coup attempt by his rivals, led by Vice President Riek Machar, he disbanded his multiethnic government on July 24, 2013, and began arresting allies of Machar.

The resulting power struggle quickly turned into an ethnic civil war, with the kin of President Kiir, a Dinka, battling members of the Nuer group, of which Machar is a member. Despite several attempts to negotiate a cease-fire, fighting has been under way since December, with thousands of people killed and hundreds of thousands forced to flee their homes.

As in Syria and Iraq, much of the fighting in South Sudan has centered around the vital oil fields, with both sides determined to control them and collect the revenues they generate. As of March, while still under government control, the Paloch field in Upper Nile State was producingsome 150,000 barrels a day, worth about $15 million to the government and participating oil companies. The rebel forces, led by former Vice President Machar, are trying to seize those fields to deny this revenue to the government. "The presence of forces loyal to Salva Kiir in Paloch, to buy more arms to kill our people... is not acceptable to us," Machar said in April. "We want to take control of the oil field. It's our oil." As of now, the field remains in government hands, with rebel forces reportedly making gains in the vicinity.

The South China Sea

In both the East China and South China seas, China and its neighbors claim assorted atolls and islands that sit astride vast undersea oil and gas reserves. The waters of both have been the site of recurring naval clashes over the past few years, with the South China Sea recently grabbing the spotlight.

An energy-rich offshoot of the western Pacific, that sea, long a focus of contention, is rimmed by China, Vietnam, the island of Borneo, and the Philippine Islands. Tensions peaked in May when the Chinese deployedtheir largest deepwater drilling rig, the HD-981, in waters claimed by Vietnam. Once in the drilling area, about 120 nautical miles off the coast of Vietnam, the Chinese surrounded the HD-981 with a large flotilla of navy and coast guard ships. When Vietnamese coast guard vessels attempted to penetrate this defensive ring in an effort to drive off the rig, they were rammed by Chinese ships and pummeled by water cannon. No lives have yet been lost in these encounters, but anti-Chinese rioting in Vietnam in response to the sea-borne encroachment left several dead and the clashes at sea are expected to continue for several months until the Chinese move the rig to another (possibly equally contested) location.

To view the Chinese drive in the South China Sea as a simple matter of nationalistic impulses would be a mistake. The riots and clashes sparked by the deployment of HD-981 have been driven in large part by nationalism and resentment over past humiliations. The Chinese, insisting that various tiny islands in the South China Sea were once ruled by their country, still seek to overcome the territorial losses and humiliations they suffered at the hands the Western powers and Imperial Japan. The Vietnamese, long accustomed to Chinese invasions, seek to protect what they view as their sovereign territory. For common citizens in both countries, demonstrating resolve in the dispute is a matter of national pride.

But to view the Chinese drive in the South China Sea as a simple matter of nationalistic impulses would be a mistake.

The owner of HD-981, the China National Offshore Oil Company (CNOOC), has conducted extensive seismic testing in the disputed area and evidently believes there is a large reservoir of energy there. "The South China Sea is estimated to have 23 billion tons to 30 billion tons of oil and 16 trillion cubic meters of natural gas, accounting for one-third of China's total oil and gas resources," the Chinese news agency *Xinhua* noted. Moreover, China announced in June that it was deploying a second drilling rig to the contested waters of the South China Sea, this time at the mouth of the Gulf of Tonkin.

As the world's biggest consumer of energy, China is desperate to acquire fresh fossil fuel supplies wherever it can. Although its leaders are prepared to make increasingly large purchases of African, Russian, and Middle Eastern oil and gas to satisfy the nation's growing energy requirements, they not surprisingly prefer to develop and exploit domestic supplies. For them, the South China Sea is not a "foreign" source of energy but a Chinese one, and they appear determined to use whatever means necessary to secure it. Because other countries, including Vietnam and the Philippines, also seek to exploit these oil and gas reserves, further clashes, at increasing levels of violence, seem almost inevitable.

No End to Fighting

As these conflicts and others like them suggest, fighting for control over key energy assets or the distribution of oil revenues is a critical factor in most contemporary warfare. While ethnic and religious divisions may provide the political and ideological fuel for these battles, it is the potential for mammoth oil profits that keeps the struggles alive. Without the promise of such resources, many of these conflicts would eventually die out for lack of funds to buy arms and pay troops. So long as the oil keeps flowing, however, the belligerents have both the means and incentive to keep fighting.

In a fossil-fuel world, control over oil and gas reserves is an essential component of national power. "Oil fuels more than automobiles and airplanes," Robert Ebel of the Center for

Strategic and International Studies told a State Department audience in 2002. "Oil fuels military power, national treasuries, and international politics." Far more than an ordinary trade commodity, "it is a determinant of well being, of national security, and international power for those who possess this vital resource, and the converse for those who do not."

If anything, that's even truer today, and as energy wars expand, the truth of this will only become more evident. Someday, perhaps, the development of renewable sources of energy may invalidate this dictum. But in our present world, if you see a conflict developing, look for the energy. It'll be there somewhere on this fossil-fueled planet of ours.

THE FIRST RUMOURS OF GERMAN GAS ATTACKS

In the early part of April, 1915, we were in the trenches opposite Messines. We enjoyed the usual morning and evening "hate"; we sniped and were sniped at; we patrolled and wired and attempted to drain away the.superfluous water, and there was much mud and humour and expectancy. It is true there were no Mills grenades or Stokes mortars or tin hats, but trench warfare was not so very different then from what it is now - with one great exception: There was no gas. And there were consequently no respirators to carry day and night. It is almost impossible now to remember the time when one did not carry a respirator in the trenches. Somehow it makes you feel quite naked to think of it and yet there we were, imagining we knew what war really was like!

The newspapers we got at that time were generally a good many days old, and censored at that, and our chief source of news about the war in other people's parts of the line was a summary of so-called information issued from headquarters, which percolated down to the battalion and, like every other summary before and since, went by the name of "Comic Cuts."

Somewhere about the middle of the month we heard that in somebody else's summary had appeared a paragraph to the effect that a deserter from the German lines up in the salient had told a cock-and-bull, story of how they intended to poison us all with a cloud of gas, and that tanks full of the poison gas were already installed in their trenches.

Of course nobody believed him. The statement was "passed for information for what it is worth." And as nobody ever believed anything that appeared in Comic Cuts in any case, we were not disposed to get the wind up about it. And then, about a week later, on April 22, 1915, was launched the first gas attack; and another constant horror was added to an already somewhat unpleasant war. Details about the attack are still somewhat meagre, for the simple reason that the men who could have told much about it never came back.

The place chosen for the first gas attack was in the northeast part of the Ypres salient at that part of the line where the French and British lines met, running down from. where the trenches left the canal near Boesinghe. On the French right was the Regiment of Turcos, and on the British left were the Canadians.

Try to imagine the feelings and the condition of the coloured troops as they saw the vast cloud of greenish-yellow gas spring out. of the ground and slowly move down wind toward them, the vapour clinging to the earth, seeking out every hole and hollow and filling. the trenches and shell holes as it came. First. wonder, then fear; then, as the first fringes, of the cloud enveloped them and left them choking and agonised in the fight for breath — panic. Those who could move broke and ran, trying, generally in vain, to outstrip the cloud which followed inexorably after them.

The majority of those in the front line were killed - some, let us hope, immediately, but most of them slowly and horribly. It is not my intention to try to play upon feelings, but those of us who have seen men badly gassed can only think with horror of a battlefield covered with such cases, over which the Germans subsequently advanced.

The Canadians on the British left fared both better and worse than the French coloured troops. Only their left appears to have been in the main path of the poison cloud, but there is little doubt that in the thickest part those who did not escape either to a flank or to the rear were killed on the field. Thousands of those in the support trenches and reserve lines and in billets behind the line were suffocated - many to die later in the field ambulances and casualty clearing stations.

Of those on the fringe of the cloud many saved themselves by burying their faces in the earth. Others wrapped mufflers round their mouths and noses or stuffed handkerchiefs into their mouths. Many of these men were saved by their presence of mind, for though gassed at the time they recovered later, after treatment in the hospitals.

It is on record that the Canadians, with handkerchiefs or mufflers tied over their mouths, continued to engage the Germans and that a number of them actually charged back through the gas cloud in an endeavour to reach the enemy. What became of them is not known.

In this way a big gap was made in the Allied lines, through which the Germans advanced. But the Canadians quickly formed a flank on the left and stoutly engaged the enemy, with such success that they first slowed up and then brought to a halt the advance of the Germans. It was this prompt action and gallant resistance that probably saved the day.

Whether the German high command had underestimated the probable effect of the gas and had arranged for only a limited objective past which the local commanders did not take the initiative to go, or whether the latter were unaware of the real weakness of the Canadian line is unknown. The fact remains that they did not press their advantage to the full. They had taken the Allied front line on a wide front, killed or captured thousands of men and taken sixty guns, and seemed to have a clear way through to Calais; but they were stopped by the pluck of a handful of Canadians. Reinforcements of men and guns were rushed up, and the immediate danger was over.

It is a matter for surmise how long the Germans had been planning and preparing their use of gas. The idea may have been a pre-war one, but it is difficult to believe that a project deliberately planned for years would not have been developed so as to make it a sure winner - for it could easily have been that. If, for example, they had made the attack over a wider front with such strong gas clouds as are now used nothing could possibly have stood against them. Every living thing to a depth of fifteen miles or more could have been killed.

On the other hand it is impossible to imagine the use of poison gas as having been decided on without better preparation having been made to meet retaliation, unless it was assumed either that the use of the gas would be decisive or that at any rate the war would be finished before the Allies could hit back with the same weapon.

In any case the preparation must have been going on for months. All the production of material, organisation of personnel and so on takes a long time. This we realised ourselves later, for though the decision to retaliate with gas was made in May it was September before an attack could possibly be made. If we assume that a like interval of four months elapsed for the perfecting of the German arrangements it means that the decision to use gas was made about Christmas 1914.

The onus of urging the Kaiser's advisers to adopt the use of poisonous gases had been laid at the door of Professor Nernst, professor of chemistry at the University of Berlin. Professor Nernst is a noted chemist, and even before the war was a notorious Pan-German and Anglophobe - one of the "Professors" who carried too much weight in Germany and whose arrogance and shortsightedness helped to lure her to her downfall. Some time after the use of gas was started Professor Nernst was made a count by the Kaiser for his "notable services" - meaning presumably the use of gas in warfare.

The actual carrying out of the gas operations was intrusted to another professor of chemistry, this being one Haber, of the Kaiser Wilhelm Physical Chemical Institute at Berlin. In 1914, long before the war started, Professor Haber and his assistants are known to have been working secretly with some intensely poisonous arsenic gases and liquids, and one of the assistants was killed and another is reported to have had his arm blown off during the researches.

Haber's particular job was to make all the scientific arrangements in the field; to decide on the gases to be used, and the quantity to employ; to study the wind directions, and decide exactly when to make the attack. In the weeks preceding the twenty-second of April, Haber was continually at the Front receiving reports from the wind observation stations and in close touch with the men in charge of the cylinders in the trenches. On several occasions during this time the attack was fixed for a certain hour, but was postponed by Haber, owing to the wind's being unsuitable.

The actual arrangements that had to be made were much more complex than the carrying out of the attack itself. First of all, decision had to be come to as to the gas to be used in the fiendish attempt. Such a gas had of course to be highly poisonous. Then it must be cheaply and easily made in large quantities; it had to be compressible, so that it could be transported easily; it must be heavier than air, so that it should keep close to the ground when first liberated; and for preference it should not be unstable, that is decompose easily and enter into nonpoisonous combinations with materials, other than man, that it should come across in its passage through the air.

Any chemist to whom such a problem is put will inform you there are very few gases that fill the bill. The German choice rested on that gas well known to students of chemistry - chlorine. Chlorine in large quantities was available from the alkali works in Germany, and it meets all the other requirements except that of not easily combining with other things. This deficiency was fortunate, for it meant that protective chemicals were easy to find when it became necessary to provide respirators to the Allied troops.

Then there was the question of transport und emission. The gas was eventually put up in steel cylinders, about thirty inches long and eight inches across and stout enough to stand a pressure of about ten atmospheres, the gas being stored in them compressed to a liquid. On opening such a cylinder the liquid boils and gives off the gas again, but this would not do for field work, because of the intense cold which is produced by the sudden expansion. This would freeze up the pipes and slow down the discharge to such an extent that the gas attack would be too weak.

To get over this difficulty the Germans fitted their cylinders with internal siphon tubes so that actually liquid chlorine was forced into the air, where it evaporated without affecting the gas remaining in the cylinder. By this means the whole of the gas in the cylinder, amounting to forty-five pounds, is emptied into the atmosphere in less than three minutes. The sudden expansion of the chlorine in the air also makes both it and the surrounding air cold and helps to keep the cloud close to the ground. The actual handing of the gas attacks was allotted to two regiments of pioneers - the 35th and 36th Pioneer Regiments, which were specially organised for this purpose. These regiments have the ordinary organisation of two battalions per regiment, with three companies and a park or transport company per battalion. The rank and file are ordinary pioneers, but the officers are specially picked and include chemists, mechanical experts, meteorologists, and other men with special scientific qualifications.

The choice of country in which to make a gas attack was a serious matter to the enemy. The gas of course will go with the wind, but it depends largely on what the country is like where the wind will go. The Germans themselves say they prefer a flat country without any marked under features and sloping gently toward our lines, just as they had at Ypres. Indeed, they went the length of saying that a gas attack could not be carried out in hilly or very broken country; and they suffered in consequence later on, through being taken unawares by the French in just such country in the Vosges when retaliation was commenced. But taking it altogether the Germans were wise in their choice of position.

Another thing that had to be considered was the outline of their own trench system, so that they would not let off the gas m such parts of the line that it would float back and gas their own troops in the neighbouring trenches. To do this they invented a "factor of safety," which represented an angle between the direction of the wind and the line of the trenches. No attack was to be made if the wind direction came within forty degrees of any trench within gassing distance. This worked very well.

Another consideration was the strength of the wind. The wind must not be too strong when the gusts disperse the gas cloud, or it will weaken it so that it loses a lot of its effect and will be blown over the enemy too quickly; nor must it be so weak that it will take a long time to reach the opposing trenches.

Another great danger in winds of too low velocity is that these are just the winds which change their direction most frequently, and anything under two miles per hour is just as likely to blow the gas back to the place from which it came. It was disregarding this principle on one occasion later on that caused the Germans numerous casualties from one of their own gas clouds. In general, however, it may be laid down that the most f avourable winds are those between four and twelve miles an hour, so that with a wind of eight miles an hour the cloud would move just twice as quickly as a man walking rapidly, and would take only twelve and a half seconds to cross No Man's Land in places where the trenches are fifty yards apart.

Let me try to give an account of the procedure of carrying out gas attacks as it was told me by a German prisoner taken not so very long ago. He said:

"I am not one of the gas pioneers, but being an engineer by trade and having been in the trenches for many weeks with the 35th Regiment of Pioneers I have got to know their methods fairly well. Indeed I assisted on one occasion in carrying cylinders into the trenches for an attack against the British. Gas is not popular with us; we have had too many mishaps, and the cylinders are a nuisance to carry into the trenches. They weigh ninety pounds and they are always carried in by the infantry. A gas regiment does not do that f or itself. It is a long carry and it is really more than a one-man load. At the most two men are allotted to carry in each cylinder, whatever the distance.

Several thousand of these cylinders must be taken into the trenches, and then we have the job of putting them in position. Deep holes are dug just underneath the parapet of the trench, and into these holes are placed the separate cylinders with the tops flush with the ground. As each cylinder is placed into position the hole is covered with a board, on top of which is placed a thing we call a 'Salzdecke,' which is really a kind of quilt stuffed with peat moss and soaked in potash solution so as to absorb any of the gases that may leak out.

"On top of the Salzdecke are built up three layers of sandbags, so that there is not much danger of the cylinders being hit by shell fragments. This also serves to hide the cylinders in case a raid is made, and the sandbags form an excellent firing step. In fact, you would never guess that the gas was ready in position to make an attack. All of this takes a long time to do, and then we have to wait for a wind that is favourable.

" It may be weeks before the right time pomes, but all the time the pioneer officers and Unteroffiziere make observations of the wind and report back to somebody at headquarters. On the night fixed for the attack all the infantry are warned beforehand. If the wind continues favourable the sandbags are taken off, the domes removed from the cylinders, and to each cylinder is attached a lead pipe which is bent over the top of the parapet into No Man's Land, with the end slightly bent up, so that if any liquid comes out it is not wasted in the ground but evaporates in the air. The end of the lead pipe is weighted with a sandbag, so that it will not kick when the gas is turned on and blow the gas back into our own trenches, as happened in one or two of the earlier attacks. It is this kind of thing that makes gas unpopular in the German Army.

"Eventually the time really does arrive for the attack, and the pioneers stand by the cylinders, of which twenty form a battery; and to each battery there are two pioneers and one non-commissioned officer waiting to unscrew the taps. A signal is given by means of a rocket. All the infantry have been eagerly waiting for this signal, which means that they have five minutes to clear out of the front-line trenches before the gas is turned on; and I can tell you they do not waste any time. Everybody makes a rush to the support trench and leaves the front line entirely to the pioneers.

'We all keep our masks ready to put on at a moment's notice, because in the earlier attack the wind on two occasions blew the gas back again into our own trenches and killed a lot of the infantry who were unprepared for its return. According to the length of time the attack is to last the cylinders are turned on from one up to five at a time, in each battery

'As soon as the taps are turned on the pioneers make for cover, but they have a good many losses from bursting cylinders, from leaks, and from the shrapnel and highexplosive shells which invariably greet the start of an attack. The promptness with which this happened at the time I was in the line made us believe that your people had known all about our gas preparations for some time. The infantry are all very glad to be away from the front-line trench when the cloud is sent over.'

FOSSIL FUELS ARE FUELING 100 YEARS OF GLOBAL CONFLICT

In this year of political discourse with its cacophony of talking heads, pundits and unsolicited opinions, facts and historical context often times get lost, if not deliberately disregarded. As it pertains to energy policy, and more specifically, foreign energy policy, as a country we can ill afford to keep the blinders on for much longer.

Our dependence on fossil fuel is fueling violent conflicts all over the world. Some oil corporations have become as powerful as states while some states have become oil corporations in disguise, and both have resorted to extreme measures to maintain power and profits. Often we choose to ignore the facts on this subject as they can be difficult to comprehend and we feel powerless to have any meaningful impact when it comes to something as extreme as global conflict.

It should be of no surprise that fossil fuel has played a significant role in global conflicts. Oil is one of the world's most important and valuable commodities and is a major source of income for the governments and corporations that control their production and distribution. The United States is the world's largest consumer of oil and past disruptions of global oil supply have damaged political reputations and cost millions of dollars to oil corporations and the overall economy. Politicians have used the concept of delivering freedom and democracy as a thinly veiled justification for protecting the 'vital interests' of the United States and its allies.

The facts presented in the timeline below outline that oil considerations have dominated U.S. foreign policy decisions and that oil has been a foundational element of global conflict. Our political leaders and oil corporations have been pursuing a path of energy acquisition reliant on aggression which has created global reactions leading to conflict for nearly a century. The abuse of power and the destruction go as far back to the early history of the oil industry in the 1900's.

I often questioned if our nation was not so dependent on fossil fuels how likely is it that these conflicts would have occurred? With our existing dependency on oil how likely is it that conflict was going to continue? And ultimately what could we do as a human race to stop the turmoil?

1904

Fossil Fuel Corporations Political Contributions Begin

The powerful influence the fossil fuel industry has had on U.S. policy has been evident since Standard Oil's contribution of $100,000 to Theodore Roosevelt's Presidential campaign fund of 1904. This contribution was equivalent to $9.8 million in today's dollar amount. Despite the controversy that this raised over a century ago the fossil fuel industry continues to contribute heavily to presidential campaigns. Since 1990 almost $500 million has been donated to presidential candidates from the oil and gas industries, while since 2010 $150 million is spent annually by fossil fuel corporations in their lobbying efforts.

1930's

Oil becomes the gateway to power and wealth...

At first, the most significant discoveries of oil came largely from the United States as it opened up its extensive territories with dynamic capitalism and technological prowess. But U.S. discovery soon peaked around 1930 and since then Middle Eastern oil has been an attraction for those in political and corporate power in the U.S. Manifesting itself in 1938 with the discovery of oil in Saudi Arabia, the attraction to oil became an obsession as a means to secure wealth and power for the elite. This period saw the emergence of a political and corporate class determined to do whatever was necessary to maintain their status. It did not take long for the conflict to begin and in its path the unmerciful and tragic loss of lives.

1941

During 1941 following the German invasion of Soviet Union, the U.S.A. cut off oil supplies to Japan. The U.S. Naval Forces represented the resistance preventing Japanese attempts to seize Southeast Asian oil supplies and raw materials in order to continue to power their military machines. With fuel supplies cut off, Japan attempted to cripple the U.S. Pacific fleet with a single strategic attack. This triggered Pearl Harbor and with it the tragic loss of life seemingly justified by oil.

1945

Oil as an exchange for military protection

To secure supplies of oil President Roosevelt made an agreement with King Abdul Aziz to provide military protection for the Kingdom of Saudi Arabia in exchange for oil. Oil made the Gulf region an integral part of the world economy and as a result, any conflict in the region was likely to involve the international community. For as long as the U.S relied on oil from the Gulf they would be involved in conflict in this region.

1953

Nations become oil corporations in disguise

Oil companies were not prepared to give up their profits without a fight and this fight was to be carried out by the U.S. and Britain. In 1953 the U.S. and Britain staged a coup d'état against the democratically elected government of the Prime Minister of Iran, Mohammed Mossadeq after he nationalized oil resources.

1960

Cuba's nationalization of U.S. oil refineries

The implementation of trade restrictions between the U.S. and Cuba resulted in the U.S. ceasing supply of its oil to Cuba, severely impacting on the economy of Cuba and driving them towards engagement with the U.S.S.R. Following talks during February of 1960 the U.S.S.R. agreed to support Cuba with supplies of oil in return for buying five million tons of sugar. In response U.S. oil companies in Cuba refused to refine Soviet oil leading to Cuba's nationalization of Texaco, Esso and Shell oil refineries. Consequently the U.S.S.R. and Cuban relations became stronger while the U.S. cut off all diplomatic relations. Ultimately attempts to protect the profits of private U.S. oil companies lent support to one of the bloodiest and most repressive dictatorships in the history of Latin America.

1973

Nixon vows to fight to protect foreign oil supplies

Throughout the 1970's, U.S. attention gradually focused on the Persian Gulf. The 1973/1974 oil crisis led to President Richard Nixon warning "...American military intervention to protect vital oil supplies."

1977

Short lived hopes for a sustainable and united future

One of the earliest and most significant political realizations that global oil was soon to become in shorter supply was a speech delivered by President Carter in April 1977.

"Our decision about energy will test the character of the American people and the ability of the President and the Congress to govern. This difficult effort will be the "moral equivalent of war" — except that we will be uniting our efforts to build and not destroy." Said President Carter. *"Because we are now running out of gas and oil, we must prepare quickly for a third change, to strict conservation and to the use of coal and permanent renewable energy sources, like solar power."*

1980

January - Carter's Doctrine

Despite an awareness of the need for alternative sources of energy just three years later President Carter's State of the Union Address outlined that military force was justified when acquiring supplies of oil from Persian Gulf.

"Let our position be absolutely clear: An attempt by any outside force to gain control of the Persian Gulf region will be regarded as an assault on the vital interests of the United States of America, and such an assault will be repelled by any means necessary, including military force," the President said in his address on January 23, 1980.

The language used by Carter inexplicably highlighted the perception that maintaining oil supplies or '*vital interests*' through conflict was now a better means of securing our energy future than pursuing renewable energy sources. This was the first formal commitment of U.S. military power in the Middle East and set a precedent for the next three decades where the loss of human life was deemed a reasonable exchange for maintaining oil supplies.

March - Activation of the Rapid Deployment Joint Task Force

Just two months later the activation of the Rapid Deployment Joint Task Force was announced with the primary objective to maintain the westward flow of oil from the Persian Gulf as outlined in Carter Doctrine.

September - Iraq attacks Iran

With their vast oil reserves, Iraq had built strategic importance for the international community and in particular for the U.S. who were keen to safeguard the supply of oil. From 1975 Iraqi oil revenues increased to an annual level of $8 billion and during the following years nearly 40 percent of oil income was used to purchase modern weapons for Iraq. In addition, Iraqi active military manpower grew to 535,000 in 1980, according to the 2009 book "Conflict and Cooperation in the Gulf Region by Joseph Kostiner.

In September 1980, led by dictator Saddam Hussein, Iraq attacked Iran in its attempts to seize the oil rich provinces of western Iran. This invasion was openly supported by the Reagan/ Bush administration with the flow of economic aid, weapons and military intelligence provided to Iraq during this period. Until its end in July 1988 the protracted war resulted in at least half a million casualties and several billion dollars' worth of damages.

1990

Oil fuels the Gulf War

In July 1990, U.S. Ambassador to Iraq, April Glaspie, knowing Iraq planned to take a portion of Kuwait, informed Saddam Hussein that the U.S. did not have a position in "Arab-Arab" border disputes, essentially giving Saddam Hussein a green light to invade Kuwait.

Just one month later, convinced that the U.S. and U.N. would not stop them, Iraq invaded Kuwait with the acquisition and control of Kuwait's oil fields Hussein's primary interest. However President Bush immediately proclaimed that the invasion "*would not stand*" andordered Operation Desert Shield in response to Iraq's invasion of Kuwait. With the free flow of oil from the Persian Gulf threatened because of Iraq's occupation of oil-rich Kuwait the U.S stepped in. This was yet another military intervention in response to the conflict caused by a global economy dependent on oil.

The U.N. and U.S. Federal Government response to the invasion of Kuwait was to levy sanctions against Iraq, with these sanctions remaining unchanged for over 10 years after the invasion. While the stated objectives of the sanctions were to respond to the threat that Saddam Hussein posed to peace and stability, it was ultimately the innocent citizens of Iraq who suffered the most. The sanctions impoverished the country and gave control of the nation's oil supply to the U.S. and its allies through the Oil for Food Program, where the United States was Iraq's biggest customer.

Despite claims that the sanctions were not intended to hurt the people of Iraq it has been identified that over one million Iraqis died as a direct consequence of the sanctions, with over half of these children. A 1999 United Nation's report outlined that since the onset of the sanctions, almost one quarter of all infants were born underweight and the same number malnourished.

1997

Peak Oil - The end of oil is in sight

It was in 1997 that the concept of Peak Oil came to the frontier with the publication of "*The Coming Oil Crisis*" by Colin J. Campbell. Peak oil is the point at which global oil production peaks and can only go down. Campbell's work highlighted that the growing Middle Eastern control of the market was likely to lead to a radical and permanent increase in the price of oil followed by physical shortages. The economic consequences of a reduced abundancy of cheap oil would impact countries in the form of rising oil prices and ultimately a loss of profits for oil corporations. The political ramifications of this would also be catastrophic, and political leaders were determined to ensure that the effects of 'Peak Oil' never materialized.

1998

Political and Corporate Responses to Peak Oil – Trans-Afghan Pipeline

Much debate focused on when peak oil would be reached, but because of its inevitable occurrence there was a necessity to move towards other fossil fuels such as natural gas. In attempts to secure natural gas a meeting was held in Houston, Texas where a delegation from the Taliban in Afghanistan visited oil company executives to discuss trans-Afghan pipeline proposals.

However on February 12th 1998 John J. Maresca Vice President of the Union Oil Company of California, a key player in attempts to secure the trans-Afghan pipeline, testified before the House of Representatives. He outlined that the Taliban must be removed from power in Afghanistan and that until a single, unified, friendly government is in place in, the trans-Afghan pipeline will not be built.

The political calming of Afghanistan, translated in military terms to having an occupational force in Afghanistan, effectively for the policing of the pipeline. Despite the obvious challenges and risks in securing the pipeline, Haliburton CEO at the time, Dick Cheney, outlined that:

"The good Lord didn't see fit to put oil and gas only where there are democratically elected regimes friendly to the United States. Occasionally we have to operate in places where, all things considered, one would not normally choose to go. But, we go where the business is."

It is also during this period that Cheney outlined the expected importance of the Caspian Basin for securing future supplies of oil. The Caspian Basin was hailed to be the savior for oil corporations with early estimates showing that the region could have up to two thirds of the world's known oil reserves.

1999

Peak Oil is Publically Acknowledged by Oil Corporates

In 1999 Cheney publically acknowledged Peak Oil in his speech at the London Institute of Petroleum and highlighted that the "*Middle East with two thirds of the world's oil and the lowest cost, is still where the prize ultimately lies.*"

2000

The Californian Energy Crisis

On May 22nd the California Independent System Operator, which manages the Californian power grid, declared the first Stage Two power alert, sparking the beginning of The Californian Energy Crisis. This was the first episode is a series of events throughout 2000 and 2001 which resulted in rolling blackouts, price volatility and poor service to the energy consumers of California.

The crisis was caused by a number of factors occurring simultaneously including regulatory failures, a shortage of electricity supply and illegal shutdowns of pipelines by Enron, the Houston based energy company. Combined these factors represented a systemic failure of California's electricity sector.

Evidence later emerged that while Californians were suffering from the chaos of rolling blackouts Enron had taking advantage of the situation to increase their profits. It was found that Enron arranged to take plant's off-line to create an artificial shortage and result in increased prices for their power, with Enron's CEO Kenneth Lay infamously stating:

"In the final analysis, it doesn't matter what you crazy people in California do, because I got smart guys who can always figure out how to make money."

This period resulted in disarray for the ordinary energy consumers reliant on vulnerable and insecure utilities for their energy needs. From January 2001 the credit rating of both Southern California Edison and Pacific Gas & Electric utilities were downgraded to junk status. A desire for Californians to gain their energy independence was beginning to emerge and the California Energy Commission's Emerging Renewables Program was launched by the State Legislature.

The Caspian Basin Oil Dream is Broken

This crisis coincided with the realization that the Caspian Basin was not going to be the solution in response to the inevitable decline of oil supplies. With 80% of the initial drilling resulting in dry wells it was clear that projections which had been made were an over exaggeration. The problem of globally diminishing supplies of oil was set to become more of a problem that previously anticipated. Regardless whatever oil that was present in the Caspian Basin was worthless until it was moved. The only route which made both political and economic sense was through Afghanistan.

Oil's dirty influence on future foreign policy

The Project for a New American Century (PNAC) was a Washington based think tank funded primarily from the energy and arms industries. Of the twenty-five people who signed the PNAC's founding statement of principles, ten went on to serve in the administration of U.S. President George W. Bush, including Dick Cheney, Donald Rumsfeld, and Paul Wolfowitz. The PNAC stated that U.S. control of Iraq transcended the issue of Saddam Hussein, outlining in their view that a "*new Pearl Harbor*" was needed to accomplish their foreign policy and military goals.

2001

Bush, Cheney and the objective of energy acquisition reliant on aggression

Shortly after the January 2001 inauguration of the Bush/ Cheney administration the very first cabinet meeting was held where initial discussions centered on how they were going to attack Iraq. Both these politicians had obvious ties to the oil industry and the energy task force of the administration soon examined oil fields which were located in the Middle East – where they were and what companies had business in them. The Bush administration had already chosen the path of war - not so much against terrorism - but by pursuing a path of energy acquisition reliant on aggression that stirred global reactions which lead to terrorism. Throughout the summer of 2001 many warnings from US allies and the CIA were received by the administration in Washington that outlined an attack was set to occur.

September 11

The September 11 attacks occur where a series of airline hijackings and suicide attacks are committed by 19 militants associated with the Islamic extremist group al-Qaeda against targets in the United States, the deadliest terrorist attacks on American soil in U.S. history. The attacks against New York City and Washington, D.C., caused extensive death and destruction. Some 2,750 people were killed in New York, 184 at the Pentagon, and 40 in Pennsylvania.

Senator Max Cleland, member of the official National Commission on Terrorist Attacks Against the United States is quoted in the New York Times on October 27, 2003 as saying;

'As each day goes by, we learn that this government knew a whole lot more about these terrorists before September 11 than it has ever admitted.'

On October 7th U.S. and British forces begin airstrikes in Afghanistan after the Taliban refuse to hand over al Qaeda leader Osama bin Laden, blamed for the 9/11 attacks. However the strategic importance of Afghanistan to securing access to Caspian Basin oil is deemed by political scientists as a contributing factor to the attacks. Afghanistan was crucial to the regional control and transport of oil in central Asia as Egypt was in the Middle East. But pipelines through

Afghanistan would allow the US both to pursue its objective of attaining one of the most lucrative markets.

Wesley Clark Revelation

A number of weeks after 9/11 Wesley Clark, a retired General of the United States Army, and former Supreme Allied Commander of NATO, reveals he was informed of a memo from the Secretary of Defense that planned to take out seven countries in five years, despite no link between these countries and the September 11 terrorist attacks. A former member of Clark's Joint Staff told him that;

"This is a memo that describes how we're going to take out seven countries in five years, starting with Iraq, and then Syria, Lebanon, Libya, Somalia, Sudan and, finishing off, Iran."

Anthrax attacks

The 2001 anthrax attacks occurred within the United States over the course of several weeks beginning on September 18, 2001, one week after the September 11 attacks and were targeted on the media and Democratic leadership. Letters containing anthrax spores were mailed to several news media offices and two Democratic U.S. Senators, killing five people and infecting 17 others. This is the catalyst to the creation of the USA Patriot Act passed in U.S. Congress.

Peak Oil as the motivator for allowing attacks

Michael C. Ruppert author of '*Crossing The Rubicon: The Decline of the American Empire at the End of the Age of Oil*' identified from his evidence that it was evident that the September attacks were not a surprise and that Peak Oil had been a primary motivation for the allowing the attacks to take place. In a November 2001 presentation at Portland State University Oregon, Ruppert outlined that without the attacks it would have been impossible for the US to invade Iraq and take over their oil fields, which gave the U.S. a dominant military position in the middle of the world's main oil production region as we passed the point of Peak Oil.

2003

U.S. invasion of Iraq - An energy war to safeguard oil

There have been many speculations as to the tactical reasoning behind the U.S. invasion of Iraq, it is evident that this conflict was, at its core, an energy war. However, notwithstanding the factors that motivated the invasion, oil remained one of the core factors for the US invasion of Iraq. Losing access to Iraqi oil presented an immense threat to U.S. interests and if this could not be prevented politically, it was likely to be done so militarily. With Iraq having the second largest supply of oil on the planet, the reality was that for all the publicity about liberating Iraq, the US military effort was in actuality about safeguarding U.S. interests in the form of oil and preventing increasing oil prices because of dwindling supplies. While it is claimed that there was no winner in this war, in reality the U.S. oil companies won it.

2004

Sullivan Solar Power Founded

A small company is founded in Southern California with aspirations to move the region away from fossil fuels entirely. This company, Sullivan Solar Power, is founded by San Diego native Daniel Sullivan.

Sullivan Solar Power pursues its mission to change the way the region and ultimately the world generates its electricity from humble beginnings as a one-man shop based in a garage, with just $2500 of capital available.

2004

Al Qaeda in Iraq becomes ISIL

In response to the invasion of Iraq by US forces in 2004, an insurgency group known as Al Qaeda in Iraq launched an offensive against coalition forces in Fallujah. After several iterations of the group and multiple battles with coalition forces, it retreated into war torn Syria in 2011 to regroup and rebuild. Al Qaeda in Iraq relaunched as ISIL, Islamic State of Syria and the Levant, and invaded northern Iraq, seizing oil assets and antiquities to fund its growth.

2010

The Arab Spring

Sparked by stoked civil unrest in Tunisia, several of the countries outlined in Wesley Clark's interview begin to fall and face severe civic unrest in what is known as The Arab Spring.

In the year since the beginning of the Arab Spring, leaders are ousted in Egypt, Tunisia, Libya and Yemen. The Tunisian Government are overthrown in January 2011 with President Zine el Abidine Ben Ali fleeing into exile.

In 2010 the U.S. and the U.N. intensify Iranian Sanctions with the objective of impacting on Iran's economy already subject to inflation, unemployment and corruption with the hope of creatingfurther political disorder.

In March 2011 violence begins escalating in Syria and the country descends into civil war as rebel brigades are formed to battle government forces for control of cities, towns and the countryside.

In August 2011 Inspired by revolts in other Arab countries, especially neighboring Egypt and Tunisia, violent protests break out in Benghazi, Libya, leading to escalating clashes between security forces and anti-Gaddafi rebels. The Libyan Civil war resulted in the overthrow of the Gaddafi government and highlighted the political chaos and civic unrest as outlined by Wesley Clark in 2001.

2014

ISIL, now known as ISIS, invades Iraq and a series of cities and strategic oil reserves fall under its control. Without oil revenue, ISIS would never achieve its objectives.

The recent funding of ISIS from oil revenues has brought the question of fossil-fuel related conflict to the present. Wide ranging research from the U.S. Department of the Treasury, U.S. Department of Defense, United Nations and UK Government has outlined that oil is a significant source of funding for ISIS providing up to 40% of their revenues. In 2014 it was producing 70,000 barrels a day worth $500m annually. International sanctions prevented ISIS from selling this oil legally, so it has resorted to unregulated underground markets. But that's not hard. ISIS tapped into long-established smuggling routes that were set up back in the 1990s. Back then, Saddam Hussein used them to circumvent United Nations sanctions previously discussed. Recent airstrikes by the U.S. led coalition have reduced the ability of ISIS to transport and refine oil impacting on their revenues, however oil is still a significant revenue generator contributing to the organization's global terrorism operations.

Conclusion

While ethnic, religious and political differences have undeniably been a significant cause of conflict over the past century it is the potential for oil profits that has fueled these wars. Without the prospective profits and power that oil promises most conflicts over the last one hundred years would either not have occurred or eventually come to an end as the revenue to buy weapons and pay fighters ran out. If we are to learn one thing from this, it is that control over oil has been a crucial factor in past global conflict and will be for future global conflict. Until oil does not bring profits to those in power then the vicious, brutal and tragic acts of the past will continue to occur, unless we break the chain.

A Better Way

Robert Ebel of the Center for Strategic and International Studies outlined to a State Department audience in 2002 that:

"Oil fuels more than automobiles and airplanes...Oil fuels military power, national treasuries, and international politics...it is a determinant of well-being, of national security, and international power for those who possess this vital resource, and the converse for those who do not."

This is not an equitable way for society to continue to develop into the future, the well-being of our nation and planet should not be determined by our access to oil. We can do better, we owe it to our children and future generations.

The Solution

It was the addiction of world leaders and oil executives to power and profits which has created the mess we as a human race are in. By ignoring the events of the past and allowing ourselves to become dependent on the one commodity that fuels this conflict we are not without blame. But we have the ability to change, now more than ever before there are ways to rid ourselves of our addiction to fossil fuels and end the dominance of oil corporations who have inflicted anguish upon millions across the world. We can power our homes and our cars with solar. We do not need the Middle East. We do not need fossil fuel corporations. We do not need corrupt politicians. We need to change.

9

Gas Wars: The First Energy Conflict in 2018

Territorial disputes over natural gas and newly discovered hydrocarbon reserves in the eastern Mediterranean basin are the reason. Up until a few years ago, the hope was that these hydrocarbon reserves would offer a real opportunity for a peaceful settlement of the Cyprus conflict. But these optimistic hopes vanished with both Turks and Greek Cypriots unilaterally speeding up exploration and drilling operations.

In 2004, the European Union had declared the Greek Cypriots the sole entity representing the island of Cyprus and accepted it as an EU member. Feeling that its hand has been strengthened following the EU decision, the Greek Cypriots claimed the right of natural resources exploration in the Exclusive Economic Zone (EEZ) around Cyprus.

Turkey, however, has been insisting that the Greek Cypriot administration in Nicosia cannot unilaterally "adopt laws regarding the exploitation of natural resources on behalf of the entire island," as it doesn't represent the Turkish Cypriots. Also, there is a separate disputed EEZ between Turkey and Greece in the eastern Mediterranean — another point of tension in the conflict. Ankara reacted strongly to the Greek Cypriots' natural gas drilling efforts in July. The Turkish army dispatched a frigate in the eastern Mediterranean to "monitor a drilling ship that is believed to have begun searching for oil and gas off ethnically divided Cyprus despite Turkey's objections," The Associated Press reported.

On Nov. 20, Egyptian President Abdel Fattah al-Sisi visited Greek Cypriot for a trilateral meeting in Nicosia to discuss hydrocarbon resources in the region. In addition to Egypt's president, Greek Prime Minister Alexis Tsipras also participated in the meeting, which was hosted by Greek Cypriot President Nicos Anastasiades. The Turkish Foreign Ministry, on the other hand, declared the outcome of the trilateral meeting to be "null and void."

However, despite Turkey's opposition, drillship Saipem 12000 sailed to carry out exploration and drilling operations on behalf of French TOTAL and Italian ENI companies in the Calypso region between March 1 and Dec. 26 in accordance with an agreement reached during the trilateral summit. Moreover, Italy, Greece, Greek Cypriot and Israel had already agreed on the construction of a gas pipeline from newly discovered fields. The project — dubbed "East-Med" — will cost some $6 billion. An over 2,000-kilometer-long (1,243-mile-long) pipeline will channel offshore reserves in the Levantine basin to Greece and Italy.

The East-Med project could be interpreted as an effort to form a regional alliance between Greek Cypriot and Greece to confront Turkey in the eastern Mediterranean. The Greek Cypriots and Greece also signed a separate agreement with Israel to channel natural gas reserves in the Mediterranean basin via an undersea pipeline. Italy's participation in this project didn't come as a surprise, as Italy has already been exploring natural gas in the Mediterranean on behalf of the Greeks. The undersea pipeline is expected to channel natural gas from Israel's Leviathan Basin and Greece's 12th plot — also called Aphrodite — to Crete, and then to Europe via Greece.

On Dec. 5, the energy ministers of Greece, Greek Cypriot and Israel and the Italian ambassador to Greek Cypriot signed an accord in Nicosia on the construction of the East-Med pipeline. The participation of EU representatives in the ceremony indicated Brussels' support for the project. In 2017, the Greek Cypriots, Israel and Greece conducted three joint exercises in March, June and November. At the beginning of November 2017, Greece and Egypt held their first joint naval exercise for the first time in quite a while.

In response, Ankara initiated its own moves and issued a navigational telex to reserve an area for military exercises. The area covers the disputed sixth, seventh, eighth and ninth blocs that the Greek Cypriots had declared as their EEZ. Ankara's declaration came at a time when Saipem 12000 arrived in the Mediterranean.

Also, the Turkish army has kept some of its forces in the eastern Mediterranean following NATO's Standing Maritime Task Forceexercise, which was conducted Nov. 7-16. The Turkish navy's TCG Gediz and TCG Barbaros frigates; the TCG Kalkan, TCG Mizrak, TCG Bora and TCG Meltem gunboats; the TCG Akar fuel tanker; and four underwater commando teams are still in the sixth bloc.

In 2018, Turkey will have its first brand-new drilling vessel, the Deepsea Metro II. According to navigation data, the ship left Norway's Hoylandsbygda port some two weeks ago and is currently sailing west of Portugal. It is expected to arrive in Turkey on Dec. 31. The critical question now is whether the Turkish navy will be providing military escorts for the new drilling vessel.

If the Deepsea Metro II is to be escorted by a Turkish navy fleet while sailing to the sixth bloc, then the affair is bound to heat up. In the meantime, the Nicosia administration also announced that drilling operations in its EEZ would begin Dec. 30 and that Saipem 12000 would join the operations as well.

Now the question is whether Turkey's Deepsea Metro II and Saipem 12000 and naval fleets escorting them will confront each other in the disputed sixth bloc.

One should also consider domestic developments in relevant countries when trying to measure the extent of a possible crisis. A possible hydrocarbon crisis is an excellent domestic political issue that all governments can use to consolidate their nationalist support base.

OFFSHORE GAS WAR BREWING IN THE EASTERN MEDITERRANEAN?

Rising tensions in the Eastern Mediterranean could have a destabilizing effect on countries in the region and the European energy market. Disputes about the right to explore offshore natural gas fields in the region are creating tensions between Cyprus, Turkey, Egypt, Israel and Lebanon. Could this ignite a new war in the region?

Optimism about the ongoing East Mediterranean offshore gas adventures could be soon confronted by a bleak reality. As the world watches the Operation Olive Branch military escapades of the Turkish armed forces in Syria's Afrin region, military skirmishes and conflicts are heating up elsewhere.

The highly publicized Iranian drone crisis over Israel not only shows the volatility on the Golan border between Syria and Israel, but also attracts attention to the gas-related security clashes offshore Lebanon, Cyprus and even Israel.

Again, Ankara has shown its appetite for confrontation when Turkish navy ships prevented a drill ship working for Italian oil major ENI to reach a disputed Cypriot offshore block. Ankara claims that possible offshore reserves are also owned by the Turkish part of the island.

Clash between Turkey and Cyprus

Offshore Cyprus is now the second battlefield between NATO members, after the Turkish confrontation with U.S. military currently supporting Syrian Kurdish fighters of the YPG around Afrin and Manbij in the north of Syria. Ankara's regional politics and power projections are no longer simply linked to perceived PKK threats (or proxies), but have again been linked to energy assets. Since last week's offshore gas discovery in Cyprus by a Total-ENI joint venture, Turkey has stepped up its military activity in the area.

On the other side of the East Med region, Egypt didn't sit still when the Cypriot-Turkish spat emerged. As was expected, due to Turkish president Erdogan's continuing pro-Muslim Brotherhood statements and his military activity in Syria and the Horn of Africa, Cairo has put its weight behind Nicosia. In a harsh statement, Egyptian Foreign Minister Sameh Shoukry, on orders of President Sisi, defended not only the Cypriot offshore gas exploration projects but also stated that the 2003 EEZ (exclusive economic zone) maritime agreement with Cyprus is valid. So any Turkish move to block this will be taken as an attack on Egypt, as well.

Exclusive economic zone

In 2003, Cairo and Nicosia signed an agreement to set up an EEZ in the eastern Mediterranean to increase offshore gas exploration. Ankara opposes these moves, as it claims legal rights on offshore resources for Turkish Cyprus, which it occupied in 1974. Turkish Foreign Minister Mevlut Cavusoglu dismissed the agreement as "null and void". Cairo, however, warned Turkey not to infringe on Egypt's sovereign rights. Although Cyprus and Egypt are supported by the European Union, Ankara continues its claims. Turkey has now begun to confront Greek vessels in other areas. At the same time, Erdogan warns international operators that they could lose Ankara's friendship.

For Egypt, the situation is considered a threat to national security. Cairo looks to further expand its offshore production, due to the ENI Zohr gas field and the latest BP offshore field. In a reaction to Turkish threats, Egyptian Major General Mamdouh Mokled stated, "We do not have to heed the Turkish statements, and we have to continue with gas exploration in the Mediterranean and avoid attempts to disrupt them." For Cairo, stability in the region is needed, as plans are being implemented to become an LNG exporter in 2020.

Those plans will be combined with Cypriot–Israeli offshore gas production. The Israeli-Turkish relationship has been ripped apart, and Israel's former plans to export pipeline gas to Turkey are over — though they were promoted by the U.S. and EU, Erdogan's current regional posture is blocking it all.

The only way for Israeli gas to become commercially attractive to be exported is in an export combination with Egypt. Ankara's strategic choices now seem to cement Egyptian-Israeli ties even more. Cyprus, as a European and NATO country, is regarded as the door to Europe, hence its strategic relevance. With the possibility of the reopening and possible expansion of Egypt's existing LNG liquefaction plans, a new Tripartite Coalition of the (Gas) Willing is being set up.

Lebanon, Israel and Syria

Threats aren't just coming from Turkey — Lebanon and Syria are suddenly also playing up. Lebanon's already struggling government, confronted by the growing power of Iran-supported Hezbollah, recently became involved in a dangerous security spat with Israel. Lebanon's move over the last weeks to tender offshore gas blocks next to the maritime border with Israel has put the latter on edge. Tel Aviv has openly warned international oil and gas companies to keep away from these areas, as it will be seen as a threat to Israeli security.

Lebanon's move comes at the same time that its main power player Hezbollah — the Shi'ite militia and political party closely aligned with Iran — has stepped up its (vocal) attacks on Israel, while substantiating its belligerent position by building up a 150,000-missile-strong military force.

Hezbollah's war fighting experience in Syria, where it has been the backbone for the survival of Syria's president Assad, is seen by Israel as an act of war — a position that was recently reiterated after an Iranian drone entered Israeli airspace and was shot down. A Syria-originated military confrontation could easily spill over to the Lebanese-Israeli theatre.

Hezbollah has also directly threatened Israeli offshore oil and gas operations. In pamphlets and a video, Hezbollah threated Israel's offshore gas platforms with attack. According to Lebanese sources, Hezbollah stated that this was as answer to Israel's objections to the Lebanese offshore tender. Hezbollah leader Hassan Nasrallah has openly claimed Lebanese ownership of the entire offshore territory.

Lebanon shouldn't take Israel's position lightly. Until now the maritime borders between Israel and Lebanon have not been settled. Military analysts fear a major confrontation. Some have warned that a major find on the Lebanese side could threaten Israel's Tamar field development, while putting pressure on the Leviathan gas field, which is expected to be onstream by 2019.

Israel has already expanded its navy to protect gas projects and shipping lines; an increased Lebanese threat will only put more emphasis on it. The Israeli navy expansion is not only for threats in the north, but also to counter Palestinian extremist Hamas movement threats to offshore projects. Hamas and Hezbollah have set up naval capabilities, including autonomous submersibles, suicide drones and scuba-diving commando units.

When looking at the facts on the ground, a war is brewing. This will put a major dent into East Med gas futures. Increased insecurity or an outright war not only threatens Israel or Lebanon, but will spill into the other countries. The year 2018 could be another showdown between Hezbollah and Israel, but at a much larger scale than before, as Hezbollah's military might has increased. Iran also plays a role, as its IRGC troops pose a threat to Israel's Golan Heights.

In the big picture, not only gas operations are threatened. Maritime threats and conflicts could hit other oil transport at the same time. A full military conflict involving the area of offshore Cyprus-Lebanon-Israel will block the oil transit routes originating in Ceyhan (Turkey). At the same time, a direct conflict between Cyprus and Turkey will also involve the Greeks, directly threatening transit routes through the Bosporus. Both could threaten transport volumes of between 1.6 million bpd (BTC pipeline) and 2.9 million bpd (Bosporus). Hedge funds would have a field day, but European consumers would be hurting.

10

Rising of Modern Warfare and Gas Attacks

THE RISING IMPORTANCE OF THE GAS SHELL

One of the most interesting things about the development of gas warfare has been the way in which the gas shell, from being the least important method of poisoning the air, has become the chief gas weapon in the German armoury.

The reasons for this extraordinary development, though various, are not far to seek. They lie chiefly in the fact that unlike the gas cloud we have not even yet approached the limit of the number or size of the gas projectiles that can be used. Nor, which is even more important, is there any limit to the variety of the poisons that can be used in gas shell.

The fact of the matter is that the gas shell is not really a gas shell at all. It is nearly always a "liquid" shell and sometimes even a "solid" shell. The term "gas shell" is used because the liquid or solid contents are atomised by the explosion of the bursting charge or are distributed round in the form of such tiny particles or droplets, as the case may be, that they act almost as a gas. In the latter case they form what might be described as a mist or smoke, but with this difference from ordinary smoke-that the gas mist or smoke is generally, though not always, invisible. Just imagine what would happen supposing a shell were filled with water. Burst such a shell with a sufficiently big charge of high explosive and all the water would be distributed into the air in the form of such finely divided spray that it would form a mist. This mist would either vapourise into the atmosphere completely or hang about like a cloud, according as the air was dry or moist. In any case, if the burster were big enough no water would be spread on the ground; nor would any big drops be formed.

This is just what happens with any of the poisonous materials filled into a shell. Indeed if the burster were big enough and carefully chosen it would be possibie to form a "gas" with treacle. With a volatile material like gasoline on the other hand all that would be needed would be a burster just big enough to open the shell.

It can be seen therefore that the choice of materials for gas shell is practically unlimited and is governed only by their being poisonous enough and by the ease of production.

Another thing in which the gas shell has the advantage over the cylinder gas is in getting surprise, which is naturally much easier to effect with shell. By the way, if the reader wishes to be counted, among those who knows, he will always speak or write the plural of shell without adding a final S. To talk of a number of shells is very civilian. which I have previously described. These new gas shell were the first of the present series of German gas shell, which are all distinctly marked with coloured crosses and named accordingly. These particular shell were the Green Cross Shell, a green cross being painted on the base of the cartridge or on the side of the shell or sometimes on both. They made their appearance on the Somme Front about a fortnight after the battle had started - that is, about the middle of July, 1916 - though a few of them had been used against the French on the Verdun Front sometime in June.

It was not long before blind or unexploded shell - "duds," we call them - were collected and sent back for examination. This is one of the disadvantages of using gas shell-your opponent can always keep track of what you are doing. Sooner or later a fuse will not function or a bursting charge will not explode and your watchful enemy carefully collects the shell, and has for examination a considerable amount of the poison material. I say "carefully collects," for it is no child's play dealing with shell which may go off in your hands

As I pointed out before, we were expecting something new to happen in the gasshell line during the whole of 1916, and had an idea that the new arrival would be something of a cyanide nature-possibly prussic acid itself. When it did come, however, it proved to be a liquid filling closely related chemicolly to phosgene and to the K-Stoff, on the slightest provocation. However, it has to be done, and as it is the gas officer's pidgin he manfully shoulders his task and the shell and has it brought in. Very frequently the fuse fails to act because a powder pellet holding up the striking needle has not burned away; but -1 remember one case where the gas officer of one of -the armies took back a big dud gas shell. It meant transporting the weighty souvenir in a not particularly well sprung car over very bumpy roads, and he was quite relieved to arrive at his destination - the field laboratory. Here it was reverently taken to bits by the experts. Imagine the gas officer's horror to find he had been bumping along for several hours in the company of a shell the powder pellet of which had burned away and whose only safety device was the weakest of weak creep springs on which the striker rested. A hard knock or a drop of six inches would almost certainly have exploded it.

The laboratory officers, who are experts at the game, may have to go up to the Front themselves to salve important duds which are regarded as dangerous and require expert attention. In one instance the officer concerned - in civil life a very celebrated professor at one of the London colleges - went up to the salient and explored about a mile and a half of trenches and finally located his prey - a fine dud 4.2-inch howitzer gas shell-out in the open.

Though the place was pretty unhealthy he "climbed the bags" and made a careful examination of the shell where it lay, finally bringing it back in with him. I forget whether he drew its sting on the spot, but in any case it was a pretty good effort, especially for a man no longer in his first youth.

Chemical analysis of the blind Green Cross Shell showed the contents to be a colourless liquid known to chemists by the extensive name of "trichlormethyleholoroformate." Its effects are just as ferocious as the name implies, and experience showed it to be very poisonous. Indeed it is as poisonous as phosgene itself. The Green Cross Shell gas "diphosgene", to give it its short name - has many effects and symptoms that make it a dangerous weapon. When dilute it has a peculiar though not particularly nauseating smell, a smell variously described as "earthy," "mouldy rhubarb", whatever that smells like, and damp hay. It is unlike the shell gases we had encountered before, it has very little effect on the eyes and causes practically no lachrymation. And this was a trap, because we had been used to lachrymators, so that many men despite the obvious smell were not particularly quick in protecting themselves because of the new symptoms.

Of course this applies only to such low concentrations as would take a long time to gas a man. In the higher concentrations the Green Cross very quickly asphyxiates-just as phosgene and chlorine do - and there is no question of whether it is deadly or not. The old Army quip about there being only two kinds of people in gas warfare, namely "The Quick and the Dead," certainly applies if you get a Green Cross Shell bursting close to you. But even for gas shell bursting some distance away immediate and complete protection is necessary because of the delayed or after effects of the gas, which are exactly similar to those of phosgene. Every care that is taken with regard to men poisoned with phosgene has to be taken for men poisoned with Green Cross gas.

Those suffering from the effects of the gas are not allowed to exert themselves at all or to take heavy meals. They are kept under close observation for at least two days, and are treated, in fact, as casualties even though they are not apparently ill. Before the need for this was understood an officer I knew was slightly gassed with shell gas but thought nothing of it. Later on he felt a bit queer, and the regimental medical officer advised him to go down to the dressing station. He walked the length of the communication trench and then mounted a push bicycle for a mile's ride to the aid post. The exertion was too much, however, and he reached the aid post only to fall dead.

The danger of not treating gassed men as casualties and resting them for a couple of days, after which they would probably be it for work again, is shown by a case where forty men were lost to the line for a considerable time though fortunately none of them died. These men were part of a working party engaged in the construction of dugouts. They were caught in a surprise bombardment, but were apparently not much affected. After completing their night's work they marched back to billets and turned in as usual. The next morning sevcral of them were so ill-nearly to the point of collapse-and the remainder were so visibly affected that the medical officer ordered the whole party to be sent down to the casualty clearing station, where they were evacuated to the base.

In still another case I remember a sergeant and twenty men of a wiring party engaged in the consolidation of a recently captured position were similarly caught by a sudden and intense Green Cross bombardment. A number of the men were gassed and felt pretty seedy, but continued their work and then withdrew. The sergeant felt no ill effects until an hour after turning in, when he woke with a bad cough and internal pain and died two hours afterward. One private went to bed without complaining at all and was found dead next morning. Another died soon after getting up. A third reached headquarters complaining of shell shock and died three hours later. I mention these cases so that my reader will realise why such great care is now taken with men who have been exposed to poison gas, and how by looking after them in this way it has been possible to reduce the number of delayed cases of death or serious illness to a minimum.

Talking of delayed effects of gas shell reminds me that at least two documents were captured during the Somme - one, of them I got myself - which were obviously notes of lectures given to officers at a German gas school or staff course. In both of these sets of notes there were references to the Lusitania, showing that the German Higher Command was trying to explain that dastardly act to its own troops by making out that the Lusitania was sunk because it was carrying phosgene shell for the Allies. This lie can easily be nailed to the board, as not a single drop of phosgene - or any other poison gas or liquid, for that matter - was shipped from America before this year, 1918. Both of the paragraphs I refer to contained a double lie, for they each asserted that the French started the use of gas shell. One of them ran as follows: "The French first started the use of gas shell with great hopes, but with little success! The most striking result was that experienced by the passengers of the Lusitania, whose rescued mostly died later."

But to return to the Green Cross Shell. These were used during the Somme Battle in enormous numbers, far surpassing anything we had had before in the extent of the bombardment. There were a great many new features about these shell quite apart from the altered nature of the gas. First of all there was the size. Until then we had had gas shell of only two sizes - 150-millimetre howitzer shell and the 105-millimetre howitzer shell. The former contained from five to eight pints of liquid according to the construction of the shell, and the latter about three pints. To these longer shell were now added shell from the ordinary field gun, or 77-millimetre gun-quite a small affair compared with the others and containing only two-thirds of a pint of liquid poison. But then, though so small, it could be fired more rapidly and accurately and could bring off an initial surprise in a way that the bigger guns could not do.

Shell of these three sizes were used then on nearly all occasions and in very large quantities. One thing that made large numbers possible was the simplicity of the shell compared with the old pattern. There was no separate lead container and the "gas" was filled straight into the body of the shell, as the - new material was unacted on by iron or steel. The head of the shell was screwed in and kept in position and perfectly gastight by means of a special cement. As very little explosive was needed to open them up and spread the contents round the noise made by the burst of the Green Cross Shell was little more than a pop - at any rate when compared with the highexplosive shell or the old tear shell. The result was that at first men were apt to regard them as duds and to delay the putting on of respirators until it was too late.

These gas shell are supposed to make a peculiar wobbling noise in the passage through the air because of the liquid inside them, and in this way to be recognisable beforehand. Personally I cannot tell any difference in the noise compared with H. E. or shrapnel of the same calibre, though I have heard thousands of both kinds; but I dare say some people can, as the belief is fairly widespread.

Of course Fritz's liberality with his gas shell caused us a lot of casualties, but not nearly so many as we might have had if he had known how to use them. The fact was 1e had not at that time got hold of the proper technique -developed later- on by the French - of concentrating his gas shell on special targets. By now, of course, he has; but at that time he still clung to the idea of being able to poison big areas with his shell gas by putting down a series of barrages over the country to be attacked. Either he had not enough shell or he chose his areas too big, for he did not produce effective concentrations anywhere but locally. If he had, our losses might have been tremendous. As it was it became rather a hit-or-miss proposition, and 1 have seen hundreds and hundreds of these shell drop into absolutely unpopulated areas of the devastated Somme battlefield.

In one case a battery of field guns came in for its share of one such promiscuous bombardment while I was there. The number of shell coming over was so great that it was like a magnified machine-gun shoot, but only a very few got on to the battery and the casualties were only two-both caused by a direct hit on one of the guns by a gas shell. If the boche had been able to concentrate his shell on and round the battery instead of giving it just the same amount as the unoccupied surrounding country the effect might have been very different.

One possible reason for the promiscuous and sometimes very casual shooting may have been the fact that the boche at that time had practically no air observation. Our flying fellows had temporarily chased his planes out of the skies and had shot down all his observation balloons. This A made it impossible for him to pick his targets, and he either had to bombard the countryside or shoot "by the map," neither method being particularly conducive to good results with gas shell.

On the other hand, one or two places that he knew were pretty certain to be occupied by our troops were given their full dose. One such place was Caterpillar Wooda big narrow spinney running off from the Fricourt Valley and so named because of its shape and the fact that on the ordnance maps, on which the woods are colored green, it looks just like a green caterpillar crawling over to the shelter of Mametz Wood. This place was continually shelled with

?-large numbers of the Green Cross Shell, and as it stood in the side of a valley the gas persisted longer there than elsewhere and built up a tidy concentration which caused a lot of trouble.

The gunners were among our chief sufferers from these gas shell, as their guns were so frequently placed in sunken roads and folds in the ground for protection against explosive shell and ae-rial observation, and these were just the kind of places that held the gas longest. In the open much less damage was done. I remember one night the first-line transport of a battalion of the Black Watch ran into a patch of country into which the boche was raining 77-millimetre Green Cross Shell, and came out with only three casualties, two of which were from a direct hit on one of the wagons, the driver being killed instantly.

It seems particularly bad luck to be killed by a direct hit from a gas shell, for the bits of shell that fly about don't do much damage in the ordinary way and don't travel great distances. Indeed it is remarkable, even in the biggest gas-shell bombardments how very few men are hurt by the fragments.

The first week or two after the advent of the Green Cross

the toll of gas-shell casualties was considerable if not alarming, but steps were immediately taken to get the situation in hand. It is in a case like this, where a surprise had been brought off, that Discipline, with a very big "D," counts for so much. Fortunately the gas discipline of the British Army was pretty good, and it was not difficult to get new instructions carried out and orders obeyed. Once they got going their effect was most apparent and the gas-shell casualties dropped from week to week until they approached a minimum.

Among the important steps that were taken were a revision of the methods of spreading the alarm, and the protection and clearing out of dugouts into which the gas had penetrated.

Mention has already been made of the slight noise caused by the explosion of the gas shell, and instructions were accordingly issued that all shell that sounded like duds were to be regarded as gas shell, and the respirators adjusted accordingly. This got over one of the elements of surprise.

A great many men, especially those in battery positions, had been gassed in their dugouts before warning of the gas bombardment had been spread. Numbers of these men were actually gassed in their sleep and were awakened too late by the choking fumes themselves. What was done was to post a gas sentry at every battery in just the same way that it was done in the trenches. Special local-alarm signals were arranged so that the sentry could wake every one in the neighbourhood without having the alarm spread beyond the limit of the gassed area. These alarms generally took the form of bells or of gongs made from big shell cases; but later on policemen's large rattles were found to be the most effective "weapon" for the purpose, and numbers of these were distributed up and down the line and in the battery positions.. It was feared at first that the noise of the rattles would be mistaken for machine-gun fire and no attention be paid to it, but this did not materialise and the rattles have done good service.

The only thing about them is that they are made of wood - and nicely pickled, easily burning wood at that. In the trenches kindling chips of any kind are eagerly sought after to make a miniature fire to warm tea or cook an egg. When men will go the length of shaving the handles of their entrenching tools to obtain dry wood it could hardly be expected that policemen's rattles would always be respected. I am afraid a number of them disappeared. With the artillery things are not so bad as fuel is easier to obtain and the rattles are therefore less liable to get lost.

THE SMOKE HELMET-ANTI-GAS SPRAYERS

THERE is no need to dwell on the execration with which the use of gas was met by the whole civilised world, and I will merely try to recount how it was taken by the men in the trenches.

The British Tommy is a difficult man to terrify, and the moral effect on the men, though quite unprotected, was remarkably small considering the terrors of the game. For two or three days all we heard about were the things we should do in the event of being similarly attacked. It appeared that great chemists from England had immediately taken up the question of providing efficient respirators, and until they came out were advising people as to emergency measures. Some of these methods seemed to us very funny. We were told, for example, that a respirator could "easily" be made by knocking the bottom off a bottle, filling the bottle with earth, and then learning to breathe with the neck of the bottle stuck in the mouth. The breath was to be taken in through the bottle and let out through the nose; but as bottles were scarce and few of them survived the attempt to get the bottom broken off there was not inuch doing.

However, we learned that handkerchiefs filled with earth and kept moist would keep some of the gas out, and by the time the first novelty had worn off we were receiving private respirators from England. These had all been made in response to an appeal by Lord Kitchener to the women of England to make respirators for the troops out of cotton wool wrapped up in muslin or veiling. The result of this was that the War Office was absolutely swamped with millions of these respirators within a few days, and most fellows in the trenches had one or two sent out by post straightaway.

Besides these, arrangements were made by the various divisions for respirators to be made in towns behind the lines; and the government factories in England got to work to turn out a simple type of respirator which had been devised by the English chemists as the quickest to make and the simplest to use. The result was that within about one month we had four or five different kinds of respirators issued to us. Most of these were simple pads of either cotton wool or cotton waste. The earlier ones were soaked in washing-soda solution, and the later ones were moistened with a special solution consisting of ordinary photographic hypo and washing soda mixed with a little glycerin.

One type that we had for a week or two in the trenches consisted of the usual pad of cotton waste together with a small wad of the same material which was kept separate. The respirators were stored in boxes let into the paradoses, or rear walls of the trenches. On the alarm being given each man in the trench made a dive for a respirator, stuffed the wad into his mouth as a first protection, and then bound the pad round his mouth and nose, the wad being afterward taken out of his mouth and stuffed round his nose so as to make a tight fit.

These practices were popular for once or twice, but when it began to be realised that the wads were not always used by the same man the novelty waned. We thought we were getting pretty smart at it when we could get every man in the trench fully protected - that is, with the tapes tied in forty seconds from the word "Go!"

Later on we had the official "black-veiling respirator," which was issued to all the British troops and which went through two or, three of the earlier attacks as the chief protection.

It was from one of these attacks delivered in the salient again, on the Twenty-fourth of May, that the first benefits of good training in the use of the respirator were seen. One of the regiments which had been on the flank of the first attack and had seen the effects of the gas and what it really meant had taken the training very seriously, and the officers had insured that every man had a respirator, kept it in good condition, and knew how to, use it in the quickest possible time should occasion rise. Other regiments were not so, good, and it was just this training or lack of it that made all the difference between heavy casualties and light casualties in subsequent attacks.

On the twenty-fourth of May the regiment mentioned above happened to be in the very thickest part of the cloud, and though the battalion on either side of it suffered serious losses they themselves came off almost scotfree. Instances of losses from insufficient education in the use of the respirator were numerous on this occasion. A lot of men took their respirators off in the middle of the attack in order to wet them with solution again; and as they did not wring them out sufficiently the respirators were difficult to breathe through and the men thought they were being gassed and repeated the dosethe result being that they could not draw air through the sodden cotton waste, and they were gassed either from pulling off the respirators altogether or from the air coming in at the side.

One very bad instance was quoted by a medical officer at an advanced dressing station which was taking in gas cases as they came down from the line. Two or three men from one battalion came in pretty badly gassed, but still able to walk. The M.O. asked them if they had respirators issued to them. They said "Yes."

"Well, why didn't you put them on?" They said: "We did put them on; we've got them on now."

And so they had - strapped across their chests! At that time respirators were generally carried by the men tied round their caps, and in some cases could not be removed in time; and the May twenty-fourth attack made it apparent that the respirators should be carried in a position ready for immediate use. For this purpose a waterproof cover was provided and the respirator kept in a small pocket inserted into the jacket, or else in a pouch slung over the shoulder.

The other bad feature about the preparations was the arrangement for dipping the respirators in solution in the trenches, as referred to above. During the attack a lot of the men dipped their respirators in water; which of course washed the chemicals out of the respirators and made them ineffectual much sooner than thev should have been. But all of these matters were remedied before another gas attack was made.

The other bad feature about the preparations was the arrangement for dipping the respirators in solution in the trenches, as referred to above. During the attack a lot of the men dipped their respirators in water; which of course washed the chemicals out of the respirators and made them ineffectual much sooner than they should have been. But all of these matters were remedied before another gas attack was made.

After the first emergency respirator had been issued every effort was made to devise ,a more effective form of protection than that given by the cotton-wool pads, in expectation of a recurrence of German attacks. As a matter of fact there were no attacks between the beginning of June and December, 1915, because the wind was unfavourable to the Germans. This was another point that they had apparently overlooked, because on investigation we found that the prevailing winds in Flanders blew from west to east, and that about three-quarters of the total winds were in our favour and against the Germans.

The long interval of the summer of 1915 gave us a splendid opportunity to develop the protection against gas which had been commenced in the spring while attacks were still being made. The most important of these developments were the invention of the celebrated "smoke helmet" and the use of sprayers for the removing of gas from the trenches. We also found out the exact value of certain other devices and methods which had been suggested for combating the gas clouds, and a lot of impossible ideas were consequently turned down.

The latter might be discussed first of all. One suggestion which was made and believed in by most people at various times - including the Germans themselves was that fires built in the trenches or on the parapet would cause such an upward draft as to lift up the gas cloud and carry it safely over our heads. Experiments showed, however, that this idea was absolutely false, because though an upward draft was certainly formed the incoming air carried with it just as much gas from the surrounding atmosphere, and nothing was gained by it. It was a long time before the Germans tumbled to this, and even many months later their own instructions on defence against gas included statements that showed their reliance on this procedure.

One suggestion which actually reached the point of being acted on was that the gas cloud could be dispersed by an explosion, and for this purpose we were provided with wooden boxes filled with black powder and with fuses attached, which we were supposed to light at the crucial moment and throw into an advancing cloud. This heroic procedure was never actually made use of, however, because experiments in the meantime agai showed that such explosions had very little effect on a cloud of gas.

Two suggestions which really did turn out to be winners were those referred to previously - the smoke helmet and the Vermorel sprayer for clearing the trenches.

The idea for a respirator in the form of a helmet to go right over the head is stated to have originated from an idea of a sergeant of the Canadians who was gassed at Ypres, who stated that he had seen some of the Germans through the gas cloud with things that looked like flour bags pulled over their heads. It was thought that something of this kind could actually be made use of, and experiments showed that it was really a practical idea, because breathing is done through a very big surface and not only through the chemicals directly in front of the mouth and nose, as in the case of the respirator. By having a big surface it is possible to have thinner material and there is, therefore, less resistance to breathing. All that is required is to tuck the helmet down inside the jacket and button the latter tightly round it at the neck, and if this is done there is little possibility of gas leaking in. As a matter of fact there is no evidence that the Germans ever did use anything of the kind.

The first types of smoke helmet were made of flannel and had a window for seeing through which was made of mica or celluloid. The helmets were soaked in the same kind of solution - hypo, carbonate of soda and glycerin - that had been employed for the respirators. Helmets of this kind were capable of standing up against really considerable concentrations of chlorine, and they were quickly recognised both by the troops and by experts as being a very big improvement on the old respirator.

These helmets were made and issued to the troops as quickly as possible and a few of them were actually used in the attack of May twenty-fourth. Men unpracticed in their use were apt to find them hot and stuffy, and, not realising that the feeling wears off, were often inclined to think that they were being suffocated or gassed. As a matter of fact well-drilled men could do almost anything while wearing the helmet, the chief difficulty being that of limited vision. After wearing the helmet for a short time the celluloid window got clouded over from the moisture in the breath but this could easily be remedied by wiping it on the forehead. In many cases also the windows got cracked or broken from the rough treatment they were bound to meet in trenches, and this was a constant danger until men learned how to fold the helmet properly so as to protect the celluloid and to place a small sheet of cardboard or thin wood over the window before folding.

"The sprayers previously mentioned were originally suggested for use against the gas cloud itself, the idea being that chemicals should be sprayed at the cloud so as to neutralise the poisonous gas and thereby purify the air. Nearly everybody with even a nodding acquaintance with chemistry wrote in suggesting ammonia for this purpose, oblivious of the fact that the chemical reaction between chlorine and ammonia in these circumstances produces a dense cloud which is most irritating to the eyes and throat, and that this together with the excess of ammonia would be almost as bad as the original gas.

"In any case it is impossible to deal with the gas cloud by spraying, because of the enormous amount of chemicals and apparatus that would be required to neutralise the attack. A cloud of chlorine from one thousand cylinders, for example, would require more than forty tons of the strongest ammonia solution obtainable to kill all the gas, even if none of the spray were lost in the ground. Besides this the spraying might have to be continued for hours, some of the attacks having lasted intermittently for more than three hours.

"As stated before, the long interval of the summer and autumn of 1915 gave the chemists and the army plenty of opportunity for thinking about the gas question, developing organisation and methods to meet attacks in the future, and making arrangements for the training of the troops so that they should be thoroughly prepared when the next attack should arrive. One of the most important things that was done was to start a big field laboratory for dealing with questions of gas warfare. And as it had already been realised that the whole basis of defence against gas was going to lie in the hands of the troops themselves by increasing their steadiness, developing their discipline, and generally accustoming them to the idea that gas was now an ordinary method of warfare, chemists and instructors were appointed for attachment to each of the British armies.

"These men were all chosen from the line. For the most part they were infantry officers who could realise the real needs and limitations of the troops, but they were picked in each instance because they had, at any rate, some chemical knowledge and could translate into practice for the benefit of the troops various chemical measures which had been adopted for the latter's safety. Their first chief job was to see that respirators and smoke helmets were issued in sufficient number; to see that they were in good condition; and then to arrange for the training of all the troops in the army in their use. This was a heroic task, to be accomplished in as short a time as possible, but by dint of speaking to large bodies of officers and men at the same time it was so far completed that all ranks were given practical instruction in the use of the helmet.

When it is realised that each of these officers had to deal with at least one hundred thousand troops it will be seen that it was no mean feat that was accomplished. What was started then has never been completely accomplished, partly because of the continual development of gas warfare and partly because it is a matter of education - which is always slow - but very largely also because of the continually changing personnel and the enormous numbers of men that have had to be trained. It was quickly seen that this was an utter impossibility, but experiments showed that a spray of the hypo solution was quite capable of removing what remained of the gas cloud out of trenches and shell holes and from dugouts into which the gas had penetrated. This of course applied only to chlorine. Arrangements were therefore made for supplying a large number of these sprayers, which are exactly the same as those used for spraying fruit trees and potatoes with fungicides, and men were specially trained in their use so that they could be employed after an attack was over. These men were officially known as the "Vermorel sprayer men," and were popularly supposed to preface all their operations with the words "Let us spray."

The sprayers were somewhat delicate pieces of apparatus to keep in good condition in the trenches, and were apt to get crusted with mud and out of order unless they were well looked after. Like everything else connected with the defence against gas, their condition in the trenches varied with different regiments according as they were well trained and disciplined or otherwise, but as a rule the sprayers were well enough looked after, and proved extraordinarily useful on many occasions after their first appearance in the line. As stated before, the long interval of the summer and autumn of 1915 gave the chemists and the army plenty of opportunity for thinking about the gas question, developing organisation and methods to meet attacks in the future, and making arrangements for the training of the troops so that they should be thoroughly prepared when the next attack should arrive. One of the most important things that was done was to start a big field laboratory for dealing with questions of gas warfare. And as it had already been realised that the whole basis of defence against gas was going to lie in the hands of the troops themselves by increasing their steadiness, developing their discipline, and generally accustoming them to the idea that gas was now an ordinary method of warfare, chemists and instructors were appointed for attachment to each of the British armies.

These men were all chosen from the line. For the most part they were infantry officers who could realise the real needs and limitations of the troops, but they were picked in each instance because they had, at any rate, some chemical knowledge and could translate into practice for the benefit of the troops various chemical measures which had been adopted for the latter's safety. Their first chief job was to see that respirators and smoke helmets were issued in sufficient number; to see that they were in good condition; and then to arrange for the training of all the troops in the army in their use. This was a heroic task, to be accomplished in as short a time as possible, but by dint of speaking to large bodies of officers and men at the same time it was so far completed that all ranks were given practical instruction in the use of the helmet. When it is realised that each of these officers had to deal with at least one hundred thousand troops it will be seen that it was no mean feat that was accomplished. What was started then has never been completely accomplished, partly because of the continual development of gas warfare and partly because it is a matter of education - which is always slow - but very largely also because of the continually changing personnel and the enormous numbers of men that have had to be trained.

POPULAR TERROR OF GAS

The final object in the training of men in defence against gas is that troops shall be able to protect themselves completely and as quickly as possible in all the multitudinous circumstances in which they may encounter the poisonous gas in the field. To attain this it is necessary to inspire confidence by letting them in as far as possible on the principles underlying the use of gas and the tactics which are adopted by the enemy; and, secondly, to bring their practical proficiency and discipline up to such a standard that they make the very best use of the apparatus that is given to them.

It must be remembered that one of the greatest difficulties in talking to people about gas is the mystery of it. Even educated people hardly understand the word "gas" in connection with war and are apt to think of coal gas and dentist's gas in consequence.

The result is that the gas of the Germans was sometimes credited with all sorts of impossible qualities of movement and deadliness, and it can hardly be realised what alarm and distrust may exist in the raw recruit with regard to gas until he has been, given some instruction. This is even as great a danger as the over-confidencee of the veteran soldier who may know just as little about it.

Mere drilling and assertion are not sufficient to inspire confidence and acquire proportion, and it was realised very early that personal experience was needed. To gain this arrangements were made, for every man to see and smell gas in concentrations that would at any rate produce severe discomfort if dwelt in for any length of time, and for each soldier subsequently to be exposed to gas while wearing a gas helmet in such a concentration that negligence in obeying orders or in using the smoke helmet correctly would lead to real danger to life. By this means confidence could be inspired in everybody, though there is always a certain danger due to recklessness among the more adventurous types.

Besides this it was necessary to give as many men as possible some idea of the common sense of the operations in which the army was being drilled. This could only be done by giving a clear idea of how the gas is used; how gas travels;

where it accumulates; how it can be removed, and so on; and under what conditions a respirator or smoke helmet protects or ceases to protect its wearer. It was on these lines that instruction was built up; and to do it thoroughly it was found that a large number of instructors were required in order to train the officers and non-commissioned officers and to get them to treat their respirators with as great respect as their rifles and to learnt to carry them through a gas-defence drill in just as smart a manner as the ordinary arms.

For this purpose special schools of instruction were started at each army headquarters, and as many regimental officers and noncommissioned officers as possible were given a four or five days' course of gas training, so that they in their turn could go back to their regiments and spread the gospel, as the responsibility for getting things done must eventually fall upon them. Not only was it found impossible to provide specialist officers for each regiment or battalion, but it was recognised that such a procedure would have a bad effect on the gas-defence measures.

Gas defence was a matter which affected everybody and was in no way to be regarded as a specialist's job; battalions were already full of specialists. Indeed the colonels were apt to complain that they had nobody but specialists to command. There were bombers, snipers, signalers, machine gunners and sanitary men. and at that time the trench-mortar personnel was also a part of the infantry battalion. With all these things the feeling was that if a job could be looked on as being a specialty it should be put on the specialist officer concerned, and nobody else worried about it much. Now if gas defence was to become Lieutenant Snook's job, it meant that it was going to be nobody else's job, and it was essential that the idea should grow up in the army that gas defence was a purely military matter and affected everybody.

What was said then is just as true today - that the defensive appliance is a certain protection if it is used properly and in time. Defence against gas is thus on an entirely different footing from defence against shells and bullets, where protection cannot be assured; and, to quote instructions on the subject: "For destructive effects gas must depend on surprise, on poor discipline or on defective appliances. Consequently gas casualties are preventable if the soldier is trained continually to exercise vigilance and is well drilled in the use and care of his respirator. "

The basis of the whole thing, therefore, was that every officer should see that the men under his command were properly instructed in defensive measures against gas attacks, and that all orders on the subject were thoroughly understood. It was then up to the officers to see that their men could get their helmets on properly in the milmmum time, and this involved considerable amount of drill practice. It was pointed out to the officers that since protection had been provided, those battalions which had been carefully instructed had come through practically unharmed, while those battalions in which instructions had been neglected suffered severely.

It was also up to the officers to explain to their men as much as they themselves had learned about gas clouds, and to impress on them, for example, that by moving to the rear they would move with the gas, and that if they got flurried they would breathe, more deeply and would run much more risk of being gassed.

Besides these questions of instruction and drilling a lot of other arrangements had to be made, so that warning of German gas attacks should be spread in the quickest possible time. Arrangements were made to install alarms of various kinds in the trenches. Of course no reliance could be placed on any method of communication which involved the use of the lungs. A man cannot blow a bugle or a whistle while he has a helmet on, and If he waited to give a signal by such a method before protecting himself he would be almost certain to be gassed. What was done was to place bells and gongs made from shell cases up and down the trenches. At first these were rather futile things, the bells generally being much too small, some of them merely cow bells. The shell cases were a bit better and are still used for local alarms; but the arrangements for giving warning were not really very good at that time. The best devices were a number of motor horns, which were obtained locally, but the supply was insufficient and there was no general issue. Later on the alarm arrangements were tremendously improved. In some cases signal lights were used, but so many different kinds of rockets were already employed. for signalling to the rear that there was great difficulty in finding a light sufficiently distinctive. There was also the danger that it could be quickly copied by the Boche, who would thus amuse himself by giving us all kinds of shocks from false alarms.

Quite as important as the provision of signals was the making of observations to see when the wind was in a dangerous quarter. This was done partly at the meteorological stations at headquarters and partly on the front line itself. The latter was regarded at the time as the most important, and orders were given that each unit in the front line should rig up some kind of wind vane and learn to ascertain the strength of the wind, so that they should be immediately prepared for an attack whenever the wind was in a dangerous quarter. Wind vanes in the trenches were of the simplest types and a great deal of ingenuity was displayed in fitting up weathercocks that would be capable of turning in really low wind - say, one with a speed of only two miles an hour. The bearings for the central rod were the greatest difficulty, but it was found that by boring out a rifle bullet a sharp pointed stick or a thick piece of wire could be got to revolve in the hollow bullet quite easily, what remained of the lead core acting as a kind of lubrication.

The greatest nuisance of these wind vanes at first was that they were made so generally obtrusive that they could be seen from the enemy's lines, and they nearly always drew fire from snipers, and sometimes actually from the artillery. Presumably the enemy thought that where the wind vanes were installed company headquarters were probably situated. The position of the wind vanes consequently had to be chosen so that the direction and speed of the wind would be measured several feet above the ground without the apparatus being too obvious. One of the simplest types of vane adopted, and one which could hardly be seen from any distance was a bit of a stick to the end of which was tied ten to twelve inches of thin thread with a tiny bit of cotton wool at the end. When the wind is blowing the direction taken by the thread shows the line of the wind fairly exactly, and the behaviour of the cotton wool in rising and falling indicates the strength of the wind. The latter, however, was supposed to be measured by reference to Beaufort's scale, which depends on the movement in wind of natural objects.

Smoke moves straight up, speed of wind is nil; smoke slants, speed is two miles an hour; the wind is felt on the face, speed is five miles; paper, etc., move about, speed is ten miles; bushes are seen to sway, speed fifteen miles; tree tops sway and wavelets are formed on water, speed is twenty miles; tree tops sway and whistle, speed is thirty miles.

All of these arrangements for training and equipment of the troops were hurried on as quickly as possible, but at the same time sight was not lost of the probability of the German's using gases different from the chlorine which had originally formed their stand-by. It was felt that a good all-round protection should be capable of keeping out not only chlorine and similar gases but also others which were quite likely to come into use.

During the whole of this time we were getting a lot of information from the intelligence branch as to materials which the Germans were making for use against us in their next gas attacks.

During the wnole ot this time we were getting a lot of information from the intelligence branch as to materials which the Germans were making for use against us in their next gas attacks. Some of this information was really farcical, but on the other hand some of it was very good and helped to confirm the conclusions to which our own scientists were coming as to the likelihood or unlikelihood of particular gases. In the former category may be classed one story which came to us containing a very circumstantial description of some experiments which were stated to have been carried out in Berlin. These trials were stated to have been made in what we considered a very proper place, namely, Hagenbeek's menagerie, where, in the presence of a large number of military representatives, a new gas was tried out.

A noncommissioned officer appeared with a tank of the gas on his back, the spraying nozzle coming out under his arm. A camel and an elephant were brought out. The noncommissioned officer advanced toward them, and at twenty paces' distance he pressed down the lever on the tank and out came some small black bubbles of gas, which floated down the wind toward the faded animals. The bubles burst, giving off a yellow vapour, and the minute this vapour came in contact with the camel and the elephant the beasts dropped down dead!

This sounded very terrible, but even in the conditions we were at the time it was not taken too seriously, and of course nothing of this kind has ever made its appearance.

Another story which commenced to make its appearance at that time, and which we have heard a great deal about ever since, was that the Germans were busy making prussic acid in enormous quantities for a huge offensive which was to finish the war. It was stated that the Kaiser had at last been persuaded to use this terrible weapon in order by its use to finish the war at once and prevent needless suffering.

When they first made their appearance stories with regard to prussic acid had to be taken a great deal more seriously than those like the "little black bubbles." For one thing we were unprotected against prussic acid, and for another it was known of course to be an extremely deadly poison. Indeed before the war it was regarded as the most poisonous vapour known, so a great deal of weight was attached to these statements, and experiments were at once put on foot to find protection against prussic acid and to see exactly how poisonous it was compared with other gases.

As a matter of fact prussic acid has not been used by the Germans simply because it is not poisonous enough. It is not so poisonous, for example, as phosgene, and a lot of captured

German documents showing the relative toxicity of different vapours always put it on a rather low basis. It was this and not a desire to avoid utter barbarity which decided the Germans not to use it. The ordinary German soldiers, just like ourselves, still consider prussic acid as the most dangerous possible material, and whenever they have a story to tell of a new gas being invented or being got ready to use against us they will tell you in awestruck tones that it is prussic acid.

The most valuable piece of information which we got was a complete set of notes of some very secret lectures given to specially selected senior officers at a conference ix. Germany. We gathered that this conference was held behind closed doors and triple lines of sentries, and all that kind of thing, and I cannot of course indicate how the information came into our hands, but there At was. It described a lot of new gases which,had been considered, and stated among other things that they intended to make a big gas attack against either the French or ourselves in Flanders in December, 1915, some time before Christmas when the wind was favourable. For this purpose they were going to use a mixture of chlorine with another gas, phosgene-the amount of phosgene to be twenty per cent of the whole.

Now phosgene had been realised by our own chemists as a very likely gas to be used. I cannot say that it is more poisonous than chlorine, but it is infinitely more deadly because it is much more difficult -to protect against and is more insidious in its nature. For one thing, though it is an asphyxiant like chlorine it is possible for a man to be only slightly gassed and think he is all right, and then, especially if he takes any exercise in between, to fall dead several hours later from heart failure.

The information was so complete that our arrangements to provide a helmet which would protect against phosgene were hastened as much as possible; and it was as well that they were, for the attack actually did come off just about the time and place mentioned, in the Ypres salient.

It was realised of course that any change in protection would have to include both prussic acid and phosgene; and this is not nearly so easy as it sounds. Phosgene is peculiarly chemically inert for such an active poison, and it was some time before a reasonable protection was found which could be incorporated in a smoke helmet. The substance actually decided upon was a solution of sodium phenate-that is, carbolic acid dissolved in caustic soda, the mixture containing an excess of caustic. This solution is quite capable of dealing with reasonable concentrations of phosgene and would successfully protect against three parts of phosgene to teil thousand of the air, which in the circumstances was quite good enough. The French also altered their protection at the same time and used sodium sulphanilate as the basis of protection against phosgene, The objections agains the sodium phenate were that it could not be absorbed into a flannel helmet owing to its destruction of the fabric, and on account of its being strongly caustic it would tend to burn the faces of the men it came in contact with. These difficulties were overcome by making the helmet of two layers of flannelette instead of one layer of flannel, and by mixing with the sodium phenate a large quantity of glycerin. This kept the fabric moist and prevented the caustic from exerting its corrosive action.

It was realised from the start that a smoke helmet containing free alkali would deteriorate considerably on exposure to air, and it was found advantageous to provide a breathing tube in the mask so that a man would breathe in through the helmet and out 'through an outlet valve; in this way the breath, which contains a lot of carbonic acid, would have no bad effect on the chemicals. The use of an outlet valve was also found to have the advantage of keeping the air purer inside the helmet and preventing the stuffy feeling which accompanied the older types of helmet.

This additional complication to the helmet was not looked upon favourably at first by the troops, but it was very quickly realised that only a little practice was required to make a man breathe quite normally in the way mentioned above, and that the advantages accruing from the alteration were very great indeed. We found that we could carry on for much longer stretches of time without being fagged out, and more exact trials by the scie-ntists showed that a man's temperature, pulse and rate of breathing did not increase nearly so rapidly if he used an outlet valve as when breathing out and in through the same material. This is largely due to what is called "dead space," which means the volume of air in between the lungs and the atmosphere and in which the air is largely composed of breath exhaled from the lungs. The smaller this space the easier it is to breathe.

This principle of using an outlet valve has been retained in all the British respirators which have been invented since and is regarded as one of the very highest importance.

Another thing which had to be taken care of was that the new helmets, which were called "tube" or "P" helmets, would gradually deteriorate on exposure to air, and would consequently have to be withdrawn from the troops in the line from time to time in order to redip them in chemicals and make them as effective as before. For this purpose large repair factories were started at the bases and were placed in charge of Englishwomen who were brought over for the purpose. These factories were organised with local labour, helped out by a little military personnel, and were capable of washing the helmets returned from the line, redipping them in new solution, and sending them back in good condition again.

This was no small job, as the smoke helmets which were sent in were generally filthy dirty, sometimes soaked in mud and sodden with water, and requiring very careful handling to be brought back into good condition. All sorts of things got back with these helmets to the repair stations, and it was not an uncommon thing for the satchels containing the helmets to be found to hold anything from a live hand grenade to the photograph of some girl, which had been stored there for safe keeping. Both then and later we always had considerable difficulty in preventing Tommy from using his helmet satchel, and later on his box respirator satchel, for these illicit purposes. He seemed to consider that if he had to carry another haversack he had a perfect right to put in it whatever he liked-rations, knives and forks, ammunition, private knickknacks of all kinds. This of course had to be stopped, owing to the damage these things might do to the respirator and the difficulty they might make in getting it out quickly.

During September and October, 1915, there were several scares as to the imminence of gas attacks by the Germans, and on one or two occasions it was definitely stated that the cylinders were actually in position in their trenches. This helped to hasten things up, and the factories in England and the repair stations in France kept themselves busy in producing the new type of helmet. A large number of them were actually issued to the troops by the time the Battle of Loose was started, and were consequently employed by our men when the first gas attacks were made, in September of that year.

It was these helmets which appeared in so many of the picture papers showing the charge of some British Territorial infantry through the gas cloud at the beginning of the battle, and there is no question about it that the men had a very fearsome appearance. With the hood over the head and the two big goggle eyes, and the outlet valve sticking out where the nose should be, small wonder that the Germans described them as "devils," and were so terrified as not to be able to put up much fight on the front where the particular charge was made.

ACCIDENTS TO THE HORNS--THE TEAR GAS SHELL

The expected German gas attack was actually made on December 19, 1915, at about 5:15 A.M., just before '"Stand to" in the morning, the venue being the north of the Ypres salient, from the canal bank at Boesinghe down to Wieltje, a distance of three miles. It was preceded by the appearance of parachute lights of an unusual kind and by a number of red rocket flares. Almost immediately afterward gas was smelt in the front trenches. In some cases a hissing sound made by the gas Is leaving the cylinders was heard and was taken as a warning by the soldiers in the trenches. In other cases the noise seems to have been deadened by rifle fire. Taking it altogether, however, there was very little warning, as the wind was favourable and the gas traveled surprisingly quickly.

There was absolutely no confusion, and the men put on their helmets at once and lined the parapets within a minute. Where the trenches were close together the men had some difficulty in getting on their helmets in time. This was particularly the case in listening posts where we had patrols out quite close to the Concertina wire. In the support and reserve trenches the arrangements for spreading the warning were not so good as those in. the front line, and a number of men were caught by the gas before they had their helmets on. Indeed in a number of cases, especially in batteries, the gas was smelt before the receipt of the warning.

The actual gas wave lasted only about half or three-quarters of an hour, but in some places the helmets had to be kept on for four hours, as the gas hung about in hollows and dugouts for a long time. This was particularly noticeable in the neighbourhood of the canal. The cloud was felt as far back as Vlamertinghe, eighty-five hundred yards behind the line, and was still visible at this

point. For at least three miles back behind the front line helmets had to be put on everywhere, and for six miles behind the line the smoke helmets were generally worn, some men who did not put them on at this distance being gassed.

The actual gas wave was accompanied by a heavy bombardment of the front line and of Ypres and the villages behind it, shrapnel and high-explosive shell and also tear shell being used, the latter shell being fired particularly against our artillery. This bombardment lasted throughout the day and most of the following night. Though our wire had been cut in many places by the artillery fire, the Germans made no serious infantry attack, and small patrols which left their trenches in a few places were immediately shot down, as our fellows were continually on the alert and had not suffered to any considerable degree.

Altogether a large number of troops were exposed to the gas but, compared with its extent, the cloud caused only a small number of casualties. This was very satisfactory after our experiences of the spring. Men who were gassed but not killed were all subsequently questioned as to the reason for their being gassed, and in each case a definite reason was forthcoming. In no single instance was the fault laid at the door of the smoke helmet, which apparently had been quite capable of standing up to the highest concentrations in any part of the cloud.

Among the reasons given for the casualties were things like the following - some men in the fire trenches did not get on their helmets quickly enough owing to the short distance between the trenches, lack of warning in the support line and insufficient practice. Some officers and men sleeping in dugouts did not have their helmets attached to them or they were caught away from their dugouts without helmets. Helmets in many cases were under the overcoats, which made it very difficult to get them and put them on quickly, as it was necessary to undo the overcoat, the top button of the jacket and the cardigan waistcoat before the helmet could be tucked in. One cause of casualties was that the "P" helmet smelt very strongly of carbolic, and a lot of men who had not had this explained to them thought that the peculiar smell was that of gas coming in and

they took their helmets off with a view to replacing them with other helmets. This of course was fatal. One sergeant was gassed through his helmet's being holed by a bullet, though he himself was not wounded. In some cases wounded men tried to remove their helmets and were gassed in this way, and it was found necessary to watch men who were hit to prevent this.

In many ways this attack of the Germans was of the greatest importance, as it displayed all of the features on which the subsequent development of the gas cloud was based. These features were: Increased concentration; the use of new material; surprise. These three things are really the basis of all gas warfare, even at the present day, whether the attacks are made in the form of clouds or by the use of gas shells or other projectiles.

The increased concentration was obtained chiefly by the reduction in the time occupied by the attack. The first attack of all lasted about one hour and a half. The next attack lasted about three hours. The one in question lasted only thirty minutes, so that if the same amount of gas was used the concentration of the cloud must obviously have been increased six times over that of May twentyfourth, as there is little doubt that the cylinders had been installed in approximately the same numbers - that is, one to a metre of front.

Probably the most important feature of the attack was the introduction of phosgene. Now there never was any actual chemical evidence of the poisons of phosgene in the German gas clouds until some of their cylinders were captured by us when they retreated on the Somme in the beginning of 1917. But unfortunately the peculiar effects of phosgene on our men who were gassed were only too apparent. There were a large number of "delayed" cases - men who thought they were only slightly gassed but who became ill or even died several hours or sometimes a day or so later from heart failure, especially if they had taken any heavy exercise in between.

In these cases there was hardly any coughing. What was really wanted was rest, but this was not realised at the time, and many men walked to the dressing stations-sometimes a mile or more-through deep mud and became quite exhausted. One officer of the Durhams had been slightly gassed at the beginning of the attack but felt perfectly all, right until about noon, when he became faint and exhausted, though not apparently seriously ill. After lying down he felt better, but inthe evening got worse again, and in walking to the ambulance to go to the field dressing station he suddenly collapsed and died. This was fourteen hours after the attack.

Another weighty piece of evidence as to the nature of the gas was given by the smell, which to trained observers was quite different from the typical chloride-of-lime smell of chlorine; and by the peculiar effects on the taste of tobacco to men who had smelt the gas. If you take a good smell of dilute phosgene and then smoke a cigarette the tobacco tastes like nothing on earth. Tommy's nearest description of the taste and smell is "mouldy hay". This peculiar effect is quite typical of phosgene and is known as the "tobacco reaction."

In the hope of getting samples of the German gas clouds for analysis a large number of gas vacuum bulbs were distributed up and down the line, and selected men were taught how to use them. This was supposed to be done by nipping off the drawn-out end of the gas bulb, whereby the contaminated air would rush in. The end was then to be closed with a hollow stopper containing wax.

To get these samples was asking a great deal. Even when packed in special boxes glass bulbs are somewhat fragile things for trench life, and the wooden boxes made excellent kindling wood, which was always'being sought for. The result is that when the cloud does come along the vacuum bulbs are often conspicuous only by their absence. Even if they are kept whole it is asking rather a lot of a man to take an accurate scientific sample during the excitement of a gas attack which is accompanied by a bombardment by explosive shells and gas shells.

For a long time none of the bulbs found their way back to the field laboratory. Eventually one did come, carefully packed in shavings and wadding. I happened to be present when it was brought in, and there was a good deal of excitement at the little prodigal's return. The bulb was taken out, but under it was found a leaf from a field service note book, on which was written: "Danger. This bulb was found in a hedge. It seems to have been dropped from an aeroplane and probably contains cholera germs. Fortunately it has not been broken."

The "surprise effect", which was mentioned above as being the third fresh feature of this new-era gas-cloud attack, took the form of making the attack in the dark and at a time when men were least preparedthat is, just before the morning " Stand to," the hour before dawn, when all troops in the trenches stand to arms. By making the attack at night, or at any rate in the dark, the boche achieved two objects: First of all, there were better wind conditions for an attack, because the night winds tend to flow down toward the earth and keep the gas cloud low-lying and thick, whereas the day the sun warms the ground and produces so many upward currents of air that the cloud gets lifted up and dissipated; in the second place it was impossible to see the cloud when it was first liberated, and this reduced the means of detecting the attack to only two - the hissing noise of the gas escaping from the cylinders and the smell of the advanced parts of the cloud.

Later on it was known that the best hours for all gas attacks, both cloud and shell bombardment, are in the night; and as a matter of fact practically all gas warfare is now carried out at night, but at that time the significance of this was not grasped, and many of our casualties were due to lack of preparedness, numbers of men being caught "on the hop" and overwhelmed.

Some most important steps in improving our protecting measures were taken as a result of the lessons learned from the attack; in fact, it may be taken that all measures in defence against gas have been learned from bitter experience, and to this extent the sufferings of the victims may be taken as having at any rate some compensating value. In such a new and strange and continually developing kind of warfare very little can be done by a priori argument. This fact we have always tried to impress on the men - that the gas warfare orders, sometimes apparently trivial and frequently wearisome and annoying, have all been made as the result of lessons learned from actual attacks.

Among the chief things that were done after the December nineteenth attack was the improvement of our system of alarms. The bells and horns in the front line had been found quite insufficient, especially for warning people in the rear; and the telephone could not be depended on for this purpose owing to the possibilities of the wires being cut by shell fire. To protect them from being cut, all wires would have to be buried at least six feet deep in the ground and this is practically impossible owing to the work involved.

It would consequently be fatal to depend on telephonic communication, especially as a gas attack is nearly always accompanied by a pretty heavy bombardment of rear lines. In one case I knew during just such a bombardment, the staff captain at a brigade headquarters was talking to one of the battalions when the whole telephone instrument seemed to burst into a sheet of flame in his hands, owing to a cut wire. The battalion concerned was isolated for more than an hour as a result, and anything might have happened in the meantime.

For these reasons it was decided to adopt for gas alarms sirens worked by compressed air, which would make a noise sufficiently loud and distinctive to be heard long dis'tances away. The type of siren which was used has been kept in use ever since in continually increasing numbers and has proved extraordinarily useful. It is known as the Strombos horn, and consists of the horn proper and two iron cylinders of compressed air charged to a pressure of one hundred and fifty atmospheres. Only one cylinder at a time is connected to the horn, the other being kept as a reserve.

The Strombos horns are mounted in the trenches in such a.way as to protect them from shell splinters as far as possible. This is generally done by packing them round carefully with sandbags, only the mouth of the horn being displayed and pointing toward the rear. Every sentry must know how and when to sound the horn. All he has to do when he realises that a gas attack is being made, or on receiving instructions from an officer to do so, is to loosen the tap on the cylinder one complete turn, when the horn will sound continuously for more. than a minute. The noise is terrific and in an enclosed space or in a quiet region it is absolutely deafening. In the trenches, however, it is none too loud, and the distances between the horns in the front system of trenches are' never more than four or five hundred yards. Farther back in the chain, toward the rear, the distances can be increased. Horns are now installed at battalion, brigade and divisional headquarters. By turning them on when the noise of those in front is heard it is possible to pass the alarm in an incredibly short space of time and thus forestall the cloud of gas to such an extent that every man in the support trenches or in rest billets or the villages behind the firing line is aware that an attack is in progress and gets ready to protect himself.

Naturally, things don't always work out exactly according to schedule. The horns are frequently damaged. In one place 1. was at, just this side of the canal, near Boesinghe, a heavy German trench mortar wrecked three of our Strombos horns within a week, and another and less suitable position had to be found for the alarm. Then there are occasional false alarms. These sometimes arise from individual men "getting the wind up" from a bombardment by gas shell and thinking that a cloud attack is being made. Others I am afraid have been more in the nature of experiments "to see how it works." After all, it must be a great temptation to a sentry to be in charge of a Strombos horn and never have the pleasure of turning it on.

False alarms are a great nuisance, however, and good arrangements have now been made to prevent their spreading. it is possible to avoid all the unnecessary disturbance to which troops are subjected by a false gas alarm. This distance is particularly objectionable in back areas.where regiments returned from the trenches are in billets. When the alarm goes everybody has to turn out-probably in the middle of the night. Sentries wake the officers and men in all the billets; messengers have to be sent post-haste to outlying villages or farms with which there is no telephonic communications; respirators are hurriedly inspected and placed in the alert position; the gas-proof curtains of cellars and dugouts are adjusted; the officers move about in the darkness to see that all their men are accounted for and ready; every one is in a state of expectancy - and then the word comes through that it is a false alarm, and the men go back, cursing, to their billets. Not only is an occurrence of this kind wearying to tired troops, but it has the old disadvantage of crying "Wolf, Wolf" when there is no wolf- the consequent determination on the part of the men not to take the next alarm so seriously.

Though it was not realised at the time, it is almost certain that the Germans started to use gas in shell almost simultaneously, and probably actually in the first attack, with the use of the poisonous gas clouds in the attacks of April and May, 1915. Many instances came to notice of men's eyes being strongly affected to such an extent that they could not keep them open. There seemed to be something in the air which made an unprotected man weep copiously if he tried to keep his eyes open, and of course if he closed them he could not see what he was doing.

These effects, and a peculiar smell which was noticed both during and after the gas-cloud attacks, gave rise to the belief that something like formaldehyde was being used by the Germans mixed with some chlorine gas. Others described the smell as. being that of chloroform or ether, but nobody could say definitely what the material actually was. It was only after a n-tunber of blind shell had been obtained and, examined that it was realised that the Germans were firing shell filled with liquid which had a powerful lachrymatory effect.

It does not appear certain whether the use of lachrymatory liquids for putting men out of action by making their eyes water is in itself contrary to The Hague Convention, as the vapours need not actually be poisonous. This was the case with the first German gas shell, as it was found that the liquid contained consisted only of a material known chemically as "xylyl bromide." The vapour of this liquid and of many similar substances has a most powerful effect on the eyes, like that of onions but much stronger. Except in very high concentrations it cannot be regarded as poisonousat any rate not in the sense that chlorine is poisonous.

Examination of the German lachrymatory shells showed that the liquid was contained inside the shell in a sealed lead vessel so that the material should not come in contact with the steel of the shell, which it destroys gradually. Shell of this kind, though termed gas shell, are not really such, as the liquid has to be broken up into fine dropletsby the explosive charge of the shell before the vapour can produce its effect. The liquid has no pressure of its own inside the shell and depends entirely on the bursting charge to get it distributed into the atmosphere.

The xylyl bromide used by the Germans was not pure, but contained a big proportion of benzyl bromide, showing that it had been made by the action of bromide on coal-tar light oil from which most of the toluene had been removed for the manufacture of the well-known high explosive, trinitrotoluene.

The effect of xylyl bromide on an unprotected man is instantaneous and remarkable. Even such small proportions as one volume of vapour diluted with one million volumes of air will at once make a man weep so copiously that he cannot possible keep his eyes open.

Obviously a material of this kind has. great military value, for though it does nol put men out of action permanently by killing them it neutralises their effectiveness to such an extent that for the time being they may be regarded as of no military :h—nportance. In strong concentrations the effect on the eyes is most powerful. I have walked into an area which was being bombarded with lachrymatory shells and suddenly got the effect just as if I had been hit in the face. Fortunately the lachrymation has no lasting effect on the eyes, and a man on getting into pure air very quickly recovers.

Throughout the spring and summer of 1915 these lachrymatory shells were used in considerable numbers, especially in the vicinity of Ypres, and at times the ramparts of that much bombarded town reeked of Iachrymatory vapoiir and nobody could stay in certain spots for any length of time with out having his eyes protected by specially constructed goggles or by wearing a gas helmet right over his head.

Taking it altogether we were not troubled nearl so much by this new type of gas as were the French in the southern part of the line. In much the same way that the gas cloud was developed by the Germans against the English the gas shell were developed chiefly against the French, and very much larger numbers were employed against the French positions than we had to contend with during the first six months or so. Later on things were more equallised in this direction. Captured German documents and statements by prisoners ,showed us that the Germans were counting very considerably on the effect produced by the lachrymatory shell, and detailed instrucfor their use in various circumstances were carefully laid down. The lachrymatory shell was known by the Germans as "T-Shell" and the xylyl bromide as "T-Stoff," and instructions were laid down 'for the use of this material. Another kind of shell was known as "K-Shell" which up to that time had not been used against us, or at any rate had not been recognised.

The T-Shell was particularly to be used against positions which it was not intended to occupy immediately, the reason for this being that T-Stoff hangs about for a long time. Some of the liquid is apt to be spread about the ground and gives off enough vapour to make the neighbourhood of the shell hole uninhabitable for many hours, and in favourable condition - for the enemy - for several days. The K-Shell, on the other hand, was intended to be used against infantry positions and strong points which it was hoped to assault and capture within an hour or two of the bombardment or on areas which it was hoped to traverse during a big attack.

The advent of the lachrymatory T-Shell incommoded us considerably, but, as it was quickly realised that the gas was not poisonous, the Tommies were not much taken back, and the "tear shell," as they were quickly called, were not considered by the rank and file to have importance, which as a matter of fact they have; but at the same time we heard rather alarming stories of the effects of gas shell as used against the French.

It was rumoured, for example, that in the Crown Prince's big advance in the Argonne, in the late spring of 1915, that such enormous numbers of gas shell had been used against the

French positions that the infantry occupying them were not only put out of action by the effect on their eyes but that the amount of gas used was so large that the French soldiers were actually anaesthetised and were taken prisoners by the Germans while in an unconscious condition.

Whether this was true or whether it was exaggerated is not certain, though it is certainly true that the Crown Prince's advance was prefaced by a hurricane bombardment of gas shell, the tactical effect of which was considerable.

Stories of this kind, however, combined with the effects which we ourselves were experiencing, made us realise that protection against tear gas was essential, and for this purpose arrangements were made to supply every officer and man in the front line with a pair of anti-gas goggles. The earliest types of these, goggles were very simple in construction, and we are told were copied from a French pattern. They consisted of a waterproof fabric lined with flannel containing a wire spring for the nose and fitted with celluloid eyepieces. By bending the wire to the shape of the nose it was possible to close the nostrils and at the same time give a reasonably good fit to the flannel on the face. In some cases the flannel was anointed with some kind of grease so as to make a still closer fit, in order to keep out small traces of gas which are quite sufficient to produce lachrymation. Later on we had a much better type of goggle backed with rubber sponge to make a tight fit to the face.

With the small numbers of gas shell used against us we had no experience of any effect on the lungs, and it was found also that the helmet form of respirator was enough to keep out, at any rate, low coneentrations of the lachrymator; but we got a rude awakening when the boche began to use his tear shells in larger numbers. Such a case happened to us in the beginning of 1916, at the celebrated village of Vermelles a little ruined town just behind the lines near Loos. The enemy tried out an attack on us over about a mile front for the purpose of bagging some of our trenches, and he attempted to keep reinforcements from coming up to counter attack him by putting down a tear-shell barrage through Vermelles and north and south of it over the roads on which our fellows would have to advance. He used thousands of his tear shells and the neihbourhood absolutely stank of them. Fortunately, it was almost impossible to put down an effective standing barrage with gas, and our reserves got through on two roads that had not been blocked effectively. The boche attack was a fizzle, but Vermelles was a little private hell of its own for that day and most of the next forty-eight hours as well.

During and immediately after the bombardment, troops passing through the village wore both goggles and gas helmets, but the concentration of lachrymator was so great that many of our fellows were sick and actually vomited inside their helmets. If you can imagine men going up to a battle with these flannelette bags over their heads and then being sick inside them, you can realise that the boche was not particularly popular with us at the time.

Besides this, Vermelles was much used by troops in reserve and was full of cellars and 'dugouts occupied by the waiting infantry and also by signallers, headquarters of various kinds, and so on. The vapours - and some of the shells themselves, for that matter - got down into these cellars and made them almost uninhabitable for days, except in those cases where they had been properly protected by double lines of blankets hung at the entrances.

About the same time in 1916 the enemy began making surprise bombardments with a new lachrymator and with the K-Shell mentioned previously, for the purpose of assisting in raids. Both of these gases rejoice in long names, the lachrymator being bromethylmethylketone, and the K-Shell gas monochlormethylchloroformate. These gases are much more poisonous and do not hang about as long as the old " T " tear gas. One such raid in which they were used was carried out at a place called La Boiselle - afterward famous as a jumping-off point in the Somme Battle.

I was not in at the raid, but heard details of it afterward. The boche rained his gas shells into the selected area and at the same time prevented re inforcements from getting up by putting down a so-called box barrage with explosive shells round the trenches to be attacked.

Our men were taken completely by surprise. Many of them were badly gassed, all were temporarily blinded; and then after a short interval the boche came in. He timed his arrival so that most of the gas had disappeared. Then there was some very fierce fighting-so fierce that a number of our men died afterward because of the exertion following on the breathing of the K-gas. But gassed and blinded men, however brave cannot fight successfully against others fresh and unaffected, and the enemy captured a number of prisoners and two Lewis guns.

Curiously enougb, during the Somme Battle a few months later we did in properly the regiment which had carried out the raid and captured the official report of the commander of the raiding party. In this report he said: "...the men of the Royal Irish Rifles created a fine impression both as regards their physique and their mode of repelling an assault. Had it not been for the use of the gas shells it would have been impossible to clear the section of trench attacked. "

Rather a fine tribute - and one thoroughly deserved! Of course surprises of this kind cannot be pulled off twice, but occurrences like this and the bombardment at Vermelles let us see that the enemy intended to develop his gas-shell industry much more than we had anticipated, and our protective measures were taken in hand so as to meet future eventualities. In fact it was about this time that the box respirator was being hurriedly developed so as to protect us against any further devilment that Fritz might send along.

CLEANING IT OUT BY FIRES-SNEEZING OF BLUE CROSS GAS

This was pretty well the position of things in July of last year, when the German use of gas shell underwent a radical development due to the advent of the so-called mustard gas. So much has been written about this gas and so many misstatements have been made concerning it that it is as well for the public to understand what mustard gas is, what it can do and what it cannot do. On the one hand, it has been credited with such impossible potency as would make it wonderful that any Allied soldiers remain at all. On the other hand, it should be realised that in mustard gas the Germans possess a very powerful weapon of war and one which they are using to a very considerable extent.

In the first place let it be said that mustard gas is not a killing gas like Green Cross, but that it is of the persistent type, like the older lachrymators. Unlike the lachrymators, however, its effects are not transitory and a man put out of action by mustard gas is going to be a casualty for several weeks and perhaps longer. Mustard gas principally affects the eyes and the lungs, but in a very strong vapour or in contact with any of the actual liquid from the shell a man Is skin may be burned very severely-even through his clothes. Alore attention has been turned to this blistering effect of the gas than to anything else, but as a matter of fact the blistering is of secondary importance and in itself does not result in the loss of many men to the line. Of course one has to be very careful. It is foolish, for example, to lea-n up against sandbags that have been spattered with the liquid or to sit in a mustard-gas shell crater. Sooner or later the skin underneath will develop a severe and possibly extensive blister, which is very painful and certain to last some time.

These burns are not dangerous, but they are most uncomfortable, to say the least, especially as they are most easily produced on the more tender parts of the skin.

Great excitement was caused at first among the Highland regiments because the story was spread about that the Scots were particularly susceptible to the mustard gas because of their attentuated clothing. As a matter of fact the kilt doesn't seem to be a source of danger at all, and Highlanders are burned no more frequently than others. Possibly the continued exposure of their legs hardens them. The chief effects of the mustard gas are on the eyes and lungs. The first thing you notice is the smell-which is slightly of garlic or mustard-and irritation of the nose and throat. Neither effect is enough to make you feel gassed, and the chief symptoms develop later on. When the gas is strong it is apt to cause sickness and some.. times actual vomiting. Later on the eyes inflame and get very sore, the lids swell and blister, but no permanent injury to the eyes takes place, though the victim may be temporarily blinded. The effects developed in the lungs are equally painful and consist of severe inflammation and bronchitis, which may take some time to get better and if not well looked after may develop into pneumonia.

It will thus be seen that for a persistent gas, though not deadly poisonous, mustard gas is a nasty proposition. First the gas does not of itself force a man to protect himself. With the old lachrymators a man either put on his mask or his eyes would smart and water so badly that he could not keep them open. With the Green Cross and similar gases a man either protects himself or dies. But with the mustard gas, though the smell and irritation may be perfectly apparent, the effect is not such as to force a main to don his mask. Yet if he does not do so and continues to live in the vapour unprotected he will certainly become a casualty. It may take half an hour, it may take several hours to come on, but come on it will.

Another particular disadvantage of the mustard gas is its persistence. It will hang about in shell holes for many hours and even for days. If it gets into a dugout it is very difficult to get rid of it, and as long as there is enough to produce the faintest smell or irritation of the nose there is enough to bring on serious symptoms eventually. This means that when it is used our fellows are forced to wear their masks for very long stretches of time.

The mustard gas is known officially by the Germans as Yellow Cross gas, and the shells are marked on the sides with bright yellow crosses and bands. The paint used for these bands changes colour in contact with the mustard-gas liquid, so that if a shell should leak it at once becomes apparent and can be taken away and buried.

The Yellow Cross gas was first used at Ypres and bombardments there were quickly followed by similar ones at Nieuport and Armentiéres. Enormous numbers of shell of all calibres were employed, including a new and larger size-the 8.3-inch howitzer shell, which holds nearly three gallons of the liquid and can be fired a distance of six miles.

At Nieuport more than fifty thousand shell were fired in one night, and equally large numbers were used in deluging the other towns. Since then the numbers used have continually increased, especially when the Boche was preparing for an attack or expecting one of ours.

Duds that were collected showed that the mustard-gas liquid was a chemical called dichlorethyl sulphide, a liquid that gives off its vapour only slowly. The shell themselves were similar to the previous gas shell except that the small one have a new type of fuse - a very simple and quick-acting fuse which bursts the shell before it can get into the ground, and consequently produces a very little crater. This of course helps to spread the gas round more than if a big hole were formed. The respirators keep out the Yellow Cross gas completely, and the blanket protection of dugouts will also keep out the gas splendidly. Of course if a dugout gets a direct hit with a mustard shell there is nothing for it but to leave it empty for some days, as the liquid cannot be removed by ventilation with either fans or fires.

A case that will illustrate what I mean was one in which a three-inch mustard-gas shell got a direct hit on a doctor's dugout and gassed him and his orderlies. Some time afterward the remaining orderlies thought they ought to send the doctor's things down the line and went in and got them out of the dugout. They noticed a faint smell but did not worry about it, and soon afterward found themselves gassed in consequence.

A fire was then placed in the dugout to clear it. In the meantime the medical sergeant secured another dugout by clearing out some infantrymen. In the. evening the infantry felt soul-sick and wanted somewhere to sleep, so they went into.the original gassed dugout and slept there. In the morning they all went down, gassed.

Where there has been no direct hit and the mustard-gas vapour gets into the dugout, it can be cleared out just like ordinary gas, by ventilation either with fans or by means of fires. For clearing dugouts a great deal of reliance is placed nowadays on building small fires inside. A dugout with two entrances can be very quickly cleared by means of fires, as a through draft is produced, which carries the gas away with it; but difficulty is frequently found in getting the necessary fuel for the fire and in keeping the stuff handy. Bundles of firewood and kindling material are supposed to be kept in the dugouts ready for use; as has already been explained, the Tommies are always on the lookout for combustible materials for their own fires, and continual inspection has to be made to see that the special supplies for ventilation are kept available. One officer told me that he always had the supplies of wood, paper and kerosene kept in an army-biscuit tin which was closed and sealed; because, as he said, no Tommy would ever investigate the contents of a biscuit tin unless absolutely forced to do so for lack of other food.

It should be realised, however, that properly protected dugouts have given perfect immunity from the mustard gas as long as the protection has remained intact, and a great deal of attention is being paid to increasing the number of the protected shelters in order to give the men the necessary rest from wearing their respirators occasioned by the extensive use by the boche of his Yellow Cross Shell. In Nieuport a special gas patrol was instituted for going the round of the town to see that blanket protection of cellars and shelters was kept in good condition, as there was always a chance that they would not be well looked after or that there was always the chance that the blankets had been taken down by some enterprising Tommy for his own personal use.

Round about battery positions the most annoying feature of the mustard gas is the length of time it persists. 1n the shell holes it can at any rate be partly destroyed by sprinkling with chloride of lime. It is rather interesting to find that in some captured German instructions great secrecy was laid on the use of chloride of lime for getting rid of the effects of mustard gas. The boche kept boxes of chloride of lime in all positions where the gas shell were stored, and issued instructions to his own, troops that "the use of chloride of lime for the protection of our own troops against Yellow Cross liquid must not become known to the enemy. Observation of the strictest secrecy is a matter of duty just as much now as it was previously. The troops will be thoroughly instructed in these precautionary measures, but nothing will be taught them as regards the nature or composition of the antidote employed."

During the present offensive the Germans have used very large quantities of mustard gas, generally for holding purposes and against our rear lines battery positions, communications and reserves. This is kept up for many hours in order to wear out the patience of our fellows and weaken them for the coming assault.

Strong points that the boche does not wish to attack are also swamped with the gas, and when Armentiéres were evacuated by the British, Yellow Cross liquid was actually running down the gutters. But in places that he intends to assault he will complete the mustard-gas bombardment against our troops some considerable time before he advances; otherwise his own troops would run into it and be forced to don their respirators.

The quantities of shell used in this preparation are enormous and supplies of the mustard gas must have been accumulated during the winter to an unexpected extent and their manufacture proceeded with to full capacity.

Take it altogether, Yellow Cross gas is very much more than an annoyance, but there is no question that good discipline and thorough appreciation and carrying out of the orders laid down for the protection of troops have reduced the losses in very much the same way that the screwed-up discipline reduced the losses after the first introduction of Green Cross Shell. One of the most objectionable features of the mustard gas is the continual care that has to be exercised to prevent casualties. It is so easy for a man whose clothing is slightly contaminated with gas to enter a dugout and contaminate the whole of the interior and all its occupants. Sentries also have to be posted to warn troops passing through or into an area that has been bombarded with mustard gas,. so that respirators can be put on. After a cold night the officers must be continually on the watch to see whether the vapours that rise from the warming of the earth by the morning sun are charged with mustard gas, and to take the necessary precautions on the slightest detection of the characteristic smell. This smell to my mind is much more like garlic than mustard, and the use of the term "mustard gas" is purely the origination of the Tommies themselves. As a matter of fact, so as not to confuse the Yellow Cross liquid with true mustard oil, efforts were made at first to prevent the stuff from being called mustard gas. But once the British Tommy decides on a name for anything, that name it is bound to have, and as he adopted the name "mustard gas" for it mustard gas it will remain for all time.

The other new material that was introduced by the Germans in the summer of 1917 and which, like mustard gas, has been in use ever since is the German " sneezing gas." For a long time high-explosive bombardments were reported on many occasions to be accompanied with violent sneezing, which at the time was laid down to the presence in the air of undecomposed explosive from the shell. As a matter of fact the sneezing was due to the presence inside the high-explosive shell of bottles containing chemicals the chief effect of which is to cause violent sneezing when small quantities get into the air. This sneezing material, or sternutator, to give it its scientific name, in this case was a solid which is atomised into tiny particles when the shell bursts. Chemically speaking, it is called diphenylchloratsine. This material is used embedded in the trinitrotoluene of the explosive shell in most cases and such shells are called Blue Cross Shell, and are marked accordingly. This is the third of the present trilogy of the German coloured-cross gas shell. The sneezing gas is also sometimes mixed in with the contents of the Green Cross Shell in considerable proportions. The idea underlying the use of this sneezing gas by the Germans was apparently partly that of getting a gas which they thought might go through our masks. In this of course they were disappointed, as the respirator keeps out sneezing gas perfectly well. The other idea underlying its use was apparently to cause such violent sneezing as to prevent men from getting their masks quickly adjusted or to cause them to sneeze them off if they had been put on.

This and all sorts of other tricks of the gas-shell business have been tried out at various times by the Germans. While putting over Green Cross or Blue Cross Shell, or both they will suddenly accompany them with violent bursts of shrapnel, the idea being that men will be so busily occupied in putting on their masks or in sneezing that they will not take the usual care in finding immediate cover from the shrapnel; or that, on the other hand, in taking cover from the shrapnel they will not get their masks on in the minimum time or will displace them in their efforts to get away.

The sneezing caused by the Blue Cross Shell is a most peculiar and violent kind. If you get the smallest dose of this stuff into your lungs you start sneezing at once. You seem to sneeze from the very bottom of your stomach upward, and feel as if the whole of your chest were going to come out with it. This may continue almost continuously for a short time; but there are apparently no after effects unless the gas has been very strong indeed, in which case there is very painful irritation of the whole of the throat and lungs which will produce bronchitis. This is the present stage of development of the German gas shell. Whether they will add another colour to their lot of Green, Yellow and Blue Cross Shell we do not know, but we are prepared for it when it does come, and in the meantime he is getting as good as he gives.

It will be news to most people to realise how the gas shell are gradually dominating the field. Some bombardments are composed entirely of gas shell. As many as a quarter of a million have been fired on the attacking front during twenty-four hours, and probably at least one-quarter of all German shell of all calibres are gas shell.

It must be remembered that there are certain things that gas shell cannot do. They cannot replace high-explosive shell for the demolition of fortified works, for example. Nor can they be used for cutting barbed wire previous to an advance; and the creeping barrage that preceded the assaulting infantry cannot be made up by gas shell. An SOS barrage in No Man's Land, to cut up an attack, also would have to be shrapnel and H. E. so as not to gas the defending troops. When all these are cut out it will be realised that the proportion of gas shell that are used against living targets must be very big indeed. It is hardly too much to assert that at the present day, of the actual methods of attacking men direct gas is the most important. It must be realised also that it can become, and is likely to become, still more important, and that the fight between the offence and the defence on both sides will continue until the end of the war.

Since December of last year the boche has been copying a method invented by the British for firing a large number of big drums of gas simultaneously. These drums are used chiefly against the front-line troops and are generally filled with pure phosgene. As each bomb contains a gallon and a half of liquid and many hundreds are fired at the same moment a good high concentration of gas is produced. Warning is given by the tremendous roar from behind the German lines when the flock of canister or rum-jar bombs starts on its way. Every man who hears the noise gets his mask on at once, even before there is any sign of gas; and if he does this there is little danger, as the respirators are quite capable of dealing with even the very high concentrations of phosgene produced. If a man keeps his head and obeys orders there is little to fear from gas. But discipline must be high. As one Tommy said: "You must be so well disciplined that when the gas alarm goes you will even drop the rum ration so as to get your respirator on in time. Beyond that it is simply a question of carrying on the work in hand while wearing a respirator, and this is entirely a matter of practice.

FLAME THROWERS

When the German Army entered on its policy of frightfulness there was none of its new and unprincipled methods which had more immediate and striking success than the use of liquid fire. And there is now none of all its methods of frightfulness which has fallen more into disrepute, and which has had less success when once the first surprise was over.

A great deal of attention has been drawn in the newspapers to the use of liquid fire, but the average man, even in the fighting forces, knows very little about the German methods and the appliances for its use. Yet Germany still has special troops trained in the use of liquid fire, and seeks continually to alter and develop the fire weapons and their tactical employment in order to take advantage of the undoubtedly terrible appearance and destructive power of the high temperature flames which can be emitted. This article is intended to show the stage to which the development has attained and the reasons for the relatively innocuous character of what is probably the most terror-inspiring method of modern warfare.

Throughout 1915 England was pouring new divisions of its National army into France. As with all new troops the procedure adopted at the time was to bring these divisions by easy stages to within a short distance of the front line, and then send them in by companies for a four day "instructional tour" in the trenches to pick up all the wrinkles and habits from the seasoned troops holding the line. After the whole formation had been put through it in this way the division would be allotted a definite part of the line, taking it over possibly from the troops with whom it had been in for instruction and allowing the latter to get out for a much needed rest, or to get "fattened up" for some impending or progressing show elsewhere.

One such new division, absolutely fresh from England and with no war experience whatever, was the target selected by the boche for his new deviltry.. The portion of line allotted to this division was on the outermost part of the Ypres salient and included the ruins of the little village of Hooge right at the point of the salient. This position had always been a hot corner - "unhealthy" in the British army parlance - and had changed hands several times. The trenches there were poor as it was almost impossible to get effective work done on them owing to their exposed position. Indeed there were many parts of the line where no movement was possible by day and the men on the posts had to lie "doggo" until night. The two lines were very close together-in many places less than twenty yards-and it was quite possible to hurl hand grenades from one set of trenches to the other. It was on this position of the line, over a front held by two battalions, that the attack was made.

After a bombardment of several days, a mine was exploded under the front line and then immediately afterward, at 3:20 A. M. on the morning of the 29th of July and without the slightest warning, the front line troops were enveloped in flames. Where the flames came from could not be seen. All that the men knew was that they seemed surrounded by fierce curling flames which were accompanied by a loud roaring noise and dense clouds of black smoke. Here and there a big blob of burning oil would fall into a trench or a saphead. Shouts and yells rent the air as individual men, rising up in the trenches or attempting to move in the open, felt the force of the flames. The only way to safety appeared to be to the rear. This direction the men that were left took. For a short space the flames pursued them, and the local retirement became a local rout. Then the flames stopped and machine guns began to take toll of the fugitives. Only one man from the front trenches is known to have returned. German infantry following up, poured into the breach in the line, widened it, took our positions as far back as Sanctuary Wood, and then consolidated.

Ten days afterward we counter attacked and won back the whole of the line concerned but at very considerable cost. Incidentally, we captured two of the German flame projectors, one of them complete, and they proved to be of the greatest possible use to, us subsequently for educating the army in the new warfare, and for inspection by our own experts with a view to their duplication for retaliation. Any one attempting to blame the troops attacked for their retirement can hardly appreciate the circumstances, and, I am convinced, over-estimates his own capacity for resistance. This attack was an utter surprise-the kind of warfare was unknown and and unheard of. Imagine being faced by a spread of flame exactly similar to that used for the oil burners under the biggest boilers, but with a jet nearly sixty feet in length and capable of being sprayed round as one might spray water with a fire hose. Personally, I am pretty sure, had I been there, that I should have hopped it if I had not been fried by the heat or frozen with terror. Later, when we knew the limitations of these things it was different, though even then it is a pretty good test of a man's nerve.

The flame projectors taken by the 14th Division in the counter attack were simple but very interesting in construction. The main part was a cylindrical vessel of steel about two feet in height and fifteen inches in diameter provided with straps so that it could be carried on a man's back. At one side about two-thirds of,the way up was a filling hole for oil, closed by a screw cap. Near the top was a pressure gauge attachment and toward the base was a lock closed by a lever handle and to which could be attached a long length of flexible hose ending in a peculiar shaped nozzle.

On examination it was found that the body of the projector was divided internally into two compartments which could be connected by opening another tap. The upper compartment was the compressor and the lower the oil reservoir. The compressor chamber was filled to a pressure of twenty three atmospheres with deoxygenated air or nitrogen. Air itself cannot be used because of its oxygen content forming an explosive mixture with the vapours from the oil, and any heating on compression, or back-flash from the flame or fuse, might make things very unpleasant for the operator. The nitrogen required for the flame projectors is carried into the field in large cylinders about 4 feet 6 inches in length and 6 inches in diameter. Several of these cylinders have been captured from the enemy since. These cylinders are actually taken into the trenches and the flame projectors charged from them there. The combustible liquid used in the flame throwers has varied in source and composition from time to time, but it invariably has one characteristic which appears to be essential for good results-it must have light or easily volatile and heavy and less volatile fractions mixed in carefully graded proportions. The heavy oil has sometimes been a petroleum product and sometimes a tarry residual oil from the distillation of wood. The light portion, which insures the jet's keeping alight was originally a light gasolene, but at one period, whether from shortage of petrol or not I do not know, the place of the latter in the mixture was taken by ordinary commercial ether.

The lighting device, fixed at the end of the flexible hose, is the most ingenious part of the whole contrivance and is so made that the oil ignites spontaneously the minute the jet is turned on, and is kept alight by a fiercely burning mixture which lasts throughout the discharge.

The nozzle is about 9 inches long and detachable so that replacement is easy. It clips into the end of the tube and is held in position by an annular ring. When the oil with its twenty-three atmospheres pressure behind it is rushed out of the jet, it forces up the plunger of a friction lighter and ignites a core of a fierce burning fuse mixture which fills the whole of the space between the central tube and an outer easing. The latter consists of a thick wick soaked in paraffin wax and fitting loosely into a thin brass case. When the nozzle is in position all that is necessary is to turn on the tap, and the stream of flame issues from the tube and can be directed at will.

The official name for this instrument we discovered was the "Flammenwerfer" (flame thrower) and it is now never known in the British army by anything else than its German name. Indeed this is one of the very few German words we have adopted as an outcome of the war, the only others I can remember being "strafe" and "Kamerad".

Flammenwerfer attacks are made by the 3rd and 4th Guard Pioneer Battalions and by the Guard Reserve Pioneer Regimentall of which troops are specially trained in flame tactics. Each battalion is composed of six companies and each company is equipped with 18 small or portable projectors similar to that described above, and with 20-22 large projectors of greater range. The latter larger flammenwerfer are built on the same principle as the former, but are too heavy to be used as mobile weapons. They are consequently built in to the trenches at about 27 yards from the opposing lines, and, if the trenches are not close enough together f or the purpose, special saps are pushed out and the flammenwerfer installed at the end. The range of these large projectors is 33-44 yards and they can cover a front of 55 yards with flames.

It is probable that in the attack at Hooge that both large and small flammenwerfer were employed. It is possible with the above equipment for a flame company to cover a total front of 1100-1600 yards. Service in the Guard Reserve Pioneers is apparently a form of punishment. Men convicted of offences in other regiments are transferred either for a time or permanently, and are forced under threat of death to engage in the most hazardous enterprises and carry out the most dangerous work. The following incident will serve to show how the German soldiers are hounded to their death in these engagements.

In the summer of last year a small flammenwerfer attack was made against our line at a point near Monchy, south of Arras. Two boches armed with flame projectors of a modified pattern were instructed fo attack one of our advanced posts which was at the head of a sap running out toward the German trenches. In broad daylight and with no covering fire worth talking about these two poor devils were forced over the top with revolvers pressed into their backs. One was shot down immediately. The other managed to get clear of his own barbed wire and then discarded his apparatus, with the intention of crawling over to us and deserting. By this time, however, he had been badly shot up - whether by his own people as well as by us, I cannot say. His left arm and his right thigh were both smashed, and he had two bullets in his abdomen. Nevertheless this man managed to crawl into our lines. and was taken care of He was sent down to a Casualty Clearing

Station in a perilous condition, but despite his terrible injuries I understand the doctors managed to patch him up, and that he recovered completely.

The portable flammenwerfer used in the attack just described was brought in by our patrols the following night, the spot where he had left it being accurately described by the wounded prisoner. It was found to be of a new pattern and other specimens of the same construction have since been captured, chiefly in the neighbourhood of Lens where they were employed by the boche in the course of abortive counter attacks against the Canadians.

In this pattern the compressed nitrogen is contained in a spherical-vessel which is contained inside a ring-shaped oil container. The whole thing looks like a life preserver and is mounted on a light frame so that it can be comfortably carried on the back. For a man who may suddenly have to get down on his stomach and crawl, the apparatus is much more compact and better fitting to the body than the original type, but it has no advantage over the older varieties as regards range or duration.

The flexible hose which carries the lighting nozzle is made of canvas and rubber, and enemy documents which have been captured show that only one tube is provided for each three reservoirs. After the discharge of one apparatus the long tube is supposed to be fitted with a new nozzle and handed on to the others in succession.

The flammenwerfer companies are divided into squads. Following the German army habit of . adopting contractions-a habit presumably forced on them by their cumbersome word-building language, the squads are designated Groftruppe or Kleiftruppe, according as they are armed with large or small projectors. The former is a contraction for Grosser-flammerwerfer- trupp (large flame projector squad), and the latter for Kleiner-flammenwerfertrupp (small flame projector squad).

In the case of attacks with the large projectors, or a combined attack with both sizes, the chief thing is secrecy of installation in the trenches. If it was ascertained or suspected that flammenwerfer were being put in, our gunners would open on the position in no time and blow the apparatus sky-high. As it is necessary to sap out to within 27 yards of our lines in order to get in a "shot," it can readily be seen that the possibilities of using the large projectors are very limited, and as a matter of fact little use has been made of them.

Attacks with the portable projectors are more possible owing to their greater mobility. But here again the essential part of the tactics and the most difficult thing to do is to get near enough the target to make the shot effective. The range is only fifty to sixty feet. The German idea is to cover the advance of the "Kleif" men by protecting machine gun fire. In an attack, the advance of the company is covered by machine gun fire from each side, converging at a point on the opposing latter for Kleiner-flammenwerfertrupp (small flame projector squad).

In the case of attacks with the large projectors, or a combined attack with both sizes, the chief thing is secrecy of installation in the trenches. If it was ascertained or suspected that flammenwerfer were being put in, our gunners would open on the position in no time and blow the apparatus sky-high. As it is necessary to sap out to within 27 yards of our lines in order to get in a " shot, " it can readily be seen that the possibilities of using the large projectors are very limited, and as a matter of fact little use has been made of them.

Attacks with the portable projectors are more possible owing to their greater mobility. But here again the essential part of the tactics and the most difficult thing to do is to get near enough the target to make the shot effective. The range is only fifty to sixty feet. The German idea is to cover the advance of the "Kleif" men by protecting machine gun fire.

In an attack, the advance of the company is covered by machine gun fire from each side, converging at a point on the opposing trenches. In the triangle thus formed the attacking force, the "Kleiftruppe" in front, then a party of bombers, and finally the raiding or attacking party take up their positions in No Man's Land and crawl as far forward as possible in the "protected area." As soon as the flame projectors are within range, the machine guns switch outward to each side, the flame is discharged and the bombers rush in and try their luck in the trench. If things go well, the infantry follows the bombmg party and proceeds to its objective.

In an attack of this kind, or a less well supported attack such as that at Arras, mentioned above, the attackers suffer from two such severe disadvantages that against well disciplined troops they stahd little chance. These disadvantages are (1) the flammerwerfer carriers have to get so near their objective that they are almost certain to be shot, and they then become a source of danger to their own side; (2) men in trenches know they are perfectly safe from frontal flame attack if they keep well down and hug the parapet side of the trench. The reason for this is that the flame will not sink down into a trench, but having little force behind it at the end of its journey is curled upward by the rising currents of hot air. The result is that any sort of head cover (unless made of wood) makes perfect protection, and a man crouching in a trench or ,even lying prone in a shell hole, is very unlikely to be more than slightly scorched at the very worst. I can vouch for this, for I have lain at the bottom of a trench with the flames playing over my head and have not been injured in the slightest, though - I confess to being very much relieved when the flame stopped. The only danger in trenches to men who keep their heads is that of "blobs" of burning oil falling from the end of the fiery stream, but this is not a very serions chance.

Another serious disability in the German liquid fire is its very short duration. The stream of flame from the portable flammenwerfer lasts rather less than one minute. It is impossible to charge up again on the spot, and the result is that once the flame stops the whole game is finished and the operators are at our mercy. Without making the apparatus of a prohibitive weight, the duration of the flame cannot be increased. Even the heavy projectors give only a flame lasting at the best one minute and a quarter.

It must be realised that it is discipline and coolness (if one may use the word) which count, and that the moral effect on unsteady troops, unaware of the fact that the appalling flames have little destructive value, may be very great indeed. When men have bolted from the trenches into the open they are an easy prey. An enfilade attack, i.e., one made from a flank, would be much more dangerous were it not for the difficulty of approach and the fact that the traverses of a fire-trench are as good protection against flame as the parapet. Only where the "'Kleif " squad can approach under cover and get in its shot at an exposed target is the flammenwerfer likely to have much success nowadays.

A certain amount of value was obtained from their use in this way in the attack on Verdun for reducing isolated strong-points, notably fortified farmhouses and broken down cottages in the ruined villages. In certain cases the flame projector carriers were enabled to approach under cover or by crawling among the ruins and heaps of debris, to within striking distance of the otherwise well protected machine gun emplacements and positions. By suddenly playing the fire jet into the loopholes, enough flame penetrated into the interior of the emplacement to put the machine gun and its crew out of action - either temporarily or permanently. This was the opportunity awaited by the covering party of bombers who would rush the post the minute the flame ceased, having made their approach while the projectors were in action. But even for special cases like these the circumstances must be so favourable and the inherent disadvantages are so great that the flarnmenwerfer cannot be counted on to attain the required result.

The low value placed by the Allies on the German flame attack can be realised from the fact that no special form of cover is provided against it. There is no special form of fireproof clothing or other protection issued to the troops, and the instructions for meeting the attack may be summarised as "Shoot the man carrying the apparatus before he gets in his shot if possible. If this cannot be done take cover from the flames and shoot him afterward..."

Bibliography

Allison, Graham: *Nuclear Terrorism: The Ultimate Preventable Catastrophe*, New York: Times Books, 2004.

Alperovitz, Gar. *The Decision to Use the Atomic Bomb*. New York: Vintage Books, 1996.

Bernauer, Thomas: *Genes, Trade, and Regulation: The Seeds of Conflict in Food Biotechnology*, Princeton, Princeton University. 2003.

Blow, Michael. *The History of the Atomic Bomb*. New York: American Heritage Publishing Company, 1968.

Bradley, John. *Learning to Glow: A Nuclear Reader*. Tucson: University of Arizona Press, 2000.

Buzan, Barry & Eric Herring: *The Arms Dynamic in World Politics,* London: Lynne Rienner Publishers, 1998.

Cochran, Thomas B. *Nuclear Weapons Databook*. Cambridge, MA: Ballinger Publishing Company, 1987.

Divine, Robert A. *Eisenhower and the Cold War*. New York: Oxford University Press, 1981.

Escobar, P.: *Globalistan: How the Globalized World Is Dissolving Into Liquid War*. Ann Arbor, 2006.

Fernlund, Kevin J. *The Cold War American West, 1945–1989*. Albuquerque: University of New Mexico Press, 1998.

Fishelson, J.: *From the Silk Road to Chevron: The Geopolitics of Oil Pipelines in Central Asia*. 2007.

Fransman M, Junne G, Roobeek A: *The Biotechnology Revolution?,* Oxford, Blackwell, 1995.

Garrelick, Renee. M.I.T. Beginnings: The Legacy of Nuclear Metals. Concord, MA: Nuclear Metals, Inc., 1995.

Gilchrist, H. L., Col., M. C., U. S. A., and Church, J. R., Col., M. C., U. S. A. *Report on Chemical Warfare in France, July 1, 1921,* 155. On file, Medical Division, Chemical Warfare Service, 1921.

Gorst, I.: *Russia Seals Caspian Gas Pipeline Deal.* 2007.

Gusterson, Hugh. *Nuclear Rites: A Weapons Laboratory at the End of the Cold War.* Berkeley: University of California Press, 1996.

Hasan-Askari Rizvi, *Chemical Terrorism and South Asia,* Albuquerque, NM: Sandia National Laboratories, February 2003.

Hoffman, Bruce: *Inside Terrorism,* New York: Columbia University Press, 1998.

Janowitz, M.: *The Professional Soldier: A Social and Political Portrait,* N.Y., The Free Press, 1960.

Johnson, R.: *Spying for Empire: The Great Game in Central and South Asia,* London, 2006.

Katik, M. : *Russia Pipeline Play Poses Dilemma for Turkey.* 2006.

Katz, M. N.: *Russian-Iranian Relations: Functional Dysfunction.* 2009.

Kaufmann, Albert R. *Nuclear Reactor Fuel Elements: Metallurgy and Fabrication.* New York: Interscience Publishers, Inc., 1962.

Laquer, Walter: *The New Terrorism: Fanaticism and the Arms of Mass Destruction,* Oxford: Oxford University Press, 1999.

Latha, J.: *Is IPI pipeline less risky than TAPI line*? 2008.

Leo Tansky, *US and USSR Aid to Developing Countries: A Comparative Study of India, Turkey, and the UAR,* New York, 1967.

Lucian, K.: *Putin Secures New Pipeline, Undermining US Plan.* 2007.

Miller, Richard L. *The U.S. Atlas of Nuclear Fallout, 1951-1962,* Woodlands, TX: Legis Books, 2001.

Moravcsik, Andrew: *The Choice for Europe: Social Purpose and State Power.* Ithaca, NY: Cornell University Press, 1998.

Norris, James A.: *The First Afghan War 1838-1842,* Cambridge, University Press, 1967.

Norton, Augustus R., and Martin H.: *Greenberg, Studies in Nuclear Terrorism,* Boston: G.K. Hall & Co., 1979.

Oksana Antonenko and Kathryn Pinnick: *Russia and the European Union.* Oxon: Routledge, 2004.

Olcott, M. B.: *The Great Powers in Central Asia*. 2005.

Piskur, M.: *The B.T.C. Pipeline and the Increasing Importance of Energy Supply Routes*. 2006.

Popescu, Nicu: *EU Foreign Policy and Post-Soviet Conflicts: Stealth Intervention*. London: Routledge, 2011.

Rashid, A.: *Taliban, Militant Islam, Oil and Fundamentalism in Central Asia*. Yale University Press, 2010.

Retzer, W.J.: *Biotechnology Workbook*, Englewood Cliffs, Prentice Hall, 1991.

Rhodes, Richard, *The Making of the Atomic Bomb*, New York: Simon and Schuster, 1988.

Stein, Arthur A.: *Why Nations Cooperate: Circumstance and Choice in International Relations*. Ithaca, NY: Cornell University Press, 1990.

Talbot, K.: *Afghanistan, Central Asia, Georgia-Key to Oil Profits*. 2003.

Trenin, D.: *Russia-Pakistan Relations*. 2011.

Warthin, Alfred Scott, and Weller, Carl Vernon: *The Medical Aspects of Mustard Gas Poisoning*. C. V. Mosby Company, St. Louis, 1919.

Weber, Katja: *Hierarchy amidst Anarchy: Transaction Costs and Institutional Choice*. Albany, NY: State University of New York Press, 2000.

Weitz, R.: *Averting a New Great Game in Central Asia*. 2006.

Xinhua. AS.: *China-Kazakhstan Pipeline Starts to Pump*, 2005.

Index

S

T

U

V

W

❑❑❑